THE LIBERTINES
BOUND TOGETHER
by Anthony Thornton and Roger Sargent

THE LIBERTINES
BOUND TOGETHER
THE STORY OF PETER DOHERTY AND CARL BARÂT AND HOW THEY CHANGED BRITISH MUSIC

ANTHONY THORNTON AND ROGER SARGENT

TIME WARNER
BOOKS

TIME WARNER BOOKS

First published in Great Britain in February 2006 by Time Warner Books

A CIP catalogue record for this book
is available from the British Library.

HB ISBN 13: 978-0-316-73234-5
HB ISBN 10: 0-316-73234-6
C FORMAT ISBN 13: 978-0-316-73259-8
C FORMAT ISBN 10: 0-316-73259-1

Printed and bound in Great Britain by The Bath Press, Bath

Time Warner Books
An imprint of
Time Warner Book Group UK
Brettenham House
Lancaster Place
London WC2E 7EN

www.twbg.co.uk

DEDICATION

To Victoria for everything. To Mum, Dad and Judy for their patience.
And to Andy F: missing you still.

Anthony Thornton

To my lovely Kerry, my parents Jill, Chris, Jan and Keith and my godson Felix.

Roger Sargent

ACKNOWLEDGEMENTS

Anthony and Roger would like to take the opportunity to thank the following people who Anthony interviewed during the course of writing this book:

Peter Doherty, Carl Barât, John Hassall, Gary Powell and Paul DuFour (aka Mr Razzcocks).

Mick Jones, Banny Pooschti, Jake Fior, Andy Lee, Roger Morton, Andy Fraser, Dean Fragile, Kirsty Wark, Paul Brownell, Alan McGee, Kirsty Ridout, Kirsty Want, Kirsten Lynn, Tony Linkin, James Endeacott, Geoff Travis, Jeanette Lee, Jim Merlis, Gwyn Mathias and Hedi Slimane.

In addition Anthony and Roger would like to thank the following people without whom this book would never have been written or published:

Stephen Jenkins, Pat Gilbert, Neil McCormick, Anthony Rossamondo, Didz, Drew McConnell, Adam Ficek, Michael and Jeff, Colin Wallace, Annalisa Astarita, Stephen King, Matt Bates, George MacDonald, Paul Reeves, Alison Philcock, Phil Whaite, Simon Evans, Terry Grimley, John Aizlewood, Peter Gunn, Jolie Lash, Rob Partridge, Ray Innes, Dominic Blore, Rik Hegarty, Kerry Swatridge, Caron Malcolm, Robert Hayden, Mr Nick Hat, Patsy Winkleman, Hannah and Rose, Alex Proud, Russell Parker, Richard Day, Bill and all at Holborn Studios, Tim Brooks, Conor McNicholas, Steve Sutherland, Neil Robinson, Tammi Iley and all at *NME*, Celia Hayley and Julian Alexander at LAW, Antonia Hodgson, Tamsin Barrack, Simon Sheffield, Caroline Hogg, Viv Redman, Maddie Mogford, Siobhan Hughes and all at Time Warner Book Group.

Roger and Anthony would like to give a special thank you to Tony Linkin whose vision and aid was immeasurable from the very beginning.

CONTENTS

PROLOGUE

IT WAS THE EVENING OF 21 MARCH 2003 WHEN A WOMAN WIELDING A CLAW HAMMER ABOVE HER HEAD BEGAN SCREAMING OBSCENITIES AT ME. THE PROFANITIES WERE PUNCTUATED WITH A SHRILL WHINE OF, 'IT'S NOT FAIR, HOW DARE THEY.' THIS WOMAN, IT WAS OBVIOUS, HAD THE MISFORTUNE TO LIVE NEXT DOOR TO A DEN OF COMINGS AND GOINGS AND PARTIES AND MUSIC. CLEARLY SHE HAD BEEN SUBJECTED TO LONG NIGHTS OF PSYCHOLOGICAL TORTURE AT THE HANDS OF BASH STREET URCHINS WITH A SOUND SYSTEM TO SPARE.

I'd been in scrapes before in my job at *NME*: soaked to the skin at Glastonbury with both hypothermia and Portishead poised to strike, and peeling my face off the sticky lager-flavoured floor of the Glasgow Barrowlands. But this was – and remains – the most scared I'd ever been. I banged at the door with a manic mixture of determination and desperation, convinced that at any moment the hammer blow would fall.

Of course, the sensible option would have been to scarper out of Bethnal Green and away from this woodchip door with 'Albion Rooms' crudely scrawled on it in biro, but after making it this far a crazy woman about to bring death on my head wasn't quite enough to deter me from what I knew would be an extraordinary evening.

The girl who answered the door calmly fixed me with a look and then shot a cooler one at the woman. In I went, ten pounds lighter – but with woodchip between me and the hammer. I scrambled up the rickety bare wooden steps and into the front room. Roger Sargent had a camera and was standing on the wrought-iron spiral stairs that dominated this tumbledown room full of books and posters. Playing through a tiny scraggy-looking amp, Peter Doherty, Carl Barât and John Hassall were entertaining a small group of people cross-legged on the floor sipping lager.

John, in striped shirt and heavy coat, sat, barely moving, his eyes closed in a deep concentration verging on trance. But out of his bass came a series of bouncing, crackling basslines, driving the music onwards with an energy in total contrast to his mannequin demeanour. Carl was swaying his head round to the music, emphasising every bar with a swagger that was half macho, half coquettish, revelling in the tinny sounds emerging from the fuzzy amplifier. He looked every bit the dandy, in leather jacket, his faithful knackered guitar picking out precise riffs that owed as much to Django Reinhardt as any of your typical guitar heroes. Glances were exchanged throughout between him and Peter; if there was a band leader, then it was difficult to tell who it was.

There was an unspoken chemistry between the two. The songs weren't announced, they materialised, filling the room with an impossibly intimate joy as they took turns to sing and, occasionally, share the mic. Peter had clearly been in the wars a little, wearing a jacket that looked as though it was going to get up and walk out, and playing chords in an equally messy way while never undermining the emotion of the songs. Beyond this, there was a twinkle of innocence in his eyes that would remain the one constant in everything that followed. Throughout all the bad times – and the countless good – it would only be extinguished once in the following two years.

Typically for The Libertines, something would go wrong. That night, drummer Gary would fail to show up, appearing later, when it was all over, a box of Tennessee Fried Chicken in his hand and a blithe attitude to it all, merely concerned that he hadn't done his bit. The whole evening was warm, inclusive and spontaneous in a way rock 'n' roll is rarely allowed to be. And it was all for twenty people who, like me, had heard about the gig through a posting on the Internet.

Five weeks previously, they'd headlined in front of 2,000 people at the London Astoria. And now they were unselfconsciously playing a gig to anyone who'd read and believed that the short post on libertines.org really was from Peter Doherty, announcing the details of a 'secret' gig the following evening at seven. Cameras were welcome and there was to be no guest list for the music industry. The address was a dingy corner of Bethnal Green.

It was Peter and Carl's flat. You know, of course, that bands don't do this sort of thing. In fact, frequently bands hate playing live, they play the minimum number of gigs for the maximum profit. You, the punter, are a necessary evil, a faceless provider of good times: a mere conduit to the party afterwards. They'd hate you if they ever met you. Yet this band were happily playing a gig at their crumbling flat for a bunch of fans who happened to have been seduced by the heady mixture of poetry, romanticism and rock 'n' roll longing that was the band's creed.

Rock 'n' roll was fifty years old, but The Libertines were doing something fresh and original. They were busting the barriers between musician and fan, and in a democratic way – it didn't depend on knowing someone or being a groupie. The cold wires of the Internet were harnessed for what The Libertines called 'a good old-fashioned knees-up'.

Needless to say, half an hour after the filthy flat filled with song, the hammer woman had her revenge and the police arrived to break it up. Heavy boots pounded on the fragile stairs. Pete looked at Carl. Carl looked at Pete. 'Time For Heroes' was abandoned and, floating on a wave of delicately strummed guitars, they sang:

When they kick at your front door
How you gonna come?
With your hands on your head
Or on the trigger of your gun

To my knowledge, The Clash, however great they were, never actually serenaded the police with 'Guns of Brixton'. But then it was already clear that The Libertines were unlike any band I had ever seen.

That night I told Roger that I didn't have a clue just what we'd got with this band. That was, it transpired, an understatement. These were people who were aware of their past but not in debt to it. If it meant making a great new tune they'd happily chuck a couple of heroes together and stand back to appreciate the sparks. But, above all, what we witnessed was a British phenomenon. They sang and were informed by a Britain that had disappeared, a land of high poetry and low comedy, of William Blake and *On The Buses* Blakey; of the Hellfire Club and Hancock; of learning and excess; literature and *The Likely Lads*. This was a band, after all, whose acceptance speech at a rock awards ceremony was Peter and Carl's tender call-and-response reading of Siegfried Sassoon's World War I poem 'Suicide In The Trenches'. From the outset, they were as at home on Radio 4 as Radio 1.

They sang with a keen British spirit that instantly bypassed the sorry Britpop clichés and clicked straight into the greatest parts of Britain's outsider past. But they did it with a precise wit that blossomed in lyrics, in person and in Peter's private diaries, The Books Of Albion. In one simple couplet they seemed to defeat the crass Americanisation of British music: 'There are fewer more distressing sights than that/Of an Englishman in a baseball cap'.

They didn't care about nu metal or Britpop. These complex people wanted to do something very simple: be in the greatest British band that ever picked up a guitar.

In the short time they existed, The Libertines accomplished the impossible: on their own they kickstarted a new British music renaissance, from Franz Ferdinand to Kaiser Chiefs to Arctic Monkeys. They erased the barrier with fans, they inspired thousands to follow, they gave away entire albums of material for free on the Internet with a determination that shocked major labels.

And where it's safer to hide under a carapace of irony rather than reveal your true feelings, they've been wincingly honest. Yet much of the media have failed to grasp the band or what they really mean, falling for live-fast-die-young clichés and trying to pin on them fabulous notions of a Sid Vicious obsession. At a time when the media has been long confident that it can spot every feint and shift of music, they've united in a strange echo of the censorious past. Headlines pleading for Kate Moss to abandon Junkie Pete have the distinct echo of the ramblings of 1960s tabloids: 'Would you let your daughter marry a Rolling Stone?'

The songs The Libertines created are the equal of anyone's in the history of British music. At the same time, they are the classic British band: a band with the finest frontline duo since The Clash and as inspirational as The Smiths. Their breathtaking live performances, teetering on the edge of disaster, were greater than those of Radiohead, Oasis or Nirvana. Original and blindingly beautiful, they blazed brightly, never compromising, never selling out.

After guerrilla gigs, crack, burglary, prison, forgiveness, addiction, *EastEnders*, Bangkok, arrest, riots, *Newsnight*, Kate Moss, two great albums, hours of material and a torturous split, Peter and Carl remain inextricably tied together, mentally if not by music; even now they find it impossible to free themselves. This is the story of Peter, Carl and The Libertines and how they changed Britain.

THE ARCADIAN DREAM

'BOTH IN THE FLOWER OF THEIR YOUTH,
ARCADIANS BOTH, AND MATCHED AND READY ALIKE TO
START A SONG AND TO RESPOND'
Virgil

CHAPTER ONE

THE ARCADIAN DREAM

FROM HAMBURG-ERA BEATLES, THE SATANIC STONES, THE FRIVOLOUS INTELLIGENCE OF ROXY MUSIC TO THE SEX PISTOLS AND THE MUSIC-HALL CAMPERY OF THE SMITHS, BRITISH MUSIC HAS ALWAYS THRIVED ON BEING THE KID IN THE CORNER WHO DEMANDS ATTENTION – SOMETHING THAT HAS TO BE WATCHED AT ALL TIMES IN CASE IT DOES THE ESTABLISHMENT, OR ITSELF, MAJOR HARM. BY THE LATE 1990S THIS HAD ALL CHANGED; THE MAJOR MUSIC-MAGAZINE COVER STARS HAD BEEN A SERIES OF WITLESS DJS AND ACOUSTIC FUMBLERS SUCH AS TOPLOADER, TRAVIS AND STARSAILOR. MUSIC WAS SLIDING INTO MEANINGLESS AOR WITH THE GENTLE GRACE OF SOMEONE SLIPPING INTO A COMA.

Of course, when you're in it, in a grand reversal of the grass-is-greener principle, it never seems quite so bad. But my god it was horrendous. I joined *NME* in November 1998 expecting a party, fun, the continuation of the rock 'n' roll dream. 'Hi,' I thought I'd say. 'Let's party like it's '67 or '77 or '89 or … hey, why the long faces?' The atmosphere at the *NME* was that of a particularly unappetising morgue. It may have been on the twenty-fifth floor of Kings Reach Tower but in spirit and lighting at least it was very much two storeys underground. Unbelievably, it was about to get worse.

The 74-year-old *Melody Maker* and the indie monthly *Select* closed within a week of each other. At the time, *NME* Editor Ben Knowles, who had only recently left *Melody Maker*, wasn't worried about his own paper. But the decline was to go into a tailspin, the clue lying in what would have been the *Melody Maker*'s Christmas issue: a portly baseball-cap-wearing misogynist arsehole, Fred Durst, at Christmas time in his own home. Nu metal was here.

Weeks later, nu metal and its sound were all over the top ten. Those who found Limp Bizkit and Durst's

grunting, big-shorted antics a little too much could enjoy the boyband metal of Linkin Park or Papa Roach. Music was not only rubbish, it was American rubbish.

Thankfully no one bothered to convey this information to Peter Doherty or Carlos Barât.

Carl Barât had enough problems without worrying about the state of British music. As a drama student at Brunel University in Uxbridge he was disappointed to find that his fellow students didn't live up to his idealistic view of what university life would be like, coloured by his unconventional upbringing – his parents were hippies. After Carl's birth in Basingstoke in 1978 his mother Chrissie had continued to live a communal, travelling existence as his father settled into factory jobs and a council-estate life. He had an itinerant childhood that included extended stays in Teepee Valley, a tented

THEY MADE A PACT TO THROW THEMSELVES INTO ETERNITY. CARL SAID TO PETER: 'IT'S EITHER TOP OF THE WORLD OR BOTTOM OF THE CANAL.'

hippy commune in south Wales. Carl's idea of university was based on what he'd read about the energetic student radicalism of the 1960s. He became disillusioned by his fellow students, who on the whole preferred simply to get drunk and get through exams.

In 1997 he did, however, fall in with a student called Amy-Jo Doherty. They ended up sharing a squat together in Richmond by the River Thames. She told Carl about her younger brother Peter who was, she said, a poet. She'd told her younger brother Peter about the amazing guitarist she shared a squat with. Peter, then just seventeen, was keen on meeting this guitar genius with a penchant for David Niven movies. He sounded like just the sort of person he could forge a musical alliance with; Peter adored The Smiths and entertained the idea, like Morrissey, of simply meeting a genius foil and making a difference.

Peter was born in Hexham, Northumberland on 12 March 1979. His father, Peter Snr, was Irish working-class stock who'd worked his way through the British Army from private to major through sheer effort, talent and hard work. As a result of his father's job, Peter had lived in London, Liverpool, Belfast, Coventry, Germany and Cyprus. He was a stern father who later on Peter would publicly fall out with, but as a child Peter adored him, his fondest memory that of being driven by his father to a Queens Park Rangers game with classic 1950s sitcom *Hancock's Half Hour* playing on a cassette – Peter Snr ran the local branch of the Hancock Fan Club.

Peter went to stay with his sister at the squat. At last, after years living in a self-contained bubble of Hancock, Queens Park Rangers Football Club and poetry, he would meet someone he could relate to. The stink of the dirty Thames wafted through the open window as Amy-Jo made ready to go to a lecture. She asked Carl to look after her brother while she was away.

Carl poked his head round the door of Amy-Jo's room and saw Peter gazing out of the window. Carl caught the smell of the room, which he assumed was emanating from Peter – it was the smell of a festering urinal. 'Great,' thought Carl. 'He's not a poet, he's incontinence in a plastic jacket.' But he braved the smell and went back to see this 'poet'.

Peter was surprised that Carl lapped up his William Blake-derived ideas of Albion and Arcadia. Carl shared his fierce pride in Britishness, which in Carl manifested itself in a love of the Edwardian wit and short-story master Saki, classic Brit movies, the theatre and music hall. They gelled instantly. Carl was a talented guitarist who had easily mastered and become bored by the Oasis tunes that fellow students always begged him to play. Peter was no more than fine on the guitar, but knew he would get better. Peter asked Carl to teach him the chords to The Smiths' 'This Charming Man'. Carl picked up his guitar and started playing Blur's 'Charmless Man' instead. He hadn't even heard of The Smiths. Peter was agog that Carl wasn't steeped in the minutiae of alternative music the way he was, but soon recognised that this was a plus.

PETER: 'That tells you how much he knew about British music. But I began to like him for that.'

Carl adored the dark vision of The Velvet Underground, The Jam, The Doors and the guitar virtuosity of Django Reinhardt. Peter loved The Smiths, Suede and Chas & Dave. Peter, like his father, adored football and QPR (he ran a literate fanzine *All Quiet On Western Avenue* in his teens); Carlos had little truck with football. Peter was forthright, talkative, confident and liable to overstate his talent; Carl was shy and constantly doubted his talent. They saw in each other something they wanted. Within minutes this closeness spilled over into competitiveness and fighting.

Carl couldn't believe that this precocious talent was a year younger than him. He was smart and although he couldn't play that well he had ideas that were intoxicating. Peter was equally smitten: he'd found his foil, a polar opposite in many respects. They saw in each other a means of escape. Carl had lost faith in university's ability to provide him with the impetus he needed and he had pretty much given up playing the guitar; Peter saw Carl as a way of escaping his humdrum son-of-a-major existence and he saw the potential of forging a creative partnership to rival his heroes The Beatles' Lennon/McCartney, The Smiths' Morrissey/Marr and Suede's Anderson/Butler.

Typically for young lads, getting a band together,

writing songs and performing is a means to an end: fame, fortune and women. By contrast, this pair were more concerned with writing great songs and becoming rivals to their heroes. The rootless, intelligent Peter had built an internal world to escape to, informed by great music and literature, classic British sitcoms and William Blake. He was intoxicated by lonely poets like Emily Dickinson, and Thomas Chatterton, dead at seventeen. Carl was obsessed with Saki, wit, charm, dandyism and music hall. Their obsessions overlapped to produce the idea of sailing 'the good ship *Albion* to Arcadia', a fondness for the gaudy trappings of musical hall and a love of literary Paris and Montmartre in particular. Perhaps Oscar Wilde, wit, raconteur and writer, was the hero they could both agree on.

Their ideas and obsessions were unusual to say the least. After all, not many mates would ensure they always had a copy of George du Maurier's Victorian page-turner *Trilby* with them at all times. This is the book that gave the world the trilby hat and the idea of a Svengali, a puppetmaster, controlling a person or people.

Peter started to visit his sister regularly and he and Carl would sit up all night, strumming guitars and talking. Peter would have to return home but would obsess about the next time they could get together to play again.

They made a pact to throw themselves into eternity. Carl said to Peter: 'It's either top of the world or bottom of the canal.' And that was that, there was no going back. Peter made his escape to London to do English literature at University College London but abandoned his course a year into it. Carl abandoned his Drama course two years in. Higher education had been a means to an end, to get to London; it was no further use to them in battling through or indeed in fighting the demons that haunted Carl in particular.

CARL: 'I didn't want to be a ghost in someone else's society, where there's no time or no direction … just drifting. I didn't want to be eating beans out of a can in a lonely bedsit in front of a flickering TV screen in fifty years. I didn't want to be the man that "could have" but didn't, which is what Peter said to me in an attempt to inspire me.'

PETER: 'Carl saved me, essentially; he looked after me after I left college. He was obsessed with the idea of being old and alone watching telly. "Death on the stairs", we called it.'

They moved into a basement flat together on Camden Road near Holloway Road, where they shared a filthy mattress, sleeping top to tail. They would be Arcadians together, they would be fellow shipmates on the *Albion*. It was death or glory. That was the plan anyway.

And that pretty much was that. Intoxicated by the idea of Albion and Arcadia, a romantic fantasy of pursuing experience, perfection and Britishness, they bonded, tightly. The Albion of Carl and Peter wasn't simply Britain or a nostalgic idea of Britain, it was an idealised Britain, a Britain of the senses and excess, of literature and hedonism. In short, not so much Britannia rules the waves as Britannia waives the rules.

They would put together a band and make all the difference. The first thing they needed, mind, was a bass player, and someone who could sing and a drummer. And a name, of course.

Steve Bedlow, or Scarborough Steve as he was more commonly known, was a neighbour of theirs. He was confident and mouthy, the perfect person to perform Peter and Carl's songs. They toyed with various names, including The Albion, but eventually the three of them settled on The Libertines, after Marquis de Sade's 'The Lust of The Libertines', extracted from his celebration of the very extremes of sexuality: *120 Days Of Sodom*. To this day no one can agree who came up with the name.

John Hassall and Johnny Borrell, who would later go on to form Razorlight, were at school together, Johnny a year above John. They'd played together and hung out. They bonded over music and getting into scrapes.

JOHN HASSALL: 'Johnny Borrell and I met Scarborough Steve, who was a regular down the pub. We used to hang out at my mum's place and then Steve came round there to drink and smoke or whatever. And he'd always go on about these two guys, Pete and Carl. He had this kind of reverence for them. He thought they were amazing guys and amazingly talented.'

Then one day he heard a knock at the door.

'It must have been '97 in the summertime. I got a knock on the front door and looked down and there was Pete stroking my cat George in the sunshine. It was a lovely summer's day. Peter with his satchel and his Farah trousers and Fred Perry T-shirt on. He introduced himself, he was very polite and very funny. We went upstairs, had a smoke; talked about music and stuff. He told me about this band he had, so the following day Pete, Carl, Johnny and Steve came round. It transpired that Steve was the singer, Carl was the lead guitar player, Pete was the rhythm guitar player and that Pete and Carl wrote the songs.'

In fact, at this stage no one was really sure who was going to do what, but one thing was certain. This was a group top-heavy with egos. Johnny Borrell would soon drift into his own projects while remaining friends.

Most bands, having assembled the personnel, then retire to the pub to discuss names for months before a single guitar is strummed. Not so with The Libertines. Two days later they played the first Libertines gig, in Carl and Peter's basement flat on Camden Road. They dragged a bunch of friends and anyone else who fancied it down from the Dublin Castle, a pub that frequently serves as the starting point for Britain's guitar bands. The band were really excited, even John, who usually preferred a devastating quip delivered in the style of a narcoleptic wise arse, picked up on the energy.

Peter, Carl and Steve had asked someone called Zack to play drums, who was never formally introduced to John.

The atmosphere was that of a debauched shindig. Candles were lit and they strummed their skiffly, acoustic gig of half-formed songs and covers. Friends and like-minded people thronged into the flat, which was full of junk-shop memorabilia, books and records. Halfway through, the electricity ran out and a hat was passed around to collect coins for the meter.

CARL: 'It was built round me and Peter. Scarborough Steve came round for a bit because neither of us had it in us to be frontmen … Still don't … hahahaha.'

Where Steve was keen to be in a band and make noise and grab attention, Peter, Carl and John discovered they were driven by a love of songwriting. John adored The Beatles and The Move and was christened king of the three-part harmony by Carl. That wasn't the half of it, though. He picked up Pete and Carl's songs straight away. In contrast, Peter saw the guitar as a means to end, didn't see himself as a musician but as a poet, and as half of a songwriting partnership with Carl. This partnership blossomed as they poured their ideas of a lost spirit of Britain into their songs: dilly boys (male prostitutes), men in white coats and love on the dole.

Within weeks they had booked themselves into Odessa studios in Clapton, east London. Steve was in Glastonbury, but they resolved to record without him. The drummer was still a problem, though. Out in Filthy McNasty's, where Peter occasionally worked as a barman, Peter and Carl were surrounded by a self-made scene of poets, musicians, writers, artists and hangers-on. A youngish, good-looking guy clocked Peter and Carl and said he had a solution to their problem: he was a drummer. They couldn't believe their luck. They eagerly enquired if he would be ready the following day. He would. The deal was done. They would record at Odessa studios and make the demo that would lift them out of their romantic but dismal world.

CARL: 'Eventually we begged, borrowed and stole to get into a tinpot studio where Gwyn Mathias who engineered The Sex Pistols helped us out. He was the loveliest fella.'

But when they turned up at Odessa studios the following day at the allotted time, the drummer wasn't there.

'They turned up at the recording studio,' recalls Gwyn Mathias. '"Where's your drummer?" I said and they said they'd met someone the night before in a pub who was going to drum. He didn't turn up, so I called a mate who lived nearby to come and help them out.'

That mate was Paul DuFour, a jazz drummer, then fifty-four, who'd played in a multitude of bands since the 1960s. He turned up and was paid a flat £50. He brought a swing to their earnest British vignettes: 'Breck Road Lover', 'Pay The Lady' and 'Music When The Lights Go Out'.

CARL: 'We were told of this legendary drummer … He

turned up and told us about the time Keith Moon had stolen his drum heads and fired a BB gun at him.'

The first was a sweeping romantic tune sung by Peter and named after the street in Liverpool where his family came from. He was still finding his voice at this time, affecting it to sound a little like Suede's Brett Anderson. 'Pay The Lady', with a lead vocal by Carl, sounded like a Rubber Soul-era Beatles with backing vocals from Peter and John and a harpsichord solo before turning into a white funk workout. But 'Music When The Lights Go Out' was the standout track, sung by Peter over a delicate backing that blossomed into a taut piece of chamber-pop with real swing. It would become the centrepiece of all Libertines performances with Paul DuFour.

Paul was impressed by this band of youngsters who played Beatlesesque songs with great hooks and managed three-part harmonies. So he took the unusual step of joining a band thirty-odd years his junior. He was a versatile, instinctive drummer with a keen sense of humour. ('They say never work with children or animals.

The Libertines were both.')

The band each had their nicknames handed out mercilessly by Carl and Peter. Peter was Bilo, Pigman or Spaniel, Carl was Biggles or Spaniel, John was Mr Lombard, and Paul DuFour, for reasons known only to Carl, became Mr Razzcocks. They were joined by Vicky Chapman, a cellist, who stayed with the band for about year.

They began gigging regularly, anywhere they could. They would play further afield than the major indie hangouts in Camden.

Roger Morton, a journalist at *NME*, was tipped off by a friend that he should check them out at a gig at the Hope & Anchor in Islington. He loved them straight away: 'They had a gang thing about them. They were good-looking and they had loads of charisma. Pete and Carlos would talk to the audience, take the piss out of them, tell jokes and muck around. They involved people in the gig, which no one else was doing. I thought: you're going to be on the cover of the *NME*. You just belong there and that's where you'll be.'

He reviewed the gig for the *NME*, lustily describing them as 'Proper London Oxfam aesthetes with dirty minds, dusty books, nice tunes and a future'.

Roger, along with his friend Andy Fraser, decided to offer their services as managers. At the same time, The Libertines were offered a management deal by John Waller, a veteran of the music industry. They decided to pick Roger; they felt he was more on their wavelength.

The gigs continued as the band grew in confidence. Filthy McNasty's was a regular venue, where they would wind down afterwards with their group of supportive friends and artists and a fellow musician called Peter Wolfe, whom Peter dubbed the Wolfman. This man had been a handsome Liam Gallagher-type in the mid-1990s when he had attempted unsuccessfully to launch a music career. Since then he had fallen into and been ravaged by overindulgence, but he always kept his dreams of music stardom alive.

Peter Doherty was doing shifts at the Prince Charles Cinema just off Leicester Square. He talked the management into allowing his band to play before the premier of *The Blair Witch Project* on 8 October 1999.

They played a proper gig in front of the scarlet velvet curtain. The front line of Peter, Carl and John, in suits and sharing two mics for the three-part harmonies of their increasingly complex songs, looked like The Beatles playing the Royal Variety Performance. They were charming and funny, and the songs were becoming better, catchier and more mature. However, even though it was a great show, it was only seen by their friends from Filthy McNasty's and the London poetry scene and those lucky enough to see the video recording.

Roger Morton decided it was time to get serious. At the beginning of 2000 he managed to get them seen by Mike Smith of EMI Publishing, who was impressed enough to give them money to demo tracks. The band recorded 'Bucket Shop' and 'Sister, Sister' (with lead vocal by John) for EMI. But the record company that had signed both The Beatles and The Sex Pistols passed on them. ROGER: 'What they were doing didn't make sense to what the label thought they should be signing. So no one had the confidence to do anything.'

The band were undeterred. They would roll into Hackney and the East End and old 1950s pubs that only old men ever went to and persuade the manager or barman or someone to let them do a gig there. They would put on a night and design posters that always suggested some sort of Byronesque orgy was happening and then they would go and play.

They played Finnegan's Wake in Islington, and basements and a kebab shop on Stoke Newington High Street; they even played an old people's home. Besuited and cheeky, they entertained the pensioners with their skiffly songs and music-hall chit-chat from Pete and Carl's music-hall alter egos Spaniel and Spaniel. CARL: 'The song we played to these pensioners losing their faculties was "I No Longer Hear The Music". Hahahaha.'

The Kings Arms in Fulham was a particularly memorable show. Spaniel and Spaniel exchanged music-hall patter as ever and, for the finale, Spaniel Carl sang 'Dream A Little Dream' and tap-danced in his shoes while Paul DuFour provided the 'tap-tap' by striking the rim of his snaredrum. To up the ante Peter took off his shirt and dropped his trousers, revealing a pair of brilliant white longjohns. Peter high-kicked as Carl tap-danced and Roger videoed the entire gig again, a wonderful record of The Libertines. They were tight. It was unfathomable that they weren't snapped up. They had songs, they were charming and funny and they looked great, yet after two years no one was interested.

Their life at that time was one of squats and parties and scraping a living hand to mouth. Despite failing to capture the imagination of a moribund record industry, the band kept their dreams alive. They did cash-in-hand jobs that frequently appalled them. On one occasion Carl secured a job handing out nibbles at a corporate event. Peter, disgusted at the thought of Carl dressed as a waiter, gatecrashed, seized the tray of vol-au-vents Carl was carrying and told him that handing out pastries was beneath him. The pair fled the do.

On another occasion, desperate for money, they came up with the idea of joining the Territorial Army to make some fast cash without having to join the full-time army. Once they'd presented themselves, the officer insisted that Carl get his foppish hair cut. He refused and they both left, without any money.

Peter recorded many of his thoughts in notebooks, which he dubbed 'The Books Of Albion'. Initially these were carefully maintained diaries of his life, but they soon developed into a forum for him to explore his thoughts and poetry. He carried his current book with him wherever he went and was not averse to pulling it out during a late night after closing time at the Foundry or Filthy McNasty's and scribbling his latest thoughts into it.

There is an almost hopeless romanticism that pervades these early books; measuring out what he should be doing, exploring his identity as a poet, writer and musician. A driven reader, Peter was also aware that if he did achieve his artistic aims and become a lyricist, poet or musician, his Books Of Albion would inevitably be read by someone. But this self-consciousness soon fades; like the family who invite a documentary film crew into their house, he's quickly absorbed into day-to-day business, only occasionally snapping out of his self-obsessed reverie. When he does, it has the flavour of a Victorian novel as penned by Joe Orton. In 2000, for example, he addresses the reader directly in a prim, starchy way redolent of the narrators of Victorian melodramas. And then having got said reader's attention, he asks if we recall the details of an anal sex encounter we had with him, and helpfully fills in the details just in case we didn't recall.

In other places, he would invite friends, and later fans, to write. In one book in 1999 Johnny Borrell lists his heroes, alongside Peter's. Johnny's are primarily the sleazier end of glam rock (Lou Reed, Iggy Pop, Johnny Thunders), Peter's are English through and through (Hancock, Blake, Wilde, Orton).

Peter told *Socialist Worker*'s Alison Philcock of Johnny: 'His mum had a mansion in Alexandra Palace and when we had nowhere to live, his mum used to fancy Carl, so we sort of crashed there. She had this boarding house for, well, it was just a mansion but it turned into a boarding house for wayward Arcadian dreamers. Steve, Carl, me,

when we were homeless we'd always stay. I was clean as a whistle actually. I had a little van there I used to have to drive him to school. He was just this little seventeen-year-old kid in a bowler hat and eyeliner, mad on the Manics and Stardust-era Bowie and the New York Dolls.'

Around this time, Roger Morton gave up managing The Libertines. He switched his attention to Johnny Borrell and would later manage him.

After two years of impasse and then the loss of their manager, things suddenly began to look brighter. Around St Patrick's Day in 2000, they met Banny Poostchi, a lawyer for Warner Chappell Music Publishing, who had worked with Oasis at Filthy's. Her boyfriend had been working with Malcolm McLaren, former manager of The Sex Pistols, on his unsuccessful bid to become London mayor. The Libertines had approached him to manage them, but he'd turned them down. Banny, however, recognised that they had something special from the off.

Banny, an Oxford graduate, was a shrewd lawyer with a passion for music. As manager she was practically part of the band, driving them onwards. It was impossible to underestimate her determination.

'They had the character, looks, style, wit, humour, originality and they could play. But could they be accepted by the culture of Britain in 2000? They were trying to resurrect a romanticised Britain which, in a sense, was in their heads. It was a life where people could be original and free-spirited. These were genuine artists, genuine poets. They lived their lives by their own rules. They crafted a scene of people through sheer determination and camaraderie – it was very similar to coffee houses in the eighteenth century or Soho in the 1950s with Francis Bacon. I tried to get them signed based on that.'

In September 2000 Carl picked out the best eight tracks they had recorded as demos in various sessions. The tracks were 'Music When The Lights Go Out', 'Hooray! For The 21st Century', 'Love On The Dole', 'Bucket Shop', 'Sister Sister', 'Anything But Love', 'France' and '7 Deadly Frenchmen'. The recording would later become the Holy Grail for Libertines fans.

BANNY: 'I was trying to do a cover in a rush. I had a picture of ballet dancer Darcey Bussell stuck on the front but I had to cut off her legs and invert them. I thought of the bingo thing. The most famous legs in England. It was appropriate that she'd be a mascot. And that's why it became "Legs 11".'

But the record industry still hadn't noticed this perfectly formed Beatlesesque band. The effect of hearing those demos now, for people who know the band through their two albums, is akin to the seismic shift in opinion that occurred when Nirvana did the MTV *Unplugged in New York* TV show. *Unplugged* revealed them to be sensitive songwriters and performers; suddenly that slightly retarded rock persona that had been projected on to them was revealed to be part of a much greater whole.

The 'Legs 11' collection is full of pastoral delights, displaying great maturity where songwriting is to the fore. Rather than punky and ragged, it's delivered precisely with great tenderness. In many ways, it's typical of a successful band's third album. The album where, after the compromises and commercial demands, they hold a record label to ransom and write and record an album that's about extending their emotional vocabulary. But this was merely a demo.

No one was biting. Banny: 'I didn't want to change them to get them signed. They were very unwilling to play the game. In 2000, people walking around in suits? It was just an anomaly.'

There were troubles internally as well. Paul DuFour was travelling down from Rugby to do gigs and John was frustrated by the lack of progress. Two years of gigging, doing gigs most weeks, and they were no closer to getting their songs beyond the usual welcoming faces of the Filthy McNasty's set. Peter was content to play for these people, for this special crowd, and for him and Carl to arrange Arcadian happenings around the East End. Secretly, John and Paul made a pact that if it wasn't working they would both leave.

The situation was brought to a head when the band got double-booked to play Filthy McNasty's and the Camden Monarch, the latter being where bands are frequently spotted and signed.

CARL: 'Peter insisted we do the gig at Filthy's because he owed somebody or something. That's when John finally had the hump. For Peter, it was better the devil you know, a good old knees-up. But the Monarch was part of the road to success.'

Peter would always put friends before success. It was important that he looked after his mates. It was a trait he would never lose. Even when he became famous he ensured that friends in bands got exposure.

JOHN: 'I decided to look after my own. I didn't know what I wanted to do. I ended up going back to college and sixth form to finally try and retake my A levels. It was actually going pretty well at the time. I was on course for some good grades for the first time in my life.'

Banny departed as well: 'In December 2000 I said I'm really sorry but I'm not going to get you signed. I think you're fantastic. But I don't think it's going to happen.'

The band disintegrated. Peter and Carl were still thick as thieves; they would go to Speakers' Corner and frighten tourists.

CARL: 'Me and Peter used to go down to Hyde Park and talk in Irish voices utter shit and then we'd ask for 5p to do a dance and the pair of us would dance this dance which involved hunched-up shoulders and swinging arms. I was always Seamus. We had these nights anyway at the Foundry on Old Street. It was almost a comedy really, vagrant artists and poets and dancers and anyone we could offer a stage to from around the world, and you know me on piano doing all the music stuff and Peter compèring. That's how we made our money, doing a raffle, stealing something from the art studio downstairs and getting money off everyone for a bit of paper torn up with a number on it. Then pulling a number or picking one at random and doing the whole Butlins number on the winner: "What's your name? Where're you from?" and getting a lame prize. I think everyone loved it. The second prize was half a gram of speed and a Charlie Manson record. It was quite good booty.'

But right then, after two and a half years and hundreds of gigs, Peter and Carl were washed up. The Arcadian dream was over. It looked like Carl's worst fears were coming true. It would be death on the stairs or bottom of the canal, after all.

PLAN A

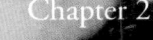

*'OUR GOALS CAN ONLY BE REACHED THROUGH A VEHICLE OF A PLAN,
IN WHICH WE MUST FERVENTLY BELIEVE, AND UPON WHICH
WE MUST VIGOROUSLY ACT. THERE IS NO OTHER ROUTE TO SUCCESS'*
Pablo Picasso

PLAN A

DESPITE HAVING NO BASS PLAYER, DRUMMER OR MANAGER, CARL AND PETER CONTINUED TO WRITE AND PLAY SONGS TOGETHER, BUT THE LIBERTINES WERE ESSENTIALLY FINISHED. PETER PUT ON MORE NIGHTS AT THE FOUNDRY, 333 CLUB AND FILTHY MCNASTY'S, COMPÈRING NIGHTS WITH NAMES LIKE 'GRANDE FOLIE LONDON'. THESE WERE PERFORMANCE POETRY IN THE LOOSEST POSSIBLE SENSE, FEATURING THE INFAMOUS WORM LADY AND HER POEMS COMPRISED OF WEIRD SEX, DELIVERED WITH A FEVERISH YELL; THESE WERE ARCADIAN ROMANTIC NIGHTS OF POETRY AND SONG WHERE ANYONE COULD HAVE A GO. IT WAS A QUESTION OF ATTITUDE.

Carl moved more into theatre, as an usher in the Old Vic on the South Bank. The dream was still alive but slumbering. Scarborough Steve and Peter jammed a bit and even managed to get a demo together.

And then The Strokes happened. In one way it was a final indignity for British music, punky forthright songs far and away better than nu metal, something you could actually fall in love with, something that Britain had always been good at. Here was a bunch of good-looking New Yorkers who were doing the job of Brits.

Peter spied the success of these skinny boys in tight suits, unable to comprehend how they'd done it where The Libertines had failed. He recorded in a Book Of Albion sadly that 'The Libertines have been dapper for years now'.

CARL: 'When people shunned us in favour of The Strokes it was quite upsetting. We thought we had everything they had and more and no one was listening.'

Banny, who was working on The Strokes publishing contract, saw her chance: 'I knew that everything was going to change now and that there was nothing in Britain to match it.'

On 28 June 2001 Banny got tickets to see The Strokes at London's Heaven. It was the hottest ticket in London – everyone wanted to go. Banny took Peter and his then girlfriend Francesca.

BANNY: 'The Strokes after-party – there were loads of people there: trendies, models and beautiful people. But The Libertines were just so much cooler than anyone else.'

Peter was inspired by the gig and also realised that everything had changed.

Banny arranged to meet Peter and Carl and offered to manage them again on strict conditions: 'Look, I'm going to get you signed in six months, guaranteed, to Rough Trade if you do exactly what I say. If you're prepared to do that I can get you a deal. If not, I don't want to waste your time.'

CARL: 'After the devastation of everything falling apart, me and Pete decided that we were going to continue and Banny decided she was going to be part of it. From that point on it was a different approach, slightly more jaded perhaps, slightly more desperate, more furious. And maybe even a bit of bitterness that our initial innocent dream hadn't been recognised or realised.'

And so Plan A was born. Banny told them to scrap everything they'd written and write a whole new set.
BANNY: 'I didn't tell them to write like The Strokes. I said you're fantastic songwriters, so why not write a bunch of songs that are similar to The Strokes and then we can get you signed. And when you're signed you can fuck off the record company and do what you want. It wasn't that I didn't think The Libertines were brilliant, it was just that I knew you had to fit in initially to sell.'
CARL: 'We still showed the depths of our schooling, that was still apparent in our songs. That's what gave it a bit of truth and stopped us from just being a copycat band. And we meant everything we did.'

Peter and Carl then wrote 'Time For Heroes', 'Horrorshow', 'Up The Bracket', 'Boys In The Band' and 'I Get Along', the last three written in Banny's flat on Copenhagen Street in Islington. Banny wanted five brilliant songs to get them signed, and she'd get frustrated when she'd turn up to rehearsals and find they wanted to play more new songs. She knew in order to get signed they'd have to play a small number of songs really well rather than twenty in a so-so way. 'Time For Heroes'

GEOFF, IN HIS TYPICALLY SOFTLY SPOKEN WAY, SAID: 'AT ROUGH TRADE WE ONLY SIGN THE BEST. AND YOU ARE THE BEST.'

was based on Peter's experiences at the 2001 May Day riots.

PETER: 'There were running battles with the police and I was part of that. I ended up with a scarf wrapped around my head and I did get hit. I think the policeman thought I was taking the piss – I was doing my hair by looking in his riot shield and he clumped me around the side of the head.'

Peter on 'Time for Heroes': 'It started off as quite a slow song and then Carl sped it up about four times and put a solo in.'

There was still the small matter of finding a bassist and a drummer. Razzcocks was considered, but was living in Holland at the time. Old acquaintance Johnny Borrell was recruited to play bass. Banny's secretary, Katie Ferry, was going out with a drummer called Gary Powell. Gary was from New Jersey in the States. He had already played for reggae artist Eddy Grant and was in another band called The Minor Birds who were on the verge of getting signed by Universal.

GARY: 'I met up with Peter and Carl at Filthy McNasty's, through Banny. She took me to meet them, and we hung out. When I met them it was just really funny. Initially, it was just about going to Filthy McNasty's. It was about going there because I lived in Angel and they were kind of homeless. They knew people there so we'd go and hang there.

'I just loved being in the company of Peter and Carl. It was literally the three of us, backs against the wall. And then it was Pete who suggested Backstreet studios, Holloway Road, an old yellow building. The first time we went in there it was me, Pete, Carl and Johnny Borrell. And the first thing we tried to play together was "Horrorshow". When we first played, because of my drum corps and concert-hall background, I used to

arrange music and all this type of rubbish, I would come up with ideas for arrangements. I remember with "Horrorshow" it was really kind of slow. And we just took the tempo up a bit and it ended up being trashy as "Horrorshow" is now.'

Banny drilled into them the need to rehearse every day and booked them into Rooz rehearsal studios. To show how serious she was, she made sure they all paid their way.

BANNY: 'But Peter never had any money, so he'd deal ecstasy to people in other rehearsal studios.'

Peter was kipping on the floor of James Mullord, who ran a small label called High Society.

CARL: 'That's when Plan A and Plan B came in. Plan B was to sign to James Mullord of High Society – that's what Pete wanted to do. I wanted to sign to Rough Trade – that was an idea that Pete had put in my head because I didn't even know who they were. It was Peter who taught me about that. That was Plan A.

'Pete wanted to do Plan B, but you can get your demos released and sold on stalls on Brick Lane or you can do it properly. He seemed inclined to do it quicker, easier: the cash-in-hand option.'

BANNY: 'I remember I was in my flat and Peter was on the phone to James [Mullord] in the process of agreeing to sign to High Society for £1000. I said, "You know what? You can fuck right off, you're wasting my time."'

So Peter turned down the offer.

In the meantime, rehearsing was going well. Although The Libertines knew they had to buckle down, they still found time to wind up Banny. On one occasion they were in Shepherd's Bush rehearsing at a studio. Banny walked in to find on the blackboard the names of the songs they were rehearsing and the words 'New Song'.

BANNY: 'I got them to play the new song. When they'd finished I just said, "That's shit."'

Peter and Carl started smirking and giggling like kids while Gary looked upset.

BANNY: 'Later I found out the "new" song was a cover of The Velvet Underground.'

On 1 October 2001, Banny phoned A&R James Endeacott at Rough Trade to see if she could get him down to see them play a showcase for him at the rehearsal studio. It was during the music industry showcase 'In The City' in Manchester, but Banny was unrepentant, insisting he should come to see them. 'I said, don't go to In The City, every other A&R twat will be going there. You have got a chance to find a unique band.'

James Endeacott is a flaxen-haired former member of 1980s wall-of-sound trance rock emissaries Loop. In a business full of sheep, he's convinced of his own music opinions and quite happy to go out on a limb or suffer ridicule in order to find something new in music he loves. Perhaps best of all, he possesses a keen sense of humour and a dislike for most of the vagaries of the music business. Bands love him. He was the perfect candidate to see The Libertines.

She arranged to pick him up from Rough Trade's offices in west London. It was done.

With everything going according to plan, Carl phoned Banny with terrible news. Johnny Borrell had gone to Wales with the Alabama 3 and wasn't returning. He tried to convince Banny to put the showcase off.

BANNY: 'I said it had to happen today. The only reason I'd blagged James was that I said I was a mate of Gordon Raphael's [The Strokes' producer]. I knew that, as Rough Trade's biggest band, he'd want to keep Gordon and The Strokes sweet.'

Banny told the band they would have to improvise. She picked James up in a flash car and gave him a big spiel about how big and important the band were. James, as an A&R man, had heard the whole 'better than The Beatles/Stones/Elvis/Clash' a thousand times before. He was impressed at her fervour, but was ready for a major disappointment.

BANNY: 'I gave them strict instructions only to play four songs. I told them if they played any more they'd fuck it up. Trying to get them not to play songs is the hardest thing in the world.'

They played their new 'Plan A' songs – which, depending on who you talk to, was 'Time For Heroes' and 'Up The Bracket' plus two of 'Never Never', 'Boys In The Band', 'Horrorshow' and 'I Get Along' – they asked James if he wanted to hear any more.

BANNY: 'He wanted to hear more, so they played the same songs again … hahaha … because they'd been drilled by me.'

Banny wasn't sure how it had gone; she thought James looked a little stunned. He asked for a CD.

They hadn't had a chance to record a demo yet, though, as they'd been working for the showcase. The only CD Banny had was 'Mocking Bird' and 'Thru The Looking Glass' with Scarborough Steve on vocals, whose vocals were a little like Liam Gallagher's – they were more in the tradition of the old Libertines. Their old friend Rabbi, a growly Irishman who looked like Gimli the Dwarf, sang 'Mocking Bird', his voice mangling the vowels, while 'Thru The Looking Glass' had a classic Tony Hancock radio show running underneath. It was a typical stroke of Libertines bad luck. James went away and listened to the CD.

JAMES: 'There were all these weird noises and samples, just completely different from what I'd seen. I was a bit disappointed, to be honest.'

CARL: 'Banny did the wining and dining to the max. It was really impressive, utterly persistent. Part of Plan A was that she'd quit her job and become the manager full-time. I mean, it was a real high-flying job at East West records. And so yeah, we were going to be blood brothers, in it together. Us two and Banny.

'She was battling as much as us. She wanted to escape from her life as much as we did from ours, I imagine.'

They heard nothing, though. Banny decided it was time for another push, at one of Peter and Carl's Arcadian nights at Whitechapel's Rhythm Factory. James, despite his disappointment, not to mention bafflement, with the demo he'd been given, was willing to give it another go.

BANNY: 'I think he'd been left perplexed and confused by this mysterious CD and wondered if the band he'd seen play in the rehearsal studio had been a strange dream.'

Banny had a massive row with Peter prior to the gig. Peter wanted to play older songs like 'Dilly Boys' and 'Love On The Dole'. He would not bend: 'This isn't just a Rough Trade showcase – this is for our mates as well.'

Banny retorted: 'This is to get you signed.'

It was a stand-off. But, ultimately, it was going to be

down to the band. Once they were onstage anything could happen. Banny knew that the band would inevitably play for too long and undo all the magic of a short, exciting set. After one last attempt to bring Peter round, she sighed and waited for the inevitable 'Good start but y'know those other songs are a bit skiffly'.

James was impressed by the turnout of people. It was a group of people divorced from the usual Camden indierati or Hoxton fashionistas. It was organic and, in James's words, 'full of freaks and mad people'. For him, used to seeing the same faces at the standard indie bars with the same bands playing, it was a revelation.

The Libertines, still without a bass player, went straight into their brand-new songs. But after playing a couple of songs, just like the first gig they'd played with John Hassall back in Camden, the electricity went off. John himself was in the audience pogoing in encouragement.

BANNY: 'It was an act of god. And James was blown away.'

James spoke to Rough Trade bosses Geoff Travis and Jeanette Lee; they agreed to give Banny money to make a demo.

But the lack of a bass player – or a bass – was still a problem. Banny, Carl and Peter headed to Andy's Guitar Shop on Denmark Street, a road where The Sex Pistols had once squatted.

BANNY: 'I didn't want to buy a bass, but I thought let's see what happens. Peter literally marched upstairs with Carl. Peter had an empty guitar case with him and he started measuring up the basses against the guitar case to see if they would fit.'

Having found a suitable specimen, Peter turned to Carl and said: 'Right, I'm going out into the street. When I'm down there, you chuck the bass out of the window and we'll leg it.'

Carl replied: 'How come I'm the one who has to be inside chucking the guitar out to you? Why don't I be outside and you chucking it to me?'

Like a youthful Lavender Hill Mob with better haircuts, they began to argue about the relative merits of who should be outside, with each of them dogmatic about their best role being the runner rather than chucker.

BANNY: 'I knew what was going to happen, so I bought the bass.'

They demoed 'I Get Along', 'Time For Heroes', 'Never Never', 'Horrorshow' and 'Boys In The Band' at Nomis studios.

On 11 December, the heads of Rough Trade, Jeanette Lee and Geoff Travis, were booked to see The Libertines in a showcase at Terminal studios, London Bridge. The band had no amplification or PA, so Banny hired new amps.

BANNY: 'They didn't have any equipment. All they had was originality, talent, humour and guitars.'

The band ran through a short repertoire for the people who could sign them. Banny was aware that she was running close to her six-month deadline promise and, so far, the only encouragement they'd had from Geoff or Jeanette was when Geoff looked at Peter and said: 'He's really very tall, isn't he?'

But at the end of the set Geoff, in his typically softly spoken way, said: 'At Rough Trade we only sign the best. And you are the best.'

Banny had pulled it off with days to spare. Plan A had succeeded. After The Libertines' three years of slog and the real possibility that Arcadia would never be reached by the weather-beaten *Albion*, they'd done it.

To celebrate, the band went to a ragged members' club called Shuttleworths, frequented by bottom-of-the-rung actors and actresses. Banny ordered loads of champagne. Peter disappeared and returned twenty minutes later with a massive bucket of takeaway fried chicken.

The twenty-first of December was to be the signing date. Peter and Carl walked all the way from east London to west London, because as always they had no money for tubes. They got lost on the way to the Ladbroke Grove headquarters and eventually turned up over an hour late, convinced they'd blown it.

JEANETTE: 'Even then you had to watch them. The pair of them were never bad, but they were always cheeky, you had to watch out for them at all times. They were like the Artful Dodger and Captain Jack Sparrow [from *Pirates Of The Caribbean*]. They were hilarious.'

The band were still without a bassist, though.

Banny phoned ex-drummer Paul DuFour. She said, 'Do you know any good bass players?' He said, 'What do you mean? There's only one bass player – John Hassall. John's the only bass player in The Libertines.'

CARL: 'Well, we ummed and ahhed but the thing is John is fucking good and he looks fucking good and so that was that. There would be no more daydreaming, it was taking it by the balls. That was the transformation that occurred, it was the new way.'

JOHN: 'I was getting calls, from mainly Carl, saying come back to the band, we're going to give it another go. I was working in a bookshop and Peter came in and he'd play me what he'd been doing. It was really sad because I loved the tunes, I'd always loved the tunes. But I'd made my decision. I didn't feel it was going to go anywhere. Then, after a few months I got a call off Carl going,

"We're going to get signed, we're going to get signed by Rough Trade." This was just when The Strokes had kicked off and I was like OK, yeah, I'll come back to the band. So I came back with my tail between my legs.

'A lot had changed since I'd been away. The manager Banny said we'd love to have you back in the band, but you can't write any songs and you can't do any interviews. And she said basically it's all about Pete and Carl. And I wasn't really in a position to argue about it, y'know?'

John is typically sanguine about it now: 'I don't know if it was Banny's idea or Pete and Carl's. I suppose I thought … I suppose I am deeply resentful of that. But I'm probably deluding myself, I was fine, actually. In fact it suited me quite well, once we'd got the machine going.'

John was back on board.

BOYS IN THE BAND

SID JAMES: 'WELL REALLY, WHEN YOU ADD IT ALL UP, IT'S . . .
A BIT TATTY, INNIT?'
TONY HANCOCK: 'TATTY? WE'RE THE HOPE-OF-THE-WORLD, MATE'
'The Poetry Society', *Hancock's Half Hour*

BOYS IN THE BAND

SO PLAN A HAD SUCCEEDED. AFTER THREE YEARS OF STRUGGLE AND HUNDREDS
OF GIGS, THE BAND WERE SIGNED. LIKE MOST BANDS THEY FELT THAT IF IT
WASN'T QUITE THE END OF THE JOB, THEN IT WAS AT LEAST TIME TO WALLOW IN
THE SECURITY OF AN ADVANCE. PETER AND CARL RENTED A FLAT TOGETHER
IN TEESDALE STREET, WHICH THEY DUBBED THE ALBION ROOMS.

The A&R James Endeacott and Tony Linkin, an experienced PR man, were both huge fans of the band. They knew they had to work fast. Roger Sargent was hired to do their publicity shots. Three came out of it: one of the band on a bed gazing wistfully at the camera, another in long coats outside a bagel shop in the East End, and the third in a studio in leather jackets, against a black background.

The Libertines were lucky. Tony Linkin's talents as a PR man lay in his passion for the bands he loves. Looking after bands and their press is more than a job to him. 'Worry worm' Tony Linkin has an innate sense of fair play and an instinctive feel for music. The band loved this delicate, greying and quiptastic man – some journalists have borrowed his putdowns to pep up their own writing. He is the antithesis of the popular image of the hard-nosed PR out to double-cross journalists. For this reason he gets the job done very effectively. And, anyway, Carl loved scooping him up and spinning him around.

Banny insisted that the long-coats shot was too reminiscent of the suits days. She wanted the world to see the leather jackets image first. Where Brian Epstein had taken four lads in leathers and put them in suits to make The Beatles more acceptable for the general public, Banny took her charges and insisted they ditch the suits and snappy dressing in favour of leathers. In forty years music's image had flipped. For this one instance, they were The Beatles in reverse.

The new signings rehearsed every day, ready to invite

TEL: 020 76'13 '12'

GIVE
WAY
VICIOUS CIRCLE

THERE ARE NO
INNOCENT
BYSTANDERS

ACISM
'TING
RSE?

I'M WIC

down key tastemakers in the press to see them. This gig would be at Cherry Jam in west London.

The gig was exactly what people wanted. James Oldham – the man who'd championed The Strokes from the very outset – led the praise. In his review, the second ever, after Roger Morton's 1999 review, he justifiably accused Britain of failing to come up with the goods musically. Although this should perhaps have been levelled at the music business in particular rather than Britain in general.

He thanked god for The Libertines and concluded: ' … [It's] the most exciting thing we've seen all year. It'll be the same when you see them.' Nestling in the midst of the prose was a line that would prove extraordinarily prophetic: ' … you don't know whether they're going to make it to the end of the song or just start punching each other.'

Accompanied by the first published picture taken by Roger Sargent, (who was just as convinced of their potential), it was The Libertines' introduction to the world. A band's first review in the *NME* is crucial; it's how bands as disparate as Oasis, Coldplay and Blur had their first break.

CARL: 'It felt like our first ever gig. There was an amazing atmosphere. Really we felt the part I think. That was our first ever *NME* thing with a picture. James wrote quite an extraordinary piece.'

From then on, things moved at a frenzied pace. Two days later, they were supporting label-mates The Strokes on a pair of rescheduled dates in Leeds and Birmingham. Signing with Rough Trade was a pretty good idea, and Banny had insisted that they have the support.

With dance music in precipitous decline and nu metal dominating the music landscape, The Libertines saw The Strokes as kindred spirits and comrades-in-arms.

The Strokes in many ways – despite being American – saved British music. They arrived at its lowest ebb in terms of sound, inspiration and intelligence. And supporting them was a massive deal for Peter and Carl, who less than a year before were lamenting The Strokes' success.

Like a couple of Artful Dodgers starring in a Powell and Pressburger adaptation of *Withnail & I*, Peter and

Carl had been lifted out of their own romantic fantasyland and couldn't believe their luck. This was the opportunity to forge an alliance and remake music in a way that rejoiced in thrills and intelligence, fun and sophistication.

CARL: 'It was amazing for us crossing the lawn at Leeds into a big canteen hall listening to the strains of *Is This It?*, the album that we'd been listening to, coming over the grass to greet us and inviting us to be a part of it. A kind of boyish feeling that I've seldom felt since.'

GARY: 'I just walked into this canteen and went, oh my god, it's the Strokes. They saw us and put their instruments down to talk to us. It was a bit wacky.'

But it wasn't to last. The New Yorkers were more aloof than The Libertines had been led to believe, and the idea of a pan-Atlantic musical alliance, with The Strokes representing the best of east-coast America and The Libertines the best of Britain, soon lay in tatters.

CARL: 'We were allowed to support The Strokes but we became a bit disillusioned. We loved their album and meeting them. We were excited to be part of it. We thought it could be an alliance: an alliance that they shunned.'

Gary puts their failure to unite down to an event in the dressing room after a Birmingham show: 'At that point I didn't know what drugs were, beyond the obvious ones. We were in the dressing room after the show and Julian [Casablancas, The Strokes' lead singer] and Pete were hanging out. People were commenting on the similarities. Pete was the Pigman back then, a little stockier. They looked very alike at the time. And Peter asked out of the blue if anyone had any crack. The dressing room went quiet and Julian says, "What are you doing that stuff for? That stuff's really retarded." And I didn't have a clue what "crack" was.

'That kind of cooled it a little bit because, in their eyes, we had crack amongst us. And if one guy's doing it,

JAMES ENDEACOTT: 'THEY WENT INTO THIS JAZZ ODYSSEY FOR TWENTY MINUTES. I HAD MY HEAD IN MY HANDS GOING, "THIS IS THE WORST NIGHT OF MY LIFE. YOU ARE DEAD."'

IN MATCHING LEATHER JACKETS, THEY
RICOCHETED OFF EACH OTHER AND THE SONGS
COMBINED SMART LYRICAL HOOKS WITH
BLISTERING PLAYING; IT WAS AS IF BRITISH BANDS
HAD FINALLY BROKEN THE TYRANNY OF
WANTING TO BE OASIS.

then you guys are letting him do it. That kind of sullied it a little bit.'

But, at this time, crack was only an occasional dalliance for Peter and, as much as anything else, the question reflected Peter's desire for a bit of mischief. Living in the moment, as always, he knew it would wind them up.

On these two dates, they were treated by reviewers with the same disdain given to almost all support acts. That's to say, if they were watched at all, it was from the bar and they certainly didn't get a review. But the dates served to get them in front of decent-sized crowds just two months after being signed, alongside a band who were cementing their reputation as the best new band on the planet.

Then, shortly after this, they were chosen to support the band with the biggest buzz surrounding them in the industry at the time, The Vines. These were Australians reared on Nirvana, whose lead singer, Craig Nicholls, was all set to be a cherubic all-conquering hero. With only 'Factory', a 7" single out, they had already been anointed as the successors to The Strokes. Deftly The Libertines had gone from supporting the band of the moment to supporting the next band of the moment. This was all fantastic – but it did appear to condemn The Libertines to being the second-best new band in Britain, with the best being from abroad.

The opening night was at the Brighton Freebutt, a pub that is the south coast venue for up-and-coming bands' first UK tours. James Endeacott wasn't concerned. He was convinced that The Libertines would blow The Vines off the stage. He hadn't bargained for Carl and Peter though.

The band, giddy with the first rush of success after years in the wilderness, decided that for their opening slot on the UK tour they'd keep things interesting. The gig became infamous.

CARL: 'It was like that Tony Hancock film, *The Rebel*, when Hancock's seen the guy's artwork at the big exhibition and he starts trying to turn pictures around to make it fresh. We'd got signed and it was, let's give it a bit of the old school here.'

JAMES ENDEACOTT: 'They went into this jazz odyssey for twenty minutes. I had my head in my hands going, "This is the worst night of my life. You are dead."'

He spoke to them sternly: jazz was out and playing a short, fast set was in. All ready for a few days later, the second night of the tour, at the Camden Monarch.

It was the first time I saw them. The chemistry between the band members was amazing, particularly between the two lead singers. In matching leather jackets, they ricocheted off each other and the songs combined smart lyrical hooks with blistering playing; it was as if British bands had finally broken the tyranny of wanting to be Oasis. They seemed a bit like The Jam and The Smiths with two frontmen. They attracted a crowd of people who'd come to see The Vines but didn't mind checking out what was going on beforehand. It was brutal and fast, a smash-and-grab raid on sensibilities that established them as a band that were exciting and original, even if everyone had eyes for The Vines.

I'd gone along to see The Vines and was knocked out by both bands, so two days later I did something unprecedented. I took time off work and booked a hotel to see them at the Bristol Louisiana. The Libertines were even better that night. They didn't just get onstage and play; the four of them came half dancing half charging through the audience to get onstage, even John. It was a magnificent entrance. And the set, in contrast to Brighton, was wonderful. Where The Vines were a one-man band, they were a gang – they were easily the most exciting new band I'd seen since I started working at the *NME* in 1998. It was a wonderful night.

Carl, however, has different memories of the gig: 'Bristol Louisiana was the gig where James Dean Bradfield (of the Manic Street Preachers) came up to us and told me he loved the gig – he was quite animated for a small bloke. I was really pleased. And he finished by saying, "Yeah, you Vines were great." After all that praise, he thought I was in The Vines. I was gutted.'

There was the chance for one last resurrection of the old days before they set off to record their debut single. In Coventry, a city where Peter had once been to school, they played a support to Six By Seven under the pseudonym Lombard & Spaniel. It served, once and for all, to put the past behind them.

WHAT A WASTER

'I THINK I SHOULD HAVE NO OTHER MORTAL WANTS, IF I COULD ALWAYS HAVE PLENTY OF MUSIC. IT SEEMS TO INFUSE STRENGTH INTO MY LIMBS, AND IDEAS INTO MY BRAIN. LIFE SEEMS TO GO ON WITHOUT EFFORT, WHEN I AM FILLED WITH MUSIC'
George Eliot

WHAT A WASTER

GARY, JOHN, PETER AND CARL WERE FIRED UP. BRIGHTON ASIDE, THEIR FIRST GIGS AS A SIGNED BAND HAD GONE REALLY WELL, AND WHILE THEY KNEW THERE WAS ROOM TO IMPROVE, THEY ALSO KNEW THAT THEY'D TURNED A FEW HEADS. MOST IMPORTANTLY, THESE HEADS WEREN'T JUST IN THE HOTHOUSE ATMOSPHERE OF LONDON – THERE WERE PEOPLE ACROSS THE COUNTRY GENUINELY EXCITED BY THEM. EVEN IF THE SHOWS WERE RAGGED, THEY GAVE IT THEIR ALL WHATEVER THE SIZE OF THE AUDIENCE.

'There was so much energy. Pete and Carl would really psyche themselves out and y'know we could be playing to ten people in a pub in Stoke and they were falling about the stage elegantly ramshackle and jumping into the crowd. We thought they were unimpressed at the time, but they must have liked it,' says John Hassall.

This energy had a lot to do with the fact they loved being on tour, bonding tightly. Peter and Carl were pulling out the acoustic guitars every night after gigs and working on new songs as well as playing old. They'd have adventures every night of the tour, partying like a couple of vaudeville heroes. Fans were surprised at how open they were and how up for a party they were. It was a blur of excess, the electrifying performances just filled them with the adrenalin for more fun and their routines clicked into seeing the sunrise most days. At a gig in Southend Peter was so tired and delirious he kept falling asleep against the pillar between songs. Sure, John's abstinence meant that he wasn't at the heart of the whirlwind so much but otherwise they were littering the UK with party debris and broken hearts.

It was time to capture this raw energy and turn it into their debut single.

Probably the most notable exponents of the British sensibility of the 1990s were Suede. They were pre-

Britpop indie darlings who in typically British form inspired the whole Britpop scene but received none of the laurels. The credit, and ultimately sales, went to Blur, Oasis and Pulp.

Suede's Bernard Butler was steeped in Britishness, a perfectionist with a vision and, what's more, experience of how to get things done as others descended into a fug of drugs and debauchery. In short, he was the perfect candidate to produce The Libertines' first single. Rough Trade, who managed him as an artist, were keen to get him on board.

Peter and John were delighted. Their hero was set to produce their record; typically Carl, with his love of The Doors and The Velvet Underground, didn't even know who he was.

CARL: 'Peter knew these people, he was quite learned in the *NME* press and its history and heroes. I always envied or admired him at least for that and I think he envied my ignorance. Bernard came in when we were doing the second set of demos and we got on. Me and Pete did our thing: the charm offensive. Playing guitars, cockney auditions and dancing and Bernard bought into it. We kind of overdid it, because of nerves and things. We didn't want him to reject us as a producer.'

They needn't have worried. Within weeks the

normally reserved and understated Bernard Butler, a man genetically allergic to hyperbole, was happy to claim that 'Peter and Carl are geniuses'.

The first single had to be something extraordinary to wake the dormant fans of British music, who were still not quite convinced that there was life after Oasis. It had to be special, a call to arms, possibly even something of a manifesto. Out of the selection of post-Razzcocks songs there were several candidates but two stood out: 'What A Waster' and 'I Get Along', at that time the best representation of what they were about.

They'd already demoed two sets of songs for Rough Trade, so recording wasn't new. But when they entered Rak studios to record the songs, they were knocked out by it: the archetypical 1970s studio set-up with a mezzanine. Carl was particularly keen on the massive talkback button which he could use to engage in fantasies of the 'once again with more feeling' variety. And it had a canteen. It was like being in the movies. It was what they'd dreamed of. But for Carl at least, the dream was overshadowed by the thought: is this going to reach anybody?

It was typical Carl pessimism. Peter displayed a mixture of bullishness and devil-may-care attitude about their prospects. But Carl worried. It was absurd really – they'd supported the two hottest bands of the year and had Bernard Butler on board.

They piled through the recording with Bernard working with them assiduously to bring out their sound, to capture the spirit of The Libertines' Albion in the magnet cage of the tape machine.

Carl laughs. 'We had to take it back and remix it because there were too many whirring and gurgling noises in it. It sounded like wandering through Margate amusement arcade. So we had to take that down. I think it upset Bernard a bit. He liked layering on sounds, it was almost like Joe Meek [eccentric British production innovator]. I very much agree with having a feedback track where you can drop in the good bits. And then there was also the speeding up and slowing down of tapes, that was my idea.'

Critics have noted that it was a prophetic single, predicting the arc of their career. But it was a little more complex than that. It was a dire warning of the consequences of blowing your chances. It was a poison-pen letter to their future selves to attempt to guilt them into action and out of the listless torpor that had always threatened to engulf them as it had so many doley characters.

News came through that the *NME* wanted to do an interview with them in time for the single, which was to coincide with the Queen's Golden Jubilee in June 2002. It was their first major interview, conducted by James Oldham in the Dive Bar on Gerard Street in Chinatown. Since closed, it was a cellar bar with a colourful history of its own. Once a gay bar, it had evolved into a romantic, dim drinking den, immortalised with a mention in the Pet Shop Boys' 'West End Girls'.

At the same time as the interview, in a perfect analogy to the violence and idealism at the heart of The Libertines, the May Day riots were kicking off just overhead. Peter and Carl rushed out to join in. Carl got whacked in the knees with a truncheon.

But before they could get back to it there was the interview itself. In this interview the seeds of all the subsequent myths and half-truths of The Libertines were sewn.

'Yeah, why the fuck do you always quote Pete?' demanded Carl. 'Every time you ask a question, he starts yapping. And another thing, why did you call him the singer? He's a scumbag.'

Perhaps most importantly they revelled in their romanticism, a romanticism that had been absent from British music for a decade. They made sure that James was aware what drove them was the pact that Pete and Carl had made: 'To sail the good ship *Albion* to Arcadia.'

For the photo shoot, Gary and John turned up to the studio on time but Peter and Carl turned up two hours late. They were competing to see who could be last, with each repeatedly phoning an exasperated Tony Linkin to

AT A GIG IN SOUTHEND PETER WAS SO TIRED AND DELIRIOUS HE KEPT FALLING ASLEEP AGAINST THE PILLAR BETWEEN SONGS.

FOR THE PHOTO SHOOT, GARY AND JOHN TURNED UP TO THE STUDIO ON TIME BUT PETER AND CARL TURNED UP TWO HOURS LATE. THEY WERE COMPETING TO SEE WHO COULD BE LAST, WITH EACH REPEATEDLY PHONING AN EXASPERATED TONY LINKIN TO SEE IF THE OTHER HAD ARRIVED YET.

see if the other had arrived yet. When they did finally show up for the shoot, Peter, dead on his feet after 48 hours without sleep, collapsed on the Union Jack Banny had hired for the event, spilling red wine over the red, white and blue.

When early fans of the band heard 'What A Waster'/'I Get Along' for the first time they were charmed by the profanity. It was rich in a stream of vulgarity that hadn't been recorded in popular culture outside of the workplace or schoolyard: 'pissed it all up the wall', 'fuck 'em', 'two-bob cunt' and, perhaps best of all, 'divvy' were all employed to delicious effect.

An often underrated British talent is the creative use and delivery of the wrongly named 'bad language'. From the soft profanity of John Gielgud's withering putdown in *Arthur* ('Well, sir, I wouldn't really know, but on the other hand go fuck yourself'), to Derek and Clive's holocaust of swearing, the British are among the greatest employers of bad language. 'What A Waster', with Peter's breathless delivery, is intoxicating. He wonderfully enunciates the profanity that revived ancient curses with the sort of vim and vigour with which Alf Garnet would deliver his 'bloody moos' in *Till Death Us Do Part*; it surpassed even the great example of *Withnail & I*. Its earthy Anglo-Saxon resonates with a power unique in British recording. This wasn't unnecessary, perfunctory, indulgent or gratuitous – these were well-rounded, carefully crafted words delivered with aplomb and ravishingly lapped up. It ranks alongside The Sex Pistols on the *Grundy Show*, except that Steve Jones had been goaded into declaring 'what a fucking rotter' out loud after muttering it under his breath. The difference this time was the revelatory joy in its delivery; it was timed and primed for maximum impact – and it worked.

The other A-side, 'I Get Along', became the climax of nearly all The Libertines gigs. It contained a couplet that simultaneously voiced The Libertines' ardent libertarian philosophy and became the

highpoint of audience interaction: 'People tell me I'm wrong [pause] fuck 'em.'

Where 'What A Waster' was chiefly Peter's vision, 'I Get Along' was chiefly Carl's – the pair of them sang lead on each of them respectively. The single showcased them both. The B-side, 'Mayday', which was half sung by both, stuffed ten minutes of aggressive verse ('First you put the tongue in/Then you put the boot in') into sixty seconds.

In retrospect it was the best British debut single since Oasis released 'Supersonic' in 1994, eight years earlier. That's how important it was. Of course, in normal circumstances, that would be an astonishing claim. However, given the paucity of British achievement in the intervening years, it was, in fact, a claim to greatness rather than genius.

The reaction to it was lukewarm. The media as a whole and printed media in particular had grown jaded. Pop columnists in the last two decades have generally been ex-writers from the weekly music press. They rightly treated the 'next big thing', in whatever form, with a marked degree of scepticism bordering on contempt, preferring to take a more ambivalent attitude to new artists.

TONY LINKIN: 'People weren't ready for the single. It was too extreme and the Londonness of it put people off. It was almost too much for people. And then there was the swearing … But then it encapsulated everything about them. It was a statement, they had to go for it.'

The single was released on 3 June, on the same day as the Jubilee celebrations, and the same day they pointedly played the ICA on the Mall opposite Buckingham Palace. They were due to play, supporting the then ascendant 80s Matchbox B-Line Disaster.

During the preposterous spectacle of Brian May playing on the roof of Buckingham Palace and Ozzy Osbourne neutered beyond self-respect, the most important band for a decade were playing across the road.

CARL: 'It was a really exciting day, everyone was buzzing – we felt part of what was going on. There was a real level of shared anticipation for a great British hope.'

Earlier in the day at the other end of the Mall, they were filmed for what was intended to be a documentary; they were hanging out in their red guard's jackets which, thanks to a promotional picture, would become synonymous with the band.

They headed down to the Virgin Megastore on Oxford Street, where Peter and Carl nicked a couple of their singles. This absurd act, including a delighted Peter standing immediately outside the main entrance happily displaying his booty, was caught on camera. It was an act that verged on the surreal: they could get as many copies as they wanted from the record company; anything they stole wouldn't be registered for the chart; it was, in short, in material terms, a pointless act. But it was a gesture that prefigured their relationship with their music on the Internet. The actual value of their music was immense but it should cost nothing. And here they led through example.

Carl laughed at the thought of it: 'Someone explained that it wouldn't chart because it wouldn't get put through the machine that registered sales, but that was lost over my shoulder as I dived out the shop.'

Two days later, The Libertines landed their first *NME* cover. Radio 1's Mark and Lard made it 'Single of the Week' but, needless to say,

the single got almost no radio play and despite efforts to stir up the idea that it had been banned, they weren't in the public consciousness so people didn't notice one way or another.

But what could be more Libertines than a grand gesture that few people were aware of? It cemented their reputation – they were adherents to an old tradition of rock romanticism. They were a band to believe in. TONY LINKIN: 'After the original Cherry Jam gig when people saw them, a load of people thought the *NME* didn't know what it was talking about. In fact, *NME* put a lot of people off the band. It probably put more people off in the media than anywhere else. At the end of the day it's not about the media though, it's about music fans. The band weren't polished but they were amazing. I've seen plenty of bands who were great to begin with but who got no better. The Libertines were brilliant but sloppy and would get better.'

So while the wider media saw The Libertines as a scam driven by a couple of motormouths, fans of new music were divided. The cynical, jaded ones thought it was just Jam-aping, London-centric retroism, while others reading the interview and hearing the single knew that something special was happening. No, they hadn't lit up the Golden Jubilee like the Pistols had ignited the Silver; but times had changed, the attitude towards the royal family had metamorphosed into one of apathy. Banned singles and anti-royalist gestures had become as old-fashioned as the three-day week and rag-and-bone men. But the seeds had been sewn: the double A-side single by an unknown band went in at number 37. Although it wasn't with quite the bang they'd hoped for, The Libertines knew that they were already the most exciting new band in Britain.

THE FIRST ALBUM

'A GOOD PUNCH
UP THE BRACKET NEVER HURT ANYBODY'
Tony Hancock, 'The Fight', *Hancock's Half Hour*

THE FIRST ALBUM

NOW THAT THE BAND HAD BEGUN TO MAKE WAVES, IT WAS ESSENTIAL TO RECORD AN ALBUM AS QUICKLY AS POSSIBLE. UNFORTUNATELY, BERNARD BUTLER WAS UNAVAILABLE TO PRODUCE IT BECAUSE HE WAS WORKING ON A SECOND ALBUM WITH HIS SOMETIME PARTNER MCALMONT. BUT BANNY DIDN'T WANT BERNARD TO PRODUCE THE ENTIRE ALBUM IN ANY CASE, FOR TWO REASONS: SHE WANTED THE BAND'S DEBUT TO SOUND LIVE, AND SHE WAS WORRIED THAT BUTLER'S STYLE COULD SUFFOCATE THE BAND'S CHARM.

Nigel Godrich, who'd worked with Radiohead and would work with Paul McCartney, was pencilled in to do it but he couldn't fit their time frame before getting back to Radiohead. Finding themselves without a producer, Banny and The Libertines despaired until Rough Trade's Jeanette Lee had an idea. As a member of John Lydon's influential post-Sex Pistols group Public Image Limited, it was her face that had adorned the cover of their third album, *Flowers Of Romance*. She suggested an old friend: Mick Jones of The Clash.

Mick Jones believes in the spirit of rock and roll: an almost indefinable thing that's easier to measure in what it isn't than what it is. It isn't processed pop, but then it's not snarling punk idiocy either; it's the spirit that can lift a ramshackle performance to the level of art; equally it's something that unfettered virtuosity can crush. In many ways, Mick is the polar opposite to Bernard Butler. Where Bernard is a perfectionist who wants to get everything right – even the wild abandon of feedback is something that is only dropped in at the right places – Mick would pick a recording with a couple of bum notes over a recording played perfectly because of the spirit, oomph and vim, a sound as live as possible.

So in many ways Mick was the ideal producer for the album; his mindset was one that gave The Libertines room to run through songs, change them, experiment and grow as performers. The downside was that it also gave them carte blanche to muck about.

Comparing The Libertines with The Clash, Jones said: 'They're a London rock 'n' roll group, which obviously appeals to me. They're very good lyrically, too. They do remind me of The Clash a little bit. There are the same elements and the tunes are really good, you can't help but get sucked in.'

Carl, having buried himself in the music of the 1960s, was as unfazed by the new producer as he was by the old.

As Carl, John and Gary sat in the third-floor studio, having just met Mick, there was suddenly an aggravated sound at the door. The door burst open and Peter revved his moped into the room, handlebars adorned with clinking carrier bags.

'Here's the beer,' said Peter. Mick Jones was instantly smitten by this charmer who'd brought his moped up to the third floor and driven in with beer just for effect. CARL: 'It was another time where it's a character [Mick] and I don't know who it is. No one could ever believe that, with both Mick Jones and Bernard Butler. They all became legendary for me afterwards. Mick was very

sincere, he instantly relaxed with me, I was expecting some aggressive punk and it couldn't have been anything more opposite. He rolled up, had a spliff, told a couple of stories and fell asleep for a bit. We played some songs together and went down the pub.'

The band worked in RAK studios in St John's Wood near to Abbey Road to record the album.

What was to become the title track, 'Up The Bracket', was soon captured. The recorded version is musically direct, adhering to Carlos's desire for a full, driving sound while lyrically laden with dense allusions. It's an extraordinarily British song featuring two dark figures on the Vallance Road, Bethnal Green (where the UK's most notorious gangland figures, the Kray twins, were brought up), and the uniquely British hand signal for 'fuck off', known as flicking the Vs and supposedly invented by British bowmen who showed contempt for their adversaries by flicking their 'two cold fingers' – if they were captured, those two fingers would be lopped off.

In the studio, Carl was adamant that the songs should be fast, aggressive and forthright. Given Carlos's tendency to mumble, Peter was surprised by this – 'Talk about a contradiction in terms.'

Their roles were practically equal at this stage in terms of writing and performing, although Peter enjoyed the idea of being Morrissey to Carl's Marr as much as the idea of being Lennon and McCartney. However, their approach was different. Even at this stage Peter was the dreamer, the character more inclined to become bored of the process of recording and want to get on to something totally new. Carlos, meanwhile, wanted to work on the songs to improve them and craft them into shape. John and Gary were still working on getting to be the kind of rhythm section that would drive them forward; providing a solid grounding to allow the other pair to spin and pirouette their way around a tune and around a stage. It was this tension in the way they approached songs that, at the moment anyway, spurred them on, providing them with the means to be greater than the sum of their parts. It was this, rather than anyone's

individual talent, that put them on a par with songwriting duos of the past.

The recording process was going strong and Plan A was working; they'd recorded the fast punky classics. The title track and 'Time For Heroes' were definite future singles. They'd done it. They'd pulled it off.

It was an album that was about Britishness and commented on Britishness. Stuffed with allusions to Hancock, the Krays and peculiar British vernacular, it contained songs that beyond their musical accomplishments provided social commentary and a sharp critique of British culture.

One of their finest songs on the album – and indeed ever – 'The Good Old Days' was a song that captures the very essence of The Libertines. It starts from a simple almost ska-like guitar line and encapsulates their shared romantic dream.

The Libertines had spent so long believing in music and the power of music that they had to have an answer to their years spent dreaming on the breadline. And 'The Good Old Days' provided it. At the other end of the scale, the sentiments that 'There were no good old days' and 'These are the good old days' were powerful expressions of dissatisfaction with the prevailing notion that all great art had already been produced. The irony that they were dabbling, not to say obsessed, with archaic ideas of Albion and Arcadia – and British comedians of the 1950s, 1960s and 1970s – was not lost on them. But that was the point. Rather than being copyists of their heroes, they were inspired by them on this quest for a creative future they called Arcadia.

'The Boy Looked At Johnny' took its title from the book penned by former *NME* journalists and *enfants terribles* Tony Parsons and Julie Burchill. They, in turn, had taken the title from Patti Smith's 'Land', a song from her classic debut, *Horses*. With its 'la, la, la' refrain it was almost Small Faces-like in its jollity, and its most memorable line 'Don't you know who I think I am?'

illustrates Peter's ability to twist a common phrase and give it a new lease of life.

'Horrorshow' was a blazing anthem, whose opening couplet had been written by Francesca. She had meant so much to Peter that there had been a time when he'd dreamt of living a *Jules Et Jim* existence with Francesca as girlfriend and Carl as friend. Francesca threatened to sue – although she had let The Libertines have the lyric. Peter's response in the press was deliberately dismissive. Francesca, who had been through so much with Peter and even bought him a guitar, became merely 'an ex-girlfriend'.

In all, the band recorded some twenty tracks in two weeks. A bunch remain in the vaults; some became 'lost' classics, some were condemned to be underappreciated as B-sides. Bizarrely a song like the fractious 'The Delaney' with its infectious 'Yeah Yeah Yeah/No No No' chorus was rescued from oblivion as fans demanded it was played at every gig. Like the rest of the album, it was

a snapshot of their intense lives living on the edge of society, but then they had an abundance of stories, images and phrases from their own experiences to raid.

Most interesting was the grimly oppressive 'Plan A'. This is the darkest song they ever recorded. Peter sings the bleak lyrics with occasional whispered backing vocals by Carl, whose searing picking drives the song. Produced by Carl, it amounted partly to a howl of disgust at the music industry for ignoring them for so long ('I read every review/No one's got a fucking clue') and partly as a secret confession about their own Plan A, embodied in its pleading motif, 'Carve it into something new'.

After her close association with Oasis, Banny was convinced that the best way to break a band, much better than supporting the hottest band or being associated with classic music stars, was to play as many gigs as possible. In all in 2002 they played about one hundred gigs. She was also convinced that as a band that disliked rehearsals it was the best way to make them tight. They continued on a huge tour playing venues that held no more that a couple of hundred people, driving around Britain in a tour van.

On 27 July they supported The Sex Pistols at Crystal Palace. Dolled up in their red guardsmen's jackets, they gave it their best shot. The Pistols' fans weren't that impressed though.

CARL: 'The crowd started signing "Yellow Submarine", in a very jeering beered-up we-used-to-be-punks sort of fashion, but I think we won them back by taking the tunics off and lobbing them into the crowd and going bare-chested. Pubescent energy and intention, that they didn't expect us to have. Later at the aftershow, I was trying to get some bugle and [John Lydon] said, "I have told your manager I am not your drug dealer and I have spoken to the proprietor and he's on his way round." He seemed to be all right though.'

A few months later they would support another of Peter's heroes: Morrissey. Peter was frantic; Carl was calm. After all, when they'd met each other Carl hadn't even known of The Smiths, although he'd grown to love them since.

CARL: 'It was a very stony serious crowd with stars in their eyes, very cult of Morrissey. When we met him he radiated a presence, like Michael Gambon [British actor of *Singing Detective* fame]. He had a kind of glow. But he was flanked by four security guards and didn't circulate a great deal. He gave us the Morrissey thumbs-up. He said that he thought "Time For Heroes" was a perfect pop song, that's a credit.'

The band then moved to Whitfield studios to mix the album. It was the same studios used by The Clash. ('It was a homecoming for Mick,' said Carl.) It was here that the public first became aware of Peter and Carl's unstable bickering ways when it was reported that, following a bust-up, Peter had gone AWOL and the rest of the band played the H2002 Festival in Scarborough without him. However, it wasn't as serious as it first appeared. The band were happy to enhance their reputation as outsiders, although Carlos was forced to learn all Peter's parts on the way to the gig.

CARL: 'That was just silly. That was just not enough sleep. It was where The Clash had done their mixing so we were on old territory for Mick. One day Mick came in and he'd been to the Victorian toyshop round the corner and he'd bought these paper masks that you put on and he bought a couple of Chinaman ones, we were doing silly voices and kung fu voices and it got a bit much. Somehow Pete managed to connect with my throat – a little unnecessarily – then we ended up bundling over the sofa. Pete disappeared and doesn't appear and we've got a date in Scarborough. So we do it without him and I'm an utter bundle of nerves and probably did quite an appalling job. I jumped him, it was still kind of loving, it wasn't a bar brawl. I think feelings were hurt more than bodies. That's the way with friends: get violent, innit?'

They were due to play the Reading/Leeds Festival on the August bank holiday. The Reading show was disastrous; Carl's amp exploded leaving Pete to carry the show for one song. He obliged with a thrashy version of 'The Ha Ha Wall', a song that was to remain unreleased for almost exactly two years. The show ended with Pete swinging a guitar at Carl and the two of them disappearing off the back of the stage in a scrum that while hugely entertaining looked a little stagey.

They slowly built themselves a reputation as a dynamic, if somewhat unpredictable, live band. Then one day, with Pete and Carl off their heads, their tour bus was pulled over on the motorway by the police. Their tour manager, Kevin O'Dwyer, went to sort out the problem.

CARL: 'We were mullered in the back trying to stash all the things we shouldn't have had. And we were a bit light-fingered – we'd learnt it from previous times – and we lifted Kevin's wallet. To our astonishment we found a police card. In a state of much paranoia we all believed that we were being investigated and spied on by Her Majesty's servants.'

The strung-out band suffered in the van until they were sent on by the police, naturally untouched, but convinced that they were public enemy number one and being driving by the UK's top spymaster.

Once they'd returned to normality and realised that

AS CARL, JOHN AND GARY SAT IN THE THIRD-FLOOR STUDIO, HAVING JUST MET MICK, THERE WAS SUDDENLY AN AGGRAVATED SOUND AT THE DOOR. THE DOOR BURST OPEN AND PETER REVVED HIS MOPED INTO THE ROOM, HANDLEBARS ADORNED WITH CLINKING CARRIER BAGS.

perhaps MI5, CI5 and the massed undercover corps of Great Britain weren't after a guitar band with one single to their name who played to a hundred people a night, they resolved to sack this veteran of twenty years of touring. Then, as a pay-off for having had a part-time policeman, they press-released his sacking, saying it was because he was too strict.

Through the Internet and some favourable media they were building a reputation as elegantly wasted bohemians who always got into scrapes, a reputation that, to be fair, was pretty close to the truth. At this stage, on the whole, The Libertines actually didn't invent anything, it just looked that way. Within a year, any inventions would be to suppress the truth of their debauchery rather than to celebrate it.

Their second single, 'Up The Bracket', was released on 30 September. To promote it they played their most important gig to date: at the 100 Club, a venue on Oxford Street that had started out as a jazz venue before becoming key in 1970s punk.

The gig marked a new stage in libertines.org, as dozens of digital pictures were posted online by people whose cameras would work in the gadget-damaging heat. It would be the Internet that would provide the breakthrough for a gig two days later at Charlie Wright's near Old Street in London. They played with a bunch of bands, including friends the Left Hand. These gigs then and in the future would serve to give their favourite new bands a leg-up; they were forging alliances with any like-minded souls. The gig itself was awful and had to be abandoned within three songs as fans engulfed the stage. But it wasn't the gig that was important, it was the fact

that Peter had advertised it on libertines.org and people had come. The fans on this messageboard were becoming a force in their own right.

'Up The Bracket' bettered 'What A Waster', charting inside the top thirty at twenty-nine; the B-sides of 'Boys In The Band' and 'Skag And Bone Man' built the mythology of dwellers in a bohemian idyll. 'Boys In The Band' with its refrain of 'Girls get them out for the boys in the band' sounded like The Jam soundtracking a late *Carry On* movie in a suitably saucy British seaside-postcard kind of way. Peter would later insist that this predominantly Carl-authored song referred to admirers getting the drinks in. In contrast to its knockabout companion, 'Skag And Bone Man' contained the most overt references to drugs yet. The title was a reference to a dealer of heroin and crack, despite being a pun on *Steptoe And Son*'s vanished rag-and-bone trade. Written in the studio, it contained a hilarious exchange after 61 seconds when it comes to a sudden stop.

PETER: *Oh shit we've fucked it all up.*
CARL: *Eh?*
PETER: *We've fucked it all up. We've missed … we've missed half the song out.*
CONTROL ROOM: *Very nice.*
PETER: *Very ni—*

And the drums crash back in. Even more than the A-side it screamed passion with a dash of fascinating ramshackleness.

After months of relentless touring the album was released on 21 October to mixed reviews. People complained that it wasn't produced well enough or more stingingly that if this was the English Strokes then roll on the real thing.

To celebrate its release they played an in-store at HMV on Oxford Street where Peter graced the stage in make-up and a rather unattractive denim miniskirt.
CARL: 'We were going to do the signing and we weren't allowed to, we were whisked straight out. But then we were throwing Libertines albums out into the audience during the gig.'

The album charted at a rather lowly thirty-five.

CARL: 'We went down the shops and there it was at nine in Our Price in Reading. And we cheered and celebrated and then we found out it was only in that shop. I think we were a bit disappointed with where the album went in. It was great to get the opus out there. It was something very precious to us. It was an epoch-making moment.'

The mixed reviews of the album and the widespread opinion that they were calculating scamsters who would at some point be unveiled as conniving rich kids or products of stage school led to suspicion. Typically, the British press had cried wolf enough times that when the real thing came around it was treated with suspicion or even contempt.

Peter detailed The Libertines' adventures in articulate, funny posts on libertines.org as they toured Europe for the first time. He wrote about being interviewed by French newspaper *Libération*, Carlos's old addiction to David Niven films and his new German flick knife that somewhat inevitably he christened 'Herr Flick' as he brandished it for the tour video camera. They'd even made the cover of German *Rolling Stone* with a picture that both James Endeacott and Jeanette Lee had hated, the picture of them in red guardsmen's uniforms. Once the German cover made it back to Britain, though, everyone wanted the picture.

They were having a glorious time ('Carlos cracks me up so much I couldn't stop laughing last night, I had to leave,' he writes of an interview with *Libération*). He revelled in the comedy set-up that Peter and Carl had perfected, combining wit and a wide range of accents, particularly Noo Yoik and Belfast.

The *NME* wanted them in the Christmas issue and Roger was dispatched to capture them in Europe looking suitably Christmassy. The Libertines considered this and decided that the most Christmassy image they could think of was frolicking in the sea in Spain.

However, back home in Blighty there wasn't much call for high-jinks. Despite the promising start to the year and hundreds of gigs, sales of the album continued to be sluggish. Banny had ensured that they played a huge amount of gigs and supported crucial people, but for many in the twenty-first century the debut album sounded a little too live in comparison to the magnificent filthy sounds of

hip hop or even the speedy metallic shimmer of The Strokes. Mick Jones had done exactly what was expected of him and produced a record that sounded timeless, but at that juncture for the general public it sounded a little too out of time. The Libertines had to be content with the fact that they weren't appreciated.

They were billed to play supporting The Vines at the London Astoria in February as part of the annual showcase of bands around the *NME* Awards. Although they were happy with the show, the omens were terrible. Their third show had been supporting The Vines and a year later they were still doing that. They were in ever greater danger of becoming inextricably viewed as the support band for everyone's favourite new band.

They had a number of fanatical fans who could see how good they were but the British public had grown suspicious of hype, and they were still dogged with a reputation for unpredictable shows that could descend into a messy tumult. It wasn't a crisis just yet, but with news of their *NME* champion James Oldham departing to form a record label, the problems were mounting.

They had time to round off 2002 with a gig on 18 December at the Rhythm Factory in Whitechapel. It was a mess. The band were out of tune, drunk to the point where they couldn't stand and managed about four songs before they stumbled offstage. I left the gig with a massive smile on my face and walked straight into a plastic chair containing the moribund figure of the band's press officer, Tony Linkin. He had his head in his hands. He knew what the band hadn't grasped, that they had to get better fast. There were already whispers in the *NME* office that perhaps this band weren't up to their original potential and would make *NME* look stupid.

As it turns out, they had to get better faster than even he had imagined. The Vines cancelled their headline slot at the *NME* Awards shows after, ironically, an onstage punch-up.

So a band with the greatest potential to be the worst band on a stage at any given show were given the opportunity to headline a massive London event. Marvellous. Really, no, that's great. Really marvellous. 2003 was destined to be a wonderful year. A really wonderful year.

THE WHOLE WORLD IS OUR PLAYGROUND

*'ELECTRONIC AIDS, PARTICULARLY
DOMESTIC COMPUTERS, WILL HELP THE INNER MIGRATION,
THE OPTING OUT OF REALITY. REALITY IS
NO LONGER GOING TO BE THE STUFF OUT THERE,
BUT THE STUFF INSIDE YOUR HEAD'*

J. G. Ballard

THE WHOLE WORLD IS OUR PLAYGROUND

NOT EVEN THE FAITHFUL WERE SURE ABOUT THIS. THEY WEREN'T SURE IF
THEY COULD PULL IT OFF. THE LIBERTINES' PLACE AS SECOND ON THE BILL HAD
BEEN APPROPRIATE, PERFECT EVEN. AFTER THE SUSPICIONS THAT HAD BEEN RAISED
THE PREVIOUS JUNE WHERE THEY'D LEAPFROGGED THE USUAL PROCEDURE TO
GET A *NME* FRONT COVER, THEY'D GIGGED, RELEASED A GREAT ALBUM AND,
ESSENTIALLY, EARNED THAT SUPPORT SLOT. THE CRITICS AND PUNDITS WHO
BELIEVED THAT BANDS SHOULD PAY THEIR DUES AND THAT ANY BAND THAT
IS LAUDED MUST HAVE SOMETHING SUSPECT ABOUT THEM WERE HAPPY TO SEE
THE NATURAL ORDER OF THINGS PREVAIL.

The fans kept hold of their tickets but they weren't so sure. Unknown to their fans, this gig could quite easily destroy The Libertines. They'd earned themselves plenty of enemies in the broader press – who, despite writing about a media that had traditionally thrived on rebellion and outsiders, were suspicious of upstarts, as no one likes to look stupid when it's revealed the emperor has no clothes.

So as the critics in the larger world circled, within the *NME* itself it was clear that this was the make-or-break point. *NME* has a reputation of building bands up and knocking them down, but in reality the *NME* will support a band they see potential in and then if the band fails to achieve that potential by not writing the required classic album or blanding out their music for commercial success then the

FANS FROM ALL OVER THE GLOBE
LOOKED ON GREEDILY, GOBBLING
UP SCRAPS FROM THE TABLE
VIA THE MESSAGEBOARDS AND
DIGITAL PHOTOS.

backlash is quite often merciless.

So if The Libertines messed this up, they could kiss goodbye to any support from *NME* and the review would be beyond merciless.

Peter was mortified; he was feeling the pressure terribly. He begged Rough Trade supremo Jeanette Lee to cancel the gig, citing illness rather than nerves. He was a wreck, he was shaking and looked pale. Jeanette faltered but knew it was for the best for them to go on. CARL: 'It's a bit fear of flying; it's out of your hands, you have to do well. I always find we're at our best under duress. We knew what we were getting ourselves into and we knew that people were happy just to scrunch us up and shove us on the fire.'

The gig, filmed by MTV UK, was a blinder. They roared through their songs, with Peter and Carl sharing the mics, the chemistry between them was particularly powerful. The other two pirouetted and fought for millimetres of space between. Between the songs Pete, Carl and John faced Gary and would suddenly turn as the song exploded into life. They were the kings of the world. The soundman Nick the Hat jollied up proceedings by interspersing the songs with sounds of insane laughter.

Even the normally sober *Guardian* were ecstatic with Betty Clarke stating: 'rarely has literacy looked so cool'. She captured possibly the very essence of the band. GARY: 'To me that's one of the memorable shows. It was one of the few shows where I started the gig playing really really hard and played that way all through the show and I didn't feel a thing it just felt so easy. It was a combination of all of us. The connection between us was so tight. Musically and non-musically it just felt so right for us to be on the stage together: Peter, Carl, John and I.'

A smiling, relieved Peter, a world apart from the sickly Typhoid Mary who'd tried to cancel the gig, was chatty and entertaining. He sought out Jeanette Lee and said simply: 'Thanks, you were right.'

Somehow, through hard work possibly or through sheer fluke, they'd nailed it. It was beginning to dawn on the wider media that perhaps The Libertines weren't just mouthy self-mythologisers. Seized with a new-found determination, they set about changing music.

But first, the day after this key gig, there was the *NME* Awards. Strangely Peter turned up early; even then he was not renowned for his punctuality. He wandered around the huge room of the Hammersmith Palais, tables carefully laid: white tablecloths, wine and starters. He nonchalantly wondered from plate to plate picking a little off each in a vacant way. Which, if memory serves, was mozzarella and tomato and breadsticks. He then swayed over to some other tables and picked bits from those as well.

The Libertines were crowned Best New Band, beating The Coral, The Vines, Black Rebel Motorcycle Club, The Datsuns and The Music. Going onstage, Peter let off a banger, waking the music business who tut-tutted at these childish antics.

But the band didn't believe that they'd walk it. CARL: 'I do wonder if the *NME* would have revoked that award if we hadn't pulled a blinder the previous day.'

Later Peter, clearly out of it, was mumbling to party-goers that he'd been bitten in a phone box for no reason: he displayed the plaster on his face as evidence and mumbled that he didn't know why it happened. Carl was on hand to shoo off unrequired and unwanted attention in an effortlessly polite manner.

With this success they went on tour to Scandinavia and then a short tour of the UK, culminating in a gig in Nottingham at the Rescue Rooms. Two days after Nottingham they were due in Hamburg to begin a European tour designed to cement their reputation. It wasn't to be.
GARY: 'There were times of feelings of brotherly love. With any sibling love there's got to be rivalry. Then we went through a bad patch on tour in England. We got on the tour bus and I went to bed. I wake up in the morning and all I can see is this brick wall and I think, Wow! We're in Germany already. We're in King's Cross. Peter got ticked off with Banny and ran off and left us. And we waited around for Peter all morning. We went looking for him and in the end we couldn't find him. We had to do this cock and bull story that Carlos had flu or else the venue would have sued us. We got a doctor to write a fake note, got it covered. All because of Pete and

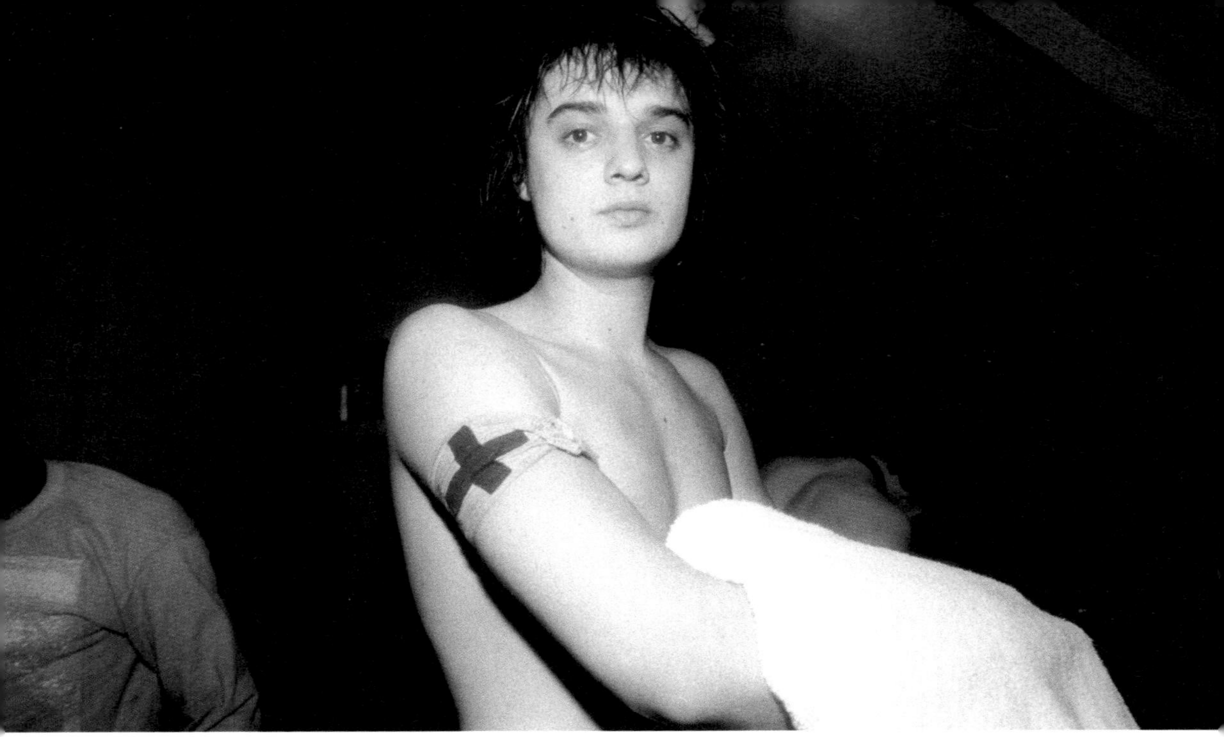
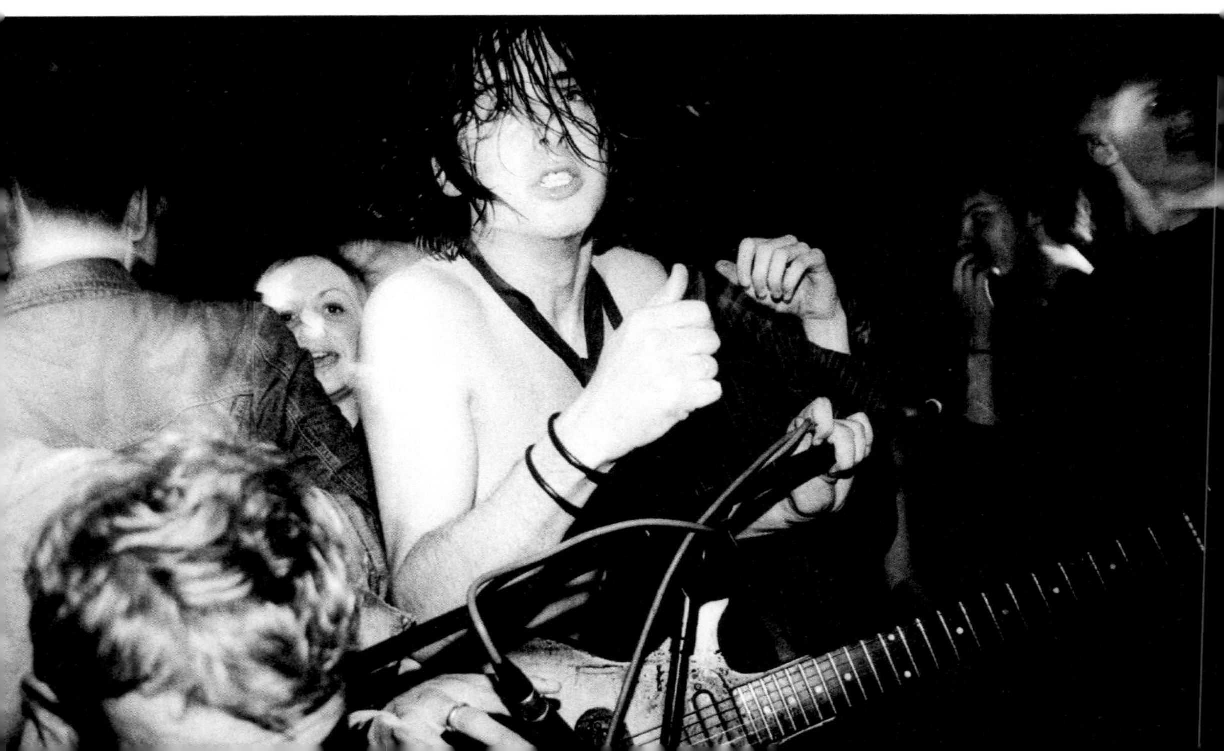

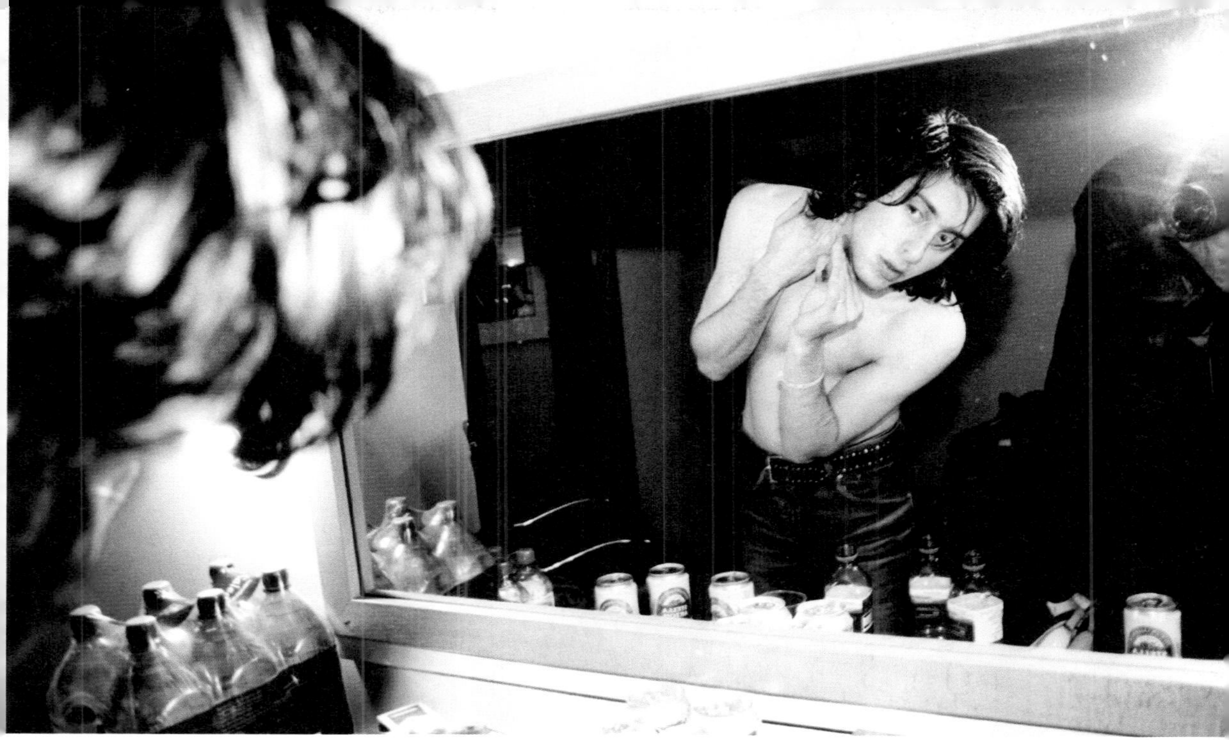

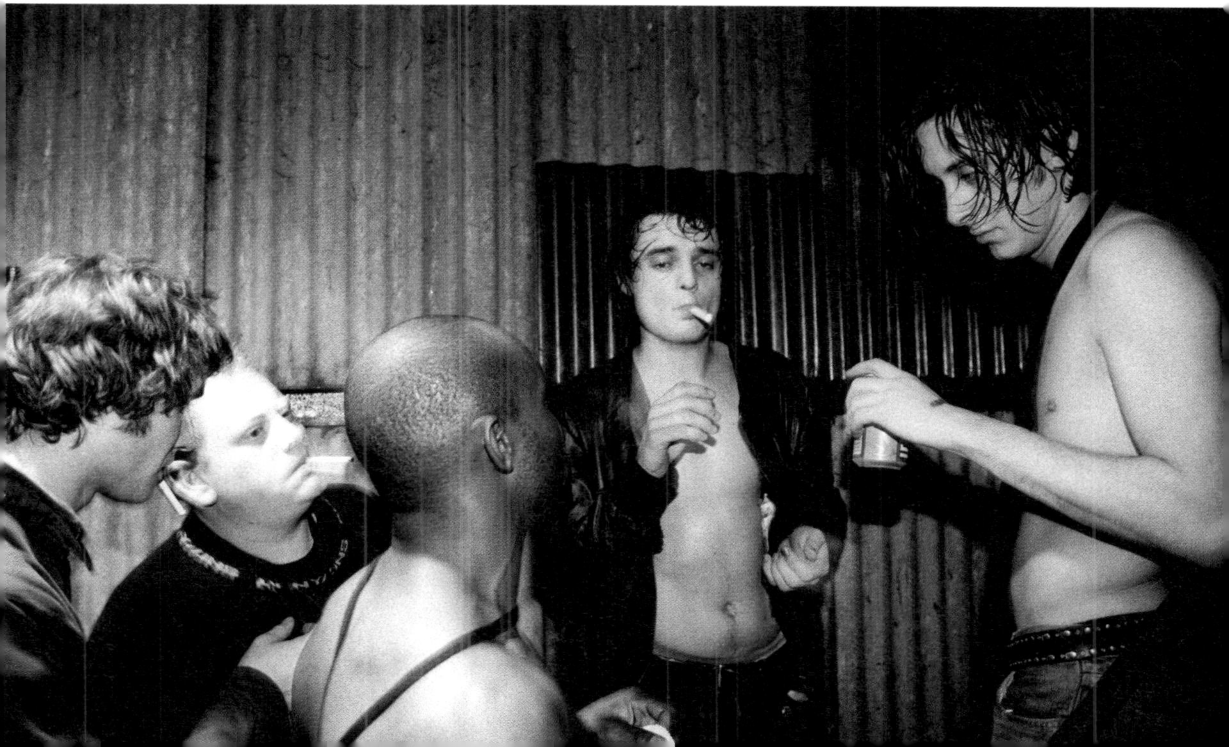

his churlish actions.'

So with a huge tour of the continent on ice, the band agreed to perform a tiny gig at the Albion Rooms, as a kind of farewell to Carlos, who was moving out. On 20 March, Peter posted the invitation on libertines.org, that would, in under fifty words, change the way that people and bands perceived the Internet.

Peter and Carl were in their element, laughing, joking and playing. For this evening it seemed as though the *Albion* had dropped anchor in Arcadia itself. Sure, Arcadia was a little threadbare and dog-eared but it was perfection: a place of song and poetry and, during 'Begging', the police.

'Whose place is it?' said the policeman who mounted the stairs.

Peter and Carl both looked like twinkle-eyed cherubs caught with their hands in the sweet jar and pointed at each other. The policeman frowned. Then they pointed at Roger. The policeman, dumbfounded and not a little circumspect at these shenanigans, said, 'Would someone like to come and speak to me who is responsible?'

With the police still well within earshot they decided to belt out The Clash's 'Guns Of Brixton'.

And as people began to file out, John sang 'Bucket Shop' with a voice and demeanour equal parts angelic.

As everyone was cleared out, photos were taken and everyone was guaranteed a kiss from Peter and Carl as they left. Peter said: 'Everything's for sale, buy it all.'

PETER AND CARL WERE IN THEIR ELEMENT, LAUGHING, JOKING AND PLAYING. FOR THIS EVENING IT SEEMED AS THOUGH THE *ALBION* HAD DROPPED ANCHOR IN ARCADIA ITSELF.

But even on first impressions people knew he was joking.

Just a matter of weeks after the Astoria gig established them as a band that really did have a future, this gig changed everything again. At a stroke they'd demolished the barrier between fan and artist. Previously this had been the realm of street theatre and performance art; the cast-iron rules of bands and gigs had been broken. The naysayers on libertines.org who'd derided those foolish enough to go on a wild-goose chase were jealous and now everyone who had anything to do with libertines.org was going to make sure they wouldn't miss another one. So when another spontaneous gig was advertised on the Web, what had been an easy-going fanbase was transformed into one desperate not to miss out again. CARL: 'You could either worry about it all night and be a queen or throw yourself into it, which is what I did. I was right behind the concept of it. I created myself a whole school of thought called Intimacy and Mechanisation. It was important to break down the barrier between the two and make everything one.

'Mechanisation is ultimately a flawed system because you can't have an artist–audience flow, it needs to be cyclical and it's chiefly one way. We broke it down again and again afterwards in the way we involved fans and were happy to pull out guitars at a moment's notice, on steps or walking through town. Just playing anywhere and any when, just for the love of playing. And letting everyone be part of it – letting people know it was special for people.

'I wanted to avoid that staleness of getting onstage, playing and leaving. It stops you being the person you were, it was something I wanted to stop. The only thing that stopped me from doing it more often was fear of

people not enjoying or accepting what I do, being made a fool of.'

The Libertines had enjoyed it as well; they got a taste for it. It was clear they were on a roll – and the best was yet to come. They announced tiny gigs at the Buffalo Bar in north London followed a day later by the Barfly.

Peter joined Carl and John onstage at the Buffalo Bar. Gary meanwhile took enormous pleasure in heckling his own band. 'Come on, play something, you fucking bastards,' he yelled before laughing himself stupid at his own joke.

Peter and Carl climbed atop stools like impish rock versions of Des O'Connor. John played a natty acoustic bass and Gary was playing bongos that really made his hands hurt. It was a different side to them. For two and a half hours they played everything they knew, some songs twice, plus a host of covers. They played a bunch of old songs including 'Music When The Lights Go Out' from the 'Legs 11' demo.
CARL: 'We did a two-hour set and broke out all the oldies and people loved it. There was a few of the hardcore who'd done their research on the Internet and knew the old songs; everyone was into it.'

They also covered Chas & Dave, The Coral's 'Dreaming Of You' (which Peter would later claim he had written). They had a passionate but ill-conceived attempt at Michael Jackson's 'Billie Jean' that rapidly collapsed. And John's crystal-clear voice was showcased on 'Sunshine Superman' by Donovan.

Then, unbidden, Peter said: 'Who wants to see Carlos dance?' There was naturally a cheer and Carl nearly knocked people flying as he went to the middle of the floor. It was cabaret time and 'Dream A Little Dream Of Me' was dusted down, his party piece from days gone by. This version owed more to Stretch Armstrong than Louis Armstrong as he cavorted ballet-like.

Peter gently teased Carl about his song, the one that ended most sets, changing one couplet in 'Plan A' to 'Sing a stupid song/Like I Get Along'. But all was still well in The Libertines.

The Strokes producer, Gordon Raphael, was in the audience hugging himself, convinced of their greatness. 'I was crying to produce their first single,' he says. 'It's like meeting The Beatles when they were eighteen years old.'

Peter and Carl planned to play all night and take everyone for breakfast nearby. At 1.15 am after three hours, just as they were about to play 'Death On The Stairs' for the third time, the visibly narked venue staff pulled the plug on the gig. If they hadn't, the chances are they'd still be playing now.

They decided to exercise their new addiction as frequently as possible. They played two gigs at the Camden Barfly at little notice for their old friends and girlfriend the Queens Of Noize, Tabitha and Mairead, who they'd known since the 1990s – Peter had dated Tabitha. In contrast to the quiet musicianly nature of the previous two outings, these gigs were packed and sweaty, passionate but brilliant. There was lots of fun had by everyone and good-natured joshing. Peter sang, 'Drummer man, can't you drum any faster?' So Carl got behind drums as Gary did a cockney knees-up all braces and a big smile before doing a hilarious hand jive like an extra from *Grease*. The second gig ended with a stage invasion.

The Albion Rooms gig was no one-off. The Web and word of mouth spread the gigs so that every fan knew about them. Fans at work, college and school would work with libertines.org in the background all day on the off chance that a gig would be announced. There was a mixture of exhilaration and dread: exhilaration at the anticipation of a new tiny gig or recent burning memories and dread at the thought of missing the announcement of one. Fans from all over the globe looked on greedily, gobbling up scraps from the table via the messageboards and digital photos; they would race home and upload them for everyone to see as soon as possible. Everyone, that is, in the burgeoning club.

The Libertines had done something fresh. These were great days, but they couldn't last for ever. Some time they would just get too big to do these gigs, as their triumphant Astoria gig would demonstrate. One day, they wouldn't be playing the back room of a pub. One day they'd only be able to squeeze fans into Brixton Academy and bigger. One day they wouldn't be able to say hi to fans they'd met a few days before.

Or, at least, that was what was supposed to happen.

*

Just before a trip to Japan and America, they played another at a pub in Islington, called Lark In The Park. The desire of fans – who were travelling from all over the country – for gigs at this point had got so mad that there was the surreal image of them queuing outside a pub in broad daylight despite the fact the pub had its usual selection of old geezers propping up the bar talking about Arsenal. Then at around five o'clock an *Evening Standard* van driven by Chev, a friend of Peter's who was gregarious and funny and utterly loyal – he would later have the unedifying role of Peter and Carl's go-between – turned up with the band's equipment inside and Peter.

Before the gig, The Libertines got together with Banny to run over the schedule for the Japanese and American trips. It was quite a tight schedule but they'd built in time for sightseeing.

As they were covering the finer points of the tour, Gary's mobile rang; it was his brother. He broke the news that his cousin had died suddenly from kidney failure.

'I was really really bothered about that. So I took a few moments and sat down and Banny said, "Are you sure you want to do the show?" and I said, yeah, I'll do the show. I need something to take my mind off it.'

Their support were their friends the Left Hand, who overstayed their welcome, convinced that the crowd loved them. In a stroke of farce, Peter had to more or less drag his friends off the stage. Scarborough Steve jumped onstage and attempted to wrestle the microphone to sing lead on 'Lust Of The Libertines'. He was about to start singing along to 'Boys In The Band' as an unasked-for encore, but Carl decided he had had his glory time and thumped him with his guitar. Someone shouted out that Peter was crap, but that just added to the enjoyable knockabout atmosphere of high-jinks and hilarity. GARY: 'Some guy called Pete crap during the show so at the end I ended up consoling Pete by the bar because somebody called him crap. I'd just had a death in the family, a close family member had died and I was consoling Pete. So we went to Japan; I missed out on his funeral.'

Chapter 7

HORRORSHOW

'IT WAS THE BEST OF TIMES, IT WAS THE WORST OF TIMES'
Charles Dickens, *A Tale of Two Cities*

HORRORSHOW

IT WAS THE BAND'S FIRST FULL TOUR OF JAPAN; PREVIOUSLY THEY'D FLOWN IN FOR TWO FESTIVAL DATES. IT'S AN EXPERIENCE THAT BRITISH BANDS ALWAYS LOVE; LIKE THE FIRST VISIT TO AMERICA, IT'S ALWAYS A WATERSHED. AND IT WAS A WATERSHED OF SORTS FOR THE LIBERTINES.

Since the previous October, Peter's prodigious drugs intake had mushroomed. He was falling heavily for harder, class-A drugs like heroin and crack, initially entranced by the romanticism of the former, which he considered to be linked to a great literary tradition, and by the latter to the fact that it was of the street. He also considered them to be a mental challenge. He rated his intelligence and strength of mind above anything else, except what he and Carl could achieve together. As someone who'd lived inside his head for his whole life, he was sure that his mind's resilience would see off any chemical threat, that addiction was for the weak-willed. Speed was a thing of the past for both of them and Carlos's personal experience drove him away from heroin and crack; he preferred the rush of cocaine.

One night in room 2322 of the Tokyo Hilton, Peter had a disturbing dream which he detailed in the latest Book Of Albion; a collision of his present life and past featuring gigs, the Albion Rooms, fighting fans, coin slots spitting out money, photos and set lists. The description is disinterested, like a scientist recording the probing of a particularly vexing microbe. He describes a gnawing pain within him that won't go away despite 'japplibertines giving me medicine', but most ominous of all is the simple matter-of-fact sentence: 'Crack

featured, of course, was it Holland?'

Opposite a page with a glued-down pink ticket that had heralded their arrival, there is an equally dispassionate contemplation of the forthcoming American tour. He was unsure whether he would actually go, and a note of weariness begins to creep in.

He explored his inner feelings, unsure initially if he agreed to do Japan just for the money. But Peter settled on the idea that it was a good farewell to Guy and John, despite the intense schedule that already included America and a host of festivals. Finally, he settled on going to America and imagines reading in cafes and coffee bars. With an almost palpable shrug, he concludes that it may as well be with the band.

He had been growing distant since the previous October. Banny had been sacked and rehired several times, each time it was on impulse for something as simple as not giving him money that would inevitably – as Peter conceded – go towards his addictions. Tensions within the group were showing, cracks that would only

... SO THEY RESOLVED TO GET THE WORD 'LIBERTINE' TATTOOED ON THEIR ARMS IN CARL'S SPIDERY HANDWRITING.

get wider under the demands of a touring schedule. With the hard drugs and travel, Peter was suffering and lashing out at his band mates. Peter thought he knew what was wrong with himself and the band at that moment. It wasn't the drugs, it wasn't the increasingly fractious relationship with Banny, it wasn't the heavy touring schedule, it was John and Gary. They weren't right. He and Carl would make an acoustic album together.

Peter was feeling more and more that the music machine was a compromise, and that he needed some sort of exit or resolution. The Books Of Albion weren't the only forum for recording observations; his relationship with the Internet was blossoming. While on tour in Japan he used it increasingly, and somewhat paradoxically, as an intimate confidante. In one particular posting he complained of loneliness and paranoia in a Japanese hotel room. It was an outpouring of grief and rage that, read in the stark white and grey tones of libertines.org, was extraordinarily distressing for fans. But come the following day things didn't seem quite so desperate, and the next postings were reflective and even-handed. The joy of the Libertine life was creeping back into them – singing and dancing on the platforms of train stations, relishing the booty (stickers, lollipops, books and scarves) that the fans massed to give them.

Success was invigorating – there was a huge contrast with their previous tour when they played the festival circuit (alongside other westerners such as the 'Stleets' and 'Mollissey', as Peter puts it). Now they were playing hour-long sets to dedicated, devoted fans. A careful reader of the diaries might notice the odd jarring note, though – Peter observes with perhaps a little relish that the name the fans are screaming is 'Peeeeter', and that Carl, as he puts it 'has the hump' about this.

On the whole, though, it seemed as if the demons that Peter was fighting had been quietened down. But the mixture of homesickness and dissatisfaction was still bubbling under the surface, and would come to a head at Penny Lane 24 in Sapporo. He and Carl had had a magnificent couple of nights on the town, but depression, boredom and the pains of withdrawal, as he struggled to get drugs in Japan, were getting worse as they flew to the north island.

The tone was set early on. As Gary tells it, a devil seemed to have got into Peter from the moment they landed.

'The promoter had paid for a girl to be a tour guide and she didn't speak very good English but it was such a beautiful city and we were driving through. Oh god, the cherry blossoms were all out; it was really really pretty. And she sang a traditional Japanese song and she had a high-pitched squeaky voice, really really cute. And Pete decided to Take. The. Piss. He just took the piss non-stop and it was like ugh don't do it, man. Leave it alone, you're making yourself look like a dick. And this girl knew she was getting the shit ripped out of her and she looked so cute and it was like oh god that's evil.'

It wasn't a good omen, and the day would get worse. The sound check was a disaster – Gary had a hangover and both the soundman and Pete took exception to his playing. Peter became incensed with Gary's playing on the riff to his new song 'Do You Know Me?'

They went through their pre-gig ritual of huddling in a foursome and dancing around but the atmosphere was still sour.

'We warm up for the show,' recalls Gary, 'and Peter's jumping around and I'm like he never jumps around what's going on here? We jump around together, have a hug and get ready but he was getting himself up for something. He kept saying, "This is going to be a good one. This is going to be a good one." I was like urrrng. Got onstage. Started with "Horrorshow". We literally got 30 seconds in, Pete's amp came down, Carl's amp came down, John's amp came down, smashed up his guitar on the floor and Peter goes offstage.'

It was a scene of chaos, and even worse it seemed like a personal attack on his band mates. He even tried to set fire to the Union Jack on Carl's amp, although interestingly, in light of the fractious atmosphere between them, he stayed away from Gary's drum kit.

The rest of the band left the stage and Peter performed 'Up The Bracket' a cappella. Before he left the stage Peter tossed his hat into the crowd and addressed them: 'Am I alone? I'm not alone, am I?'

They bellowed, 'No!' And Peter exited.

This was the first time since the Scarborough no-show

the fans in the venue attempted to understand what had happened.

Somehow the roadies managed to get a working amp and guitar together, so Peter and Carl left the bar and returned to the stage with Peter on Carl's shoulders. Gary and John initially refused to return so Carl took a seat behind the drums and they swapped over to do a clutch of songs including 'I Get Along', 'Boys In The Band' and 'Time For Heroes'. By the end all four of the band were onstage, but they kept getting electric shocks from the wrecked equipment.

Gary was particularly furious. 'We came offstage, went to get a shower and I stood up to get something. And Pete comes up to me and says, "Sorry, Gary," and I went, "Why are you sorry?" and he looked at me and he went, "I dunno." And I went, "Well, don't apologise," and walked out. I thought, typical.'

Despite the wreckage Peter had caused, Carl rallied round him, and afterwards the duo stood outside the venue and signed everything for every fan even as the tour manager was trying to get them away. When it was all over, Peter and Carl hit Sapporo for the night of their lives – 'it was like the Marx Brothers crossed with Chaplin' wrote Peter – and they took their frustrations out on poor waiting staff. It seemed as though the band was back to normal, and even Gary, having spoken to Peter, thought things were sorted out, that they were 'cool'.

But Peter wasn't cool. He recorded in the Book Of Albion that he wanted some dulling opiate to allow himself to sleep. And his depression was wearing away on his mind. He felt isolated from humanity; unable to imagine a single person he'd want to talk to.

At this point, what seemed like great news reached Peter in Japan. Wolfman had been missing for some time, and was even rumoured to be dead, but Pete discovered

that the band's rifts had been so visible in public. Carl was furious with Peter, but typically not over the destruction of the equipment and the short set, but over unshared glory.

'You could have come and got me for the stage dive. Promise me you won't do that again or you're on your own.'

'All right,' said Peter. 'I'm on me own.'

'I mean onstage, Peter.'

'Aaaah!'

Peter was over the moon at the chaos and confusion around him and made a display of cutting his chest with a knife as Banny looked on, paralysed. Carl and Peter regrouped in a bar across the road as

he was very much alive, shacked up in a flat in Chelsea and being sponsored by a man called Jake Fior. That flat would be pivotal in The Libertines' future.

Jake was a bookseller with a shop in Exmouth Market, near Filthy McNasty's. A dandyish Svengali in bookseller's threads, floppy of fringe with twinkly eyes and a disarming turn of phrase, Jake has two odd claims to comedy-related fame in his past: in the mid-1980s he played bass in a Bon Jovi-style AOR metal band with *The Office*'s Ricky Gervais called The Savage Hearts, and his acerbic bookshop management style was the model for Dylan Moran's misanthropic drunk Bernard in *Black Books*.

In Japan they had time to see The Coral play a blinding gig and resolved to record a song with them. Peter considered roping them in for the crucial shoop-shoop backing on the new song, 'What Katie Did'. The long flight home with stopovers and a little time off was calming for Peter; the desire to sack John and Gary faded

and he composed a poem that contained a rhapsody to the Flophouse, a place 'where one can buy oblivion'. His anticipation rose as he wrote about the crack he would smoke through a wire mesh on a bottle.

After the band landed, Peter headed straight back to a hotel in Whitechapel where he met Wolfman and some like-minded souls to share a room. The next entry in the Books Of Albion was succinct. He recorded the precise year, date and time that the drugs he craved kicked in.

With Japan out of the way and the band still existing, America was the next port where the *Albion* would drop anchor. They were accompanied on the trip by James Endeacott, concerned that Peter was getting out of control.

Their notoriety had, courtesy of the Internet, already been beamed into the artistic capital of America. Sure, they weren't played on the radio yet but music fans had got hold of their music and read their lyrics and their touchstones and knew that this band were intelligent

and musically brilliant. The Donnie Darko bookish outsiders loved them before they even landed. It was a cerebral reaction as much as it was a genuine outpouring of passion. The concept of Albion and Arcadia had hit a nerve in America and especially in New York which ironically it had taken much longer to find in Britain.

The sense of just controlled violence that had been present at concerts in the UK had, via the Internet, translated a quintessentially English band into the heart of America, and those who knew about it were ready for cathartic rock 'n' roll thrills.

The first gig in America had to be cancelled after Peter's grandmother died. He flew home for the funeral but had to return immediately for their next gig, at the prestigious Coachella Festival in Indio, California. This is a festival that in spirit has modelled itself on the UK's Reading Festival. Its music choice is eclectic, its impressive bands have included The Cure, Oasis, The Pixies, Kraftwerk, Coldplay and Nine Inch Nails, and it is often the place where new talent gains a foothold in the public consciousness. It was an important trip, and one that they felt was symbolic.

CARL: 'I hoped it [America] was going to go a bit further. I'd always had a fascination with America and I'd always been a movie addict. And to go to the place where in everyday life I'd spent so much of my childhood – it was something I desperately wanted. But having wandered London streets for years, I didn't want to go over there a tourist, I wanted to go over there as someone who had a plan and who was going to do something. It was setting foot in a brave new world.'

Peter and Carl had a great time at the festival, hanging out with Johnny Marr and Primal Scream. But their much vaunted headline slot in one of the main tents was set for a disappointment. Groove Armada overran their set, and The Libertines went on at 11.50 p.m., fifty minutes after the curfew.

CARL: 'They pulled it after two songs – pulling the plug and cutting the electric out of the entire tent – it was pitch black. And we played one song without the PA and we were shouting the song at the crowd. The next day, though, I got to meet Tim Burgess of The Charlatans. He is that corner of a foreign field that'll be forever England. If you happen to be in LA, that is.'

They stopped at Seattle for one date before flying to New York. Gary had been there before, but for the others it was their first ever visit. On the surface, the band were ecstatic – everything was going to plan; they'd even managed to secure a live performance on the David Letterman show, the key chat show in the US.

But after the respite from the worst of the madness in LA and Seattle (where they played Crocodile Café), in New York it was off from the start. Roger Sargent had scraped together enough money to go and join them, and when he got there the band was in disarray.

'Wolfman had told Peter that if he wanted to score drugs on the streets of New York he should talk to the homeless, so when the band were supposed to be doing a sound check we turned round and Peter was just walking off into the distance going up to homeless person after homeless person in the Bowery.' And of course he was successful, making contact with a crack dealer, Chris, who became his drug buddy.

Their first New York show was at CBGBs, spiritual home of the American New Wave of the 1970s. The show itself was a little rough around the edges, frequently teetering on the edge of disaster, but there was an edge of excitement there that was totally at odds with the way rock 'n' roll was presented in the US. This wasn't slick or marketed, it felt and looked real.

Between gigs the band had convinced Rough Trade to stump up time for recording a new bunch of songs. It was to be a mixture of works in progress and some old stuff. They were booked into Sorcerer studios on Mercer Street, where Norah Jones had recorded her multi-platinum debut album in October 2000.

At first the sessions went well. It was impromptu so neither Gary nor John made it. Peter and Carl recorded a number of new songs, including an acoustic version of one of their best from their debut, 'The Good Old Days'. On drums was a local tailor and blagger, 'Spiky Phil', part of the social circuit of New York. Aside from a new Peter backing vocal that paraphrased Elvis and The Smiths with a reference to 'his latest flame', it contained a notable ad lib in the middle. On the new version where Peter and Carl sing 'a list of things we said we do tomorrow' Peter whispers, 'Get a tattoo.' It was something they'd thought about before. And so they resolved to get the word 'Libertine' tattooed on their arms in Carl's spidery handwriting. It was to be a bond to illustrate their belief in the band and each other. The execution was of course a little more complicated, since they wanted to do it after a gig, around midnight. It was to become one of those many fruitless searches.

But the next day they managed it – the pair of them were Libertines. It was indelibly inked upon their bodies.

The next gig, at the Bowery Ballroom, was again incredible. The band were on good form, having a great time. There was a line of New York girls in the front row looking adoringly at Peter and Carl. The only low point came when Peter pulled Chris the drug dealer on to sing. Roger recalls: 'He couldn't sing and he was probably the only black man in New York without a sense of rhythm.'

The crowd had no idea what was going on. But Peter knew that this act of randomness, meeting someone, befriending them and getting them onstage, was all part of being a Libertine. He was convinced that Carl would come round, surely.

Damon Albarn had a reserved table on the balcony. He came backstage afterwards to say hello. It was an odd moment, the meeting between the king of old Britpop and the troubadours of the new Albion. Roger witnessed the rather tense exchange.

'I wonder if it was fear on Peter's part. Peter was very kind of aloof, no interest in him at all. Damon walked in and walked over and put his hand out for Peter to shake. For two long moments, Peter didn't even look up. And then he did look up. And you could see he was thinking, Shall I? Shan't I? Shall I? Shan't I? and eventually he went, "'ello, mate," and carried on talking to someone else.'

Damon had advice for them: on how to treat your audience in a way that was tantamount to the old adage

'treat 'em mean and keep 'em keen'. But it wasn't what The Libertines were about. As Carl said: 'But we like our audience.'

Damon sounded like some kind of old army officer, handing out crumbs of truth to the new guard. It was slightly tragic. In one last gesture of comradeship Damon gave Carl his Kangol hat. Carl threw it away.

And this triumphant night was perhaps the last of the glory days in America. The following day there were signs of trouble. Pete refused to get up for the early-morning flight to Philadelphia, hiding in his room and saying, 'I'm not going, I'm not going.'

Gary, hanging on to his professionalism, was exasperated. 'He wanted to spend time with Carl. He just wanted to hang out with Carl, which was fair enough. But we were kind of working. We had a show to do – let's be professional about this, at least for a little while. So we ended up leaving late so Pete and Carl could hang out together.'

Between Pete and Carl – tattooed up and bonded over their new songs – it was again going well. When they finally reached Philadelphia they finished what Peter proclaimed was their new anthem, 'Don't Look Back Into The Sun'. Things were back on course; things were going to go well. But the others, once again, were feeling excluded.

It was just when Gary's exasperation was reaching its limit that he finally had a proper conversation with Pete.

GARY: 'Peter came up to me and said, "What are you doing now? Do you want to hang out?" And as soon as he said it, I knew he had something he wanted to tell me.'

Gary said he was going to get wine and invited Peter along. The pair got back. After a shower Peter got his guitar out and they had a singsong and goofed around.

GARY: 'And then I was just asking him, "Are you happy?" "I don't know." "What do you want to do generally?" "I don't know." "Well you need to take some time for you because right now you seem to be somebody who's at loggerheads with themselves about everything in general." We had a really, really good chat about it and I think even though he had it in his mind I think that's where the whole Babyshambles band ended up coming together. Even though we never told anyone else that we spoke about it. He needed an outlet. He never told anyone else about it.'

But back in New York, even for Carl, Pete was once again taking it too far, basking in his fame and playing host to his vagrant friends.

Peter thought this was the real Libertine

adventure, though. Couldn't Carl and everyone else see? This was real life. This was the stuff of Albion and Arcadia after all, and as the patron saint of Arcadia, William Blake, observed: 'the road of excess leads to the palace of wisdom'. But suddenly it was getting difficult; Peter's new friends were inviting more friends up to his room – he didn't know all these characters. And yeah it was fun but there was an edge. There was a whiff of malevolence merging with the crackle of foil and the aroma of burning heroin. There was a flicker of the possibility of serious violence. And it may have been the drugs but this suddenly seemed bad, really bad. Peter was, finally, scared – what did Blake know?

CARL: 'At one point he came up to my room and he was in tears and I went and kicked some very heavy characters out of his room in the hotel. He'd had enough. I mean, I cacked myself; I think the only thing that saw me through it was my anger and frustration that my dear dear friend

had ended up in the situation with these parasites, y'know. Thankfully with that to guide me I was oblivious to the potential risk with a bunch of very high, very mean people. I just told everyone to leave. They were very reluctant. Eventually I got them all out. Peter was very grateful and quite touched that I'd done it.'

It had all been out of control but now it was fine. Peter was thankful that they'd gone and he calmed down. It'd got out of hand, but now it was going to be fine. Carl would look after him, a few drinks, chat, play the guitar; play the new anthem through again, 'Don't Look Back Into The Sun'. Then Peter retired to bed, grateful. The two of them bonded; they'd stood up to the dark forces and won. Peter slept easily, ready for tomorrow and new adventures.

But of course it wasn't fine. The next day the drug buddies were back, in the studio and frolicking on the roof with a video camera. Carl's boiling point came when he found them singing along to one of his own songs. 'C'mon,' said one of them, 'don't be like that, join in. I'll teach you the words.' It was at this point that he left, seething, and Pete finished off the session alone with a medley of his own and his favourite songs. These sessions contained all of the current works in progress.

So on the one hand they were staking their claim as the cream of the underground, yet the band were riven with problems. New York should have been the time of their lives, and quite often, outwardly, it was. But Roger was getting a

PETER WAS FEELING MORE AND MORE THAT THE MUSIC MACHINE WAS A COMPROMISE, AND THAT HE NEEDED SOME SORT OF EXIT OR RESOLUTION.

different view from his ringside seat. 'It was possibly the most upsetting time to be around the band. It wasn't that anyone had any animosity towards Peter – they were more bemused and felt estranged and cut out of his world. He wasn't doing it deliberately. He just thought that he was carrying on in this spirit of this great adventure. He thought it was romantic that he'd hooked up with this talentless drug-dealer idiot.'

They had one important thing to do, the David Letterman show, and they did it in Libertines style.

John recalls a classic Libertines moment. 'We were in our red jackets waiting for the gig. And an announcement goes out over the tannoy: "Could Marilyn Manson please come down to the stage door." Marilyn Manson – whose real name happens to be Brian – walks past the band's dressing room looking like a fucking monster – he's really tall and is wearing the whole gear and had all these big bouncers around him. As he walked past the dressing room, Pete and Carl were yelling, "Brian, Brian, Brian!"'

Pete and Carl ran after him, but as they got to the elevator the doors closed. So without a thought they ran down to the next floor and pressed the button. The door opened and there was Marilyn Manson and his entourage standing in the elevator. Pete had an acoustic guitar and as the door opened, Pete started playing. They looked him dead in the eye and sang: 'We'll meet again, don't know where, don't know when.' Marilyn Manson – seven foot

tall, white-faced, freakish – looked at them as the elevator doors shut. 'Funny guys,' he said. 'Funny guys.'

The most memorable part of a thoroughly memorable performance, perhaps, was Carlos's changing of the 'fuck 'em' lyric to the far more appropriately American and uncensorable, 'your mother'. There was something uniquely appealing about an English twang enunciating American slang.

CARL: 'That was always one of my silly dreams. I always wanted to play a theatre on Broadway and I did and it was seen by about sixty million people. It was quite something. And it was my song as well (hahaha).'

They'd succeeded in, if not conquering America, which was impossible in a small series of dates, then at least making a substantial beachhead into US consciousness. But the frustrations were getting worse – Gary was furious when Pete's unreliable behaviour screwed

up a planned visit to his American family, and Pete's slide into drug use was getting far far worse.

CARL: 'I went into a room trying to find Pete and found a guy preparing to stick needles into my good friend's arm. I didn't want that, I freaked out and smashed all the syringes and needles against the wall. Y'know, I restrained myself in a very dignified fashion from pulling this guy's throat out, and then I got in a taxi and left. And of course I did the rounds and asked everyone to keep an eye on him, the record company and people I knew out there and even the junkies – I knew they didn't give a shit, I had to try through. And I flew back home. And I left part of me back out there. Things changed then, pretty much irreparably. I may have smashed up a handful of syringes and scared some guy but as soon as I'm out the room it doesn't matter any more. Pete's only in there because he wants to be in there.'

INNOVATION AND THE RAPTURE

'AND THERE STALKS DISCORD DELIGHTED WITH HER TORN MANTLE'
Virgil

INNOVATION
AND THE RAPTURE

BEFORE PETER LEFT NEW YORK HE RESOLVED TO UNDERTAKE ONE LAST MAGNIFICENT GESTURE. HE WOULD GIVE ALL OF THE TRACKS HE AND CARL HAD RECORDED AWAY. HE SET ABOUT CONTACTING A FAN, SAYING HE WAS GOING TO GIVE HER SOME PICTURES FOR HER WEBSITE. THE FAN, HELEN HSU, GOT MUCH MORE THAN SHE BARGAINED FOR.

He arranged to meet her in the lobby of the Chelsea Hotel just after noon. He handed over the three CDs that comprised the sessions.

She eloquently described the booty in a document that accompanied the MP3s she uploaded. 'They are the scrap pages riddled with coffee stains and cookie crumbs, and ash on the carpet. They are unfinished letters to friends and enemies. This music is the stumbling and fumbling towards an idea, like-minded people in a room vibrating to their own frequency. It is musical stream of consciousness and raw inspiration.'

She continued: 'It's not about making and selling records, it's about communication, opening the door to the attic and letting us all in. We are offered a glimpse into their mad world, an invitation to visit a while, a tender postcard from their journeys thus far. In the vast landscape of cynicism and ultracool, they have redeemed hope, housed in Arcadia, trafficked on the Albion. I thank them. And I thank Peter for trusting a stranger, I hope I made good.'

It's fair to say, she did make good. She posted the original discs to Rough Trade the following Monday.

Here were three whole CDs of almost totally new material – a genuine snapshot of a band in creativity. The fans were ecstatic. Few asked who the terrible singer was on 'That Bowery Song', they were too grateful to have three CDs of new material.

There was a twenty-minute unedited track that was

Peter playing his favourite songs. It was a rare moment of calm in New York.

JAMES ENDEACOTT: 'I went into the studio, and Peter hadn't seen me, so I hid and watched him play through all these songs; it was beautiful, he was content, calm, totally lost in the music.'

Somehow, there was barely a hint of the conflict and atmosphere of dread in the recordings; in fact, these were precious. Many fans prefer the versions on what was to become known as the Babyshambles Sessions to the final recorded versions on the second album.

Not content with forging a unique relationship with fans, Peter had subverted the recording process itself, letting the fans have a glimpse below decks at the *Albion*, producing a snapshot of the recording process in mid-curve. This is the kind of thing that, if it's ever revealed at all, is on expensive box sets released decades after a band's demise. It's certainly not done with brand-new songs that hadn't even been heard live.

John and Gary were ambivalent about this release of material, and Peter was pleased that Rough Trade, while

PETER HAD SUBVERTED THE RECORDING PROCESS ITSELF, LETTING THE FANS HAVE A GLIMPSE BELOW DECKS AT THE *ALBION*, PRODUCING A SNAPSHOT OF THE RECORDING PROCESS IN MID-CURVE.

not swinging from the rafters, tolerated it. Carl was more positive, but was irritated that the material had been christened the Babyshambles Sessions, particularly given the confusion that would subsequently arise.

After three weeks in America, Peter was the last Libertine to return to the UK, but his destructive behaviour was to cast a long shadow.

The band perhaps should have taken stock at this point, but their schedule dictated they return to the studio. Once back in London, the band settled in to record 'the new Libertines anthem' 'Don't Look Back Into The Sun' as their new single. This recording would also mark the return of Bernard Butler as producer. Banny and the band believed that after the smash-and-grab energy of the debut album it was time to produce a different sound that would appeal more to the radio. Gary was dismayed, as he'd not been a fan of Bernard's production on 'What A Waster'. Bernard, meanwhile, wanted to get the work done and simply wouldn't take what he saw as antics from Peter. Just as Peter's intake was growing to obscene proportions, drugs were banned from the studio.

Peter wanted Carl to join him in his hedonistic pursuit of pleasure and experimentation. He thought it was the next step in giving your all to the Arcadian dream. CARL: 'It was heartbreaking and he was angry that I wasn't going along. I'd seen with previous experience that it was a very different thing. I'm lucky I had that experience because the attempt to take it onward would have left me six feet under. Peter does have an amazing constitution that I don't have and I'm much more a victim of my demons.'

This pursuit of the dream, however, led Peter to turn up late and dishevelled or not turn up at all. In the midst of all this and to the annoyance of the band he announced another gig, this time at Gunter Grove off King's Road, the Wolfden where Wolfman's new Svengali Jake Fior had housed his new charge.

Gunter Grove had once upon a time been a run-down part of town. In 1978 John Lydon had bought a house at 45 Gunter Grove with the money made from the final Sex Pistols US jaunt. He'd lived there with Public Image

Limited; a band that had imploded as drugs tore them apart. In recent times it had become much more upmarket, attracting the moneyed set of Chelsea.

This would be the venue for the next guerrilla gig. Peter was desperate to play the new songs that had been captured at the sessions in New York. It was announced via libertines.org that the gig would be at 1A Gunter Grove and that attendees would have to crawl through a window. Attendees were told to bring blankets and that the entry fee included a kiss, music and a place to kip.

Peter was insistent that Carl should come along. Given that this was the first time The Libertines were to play the UK in any way since they left for Japan, fans were ready in abundance. They queued up early and packed the place out.

Peter had also been talking to a young band from Hull called The Paddingtons and they were invited down for the occasion. This was typical of Peter's generosity; he would go out of his way to encourage new bands. Many bands were catapulted into a small degree of fame by Peter's endorsement – some it must be said, probably beyond the realm of their abilities.

The Paddingtons had played Scarborough Steve's squat a couple of weeks previously where, essentially, they had been a Libertines covers band, playing 'Time For Heroes' among others. Peter had taken a shine to them and insisted that they play Gunter Grove. As a result they drove down all the way from Hull to play this glorified house party.

Within two years The Paddingtons would feature in *Vogue* and play a gig for the head designer of Christian Dior.

Peter always looked after the bands who were around and made a fuss of them. He always made sure they got attention. Where people have a talent, he gives people an opportunity. For Peter it was never just about The Libertines, it was about the fans.

Two such fans, Kirsty Ridout and Kirsty Want, had followed the band to a number of gigs including the Albion Rooms and Buffalo Bars gigs. They were both passionate about The Libertines and about music in general, and they were always immaculately turned out, being queens of vintage clothing. Kirsty Want with her

long raven hair was mistress of the 1940s and 1950s while Kirsty Ridout preferred Swinging Sixties garb to go with her bob. Together they presented a formidable force. They had become friendly with Peter and he'd convinced them to set up and run babyshambles.com for him. Within six months, at Peter's behest, they would be running The Libertines fan club and the band's official site.

Gary Powell turned up at six o'clock with Banny and chatted to fans outside; he seemed good-natured and happy. In fact it was a last-ditch attempt to persuade Peter to return to the studio and finish off the session. Gary spoke to Peter but couldn't persuade him out of the idea; Gary left, but Peter remained convinced that the rest of the band, or at least Carl, would still come.

Peter entrusted the Kirstys with the Books of Albion that night. And told them to put them all up on babyshambles.com. Not only did he intend to share music with the world, he wanted to share himself. These books contained his personal writings and he did nothing to censor them. It seemed a dangerous thing to do – the music was the start, but now he was giving himself totally to strangers.

Despite the fact that numbers were limited, it was clear that this shabby-looking flat was overflowing. Peter was warm and friendly with everyone, insisting that they daub poetry on the walls. Many were happy to oblige. At around eight o'clock, after phoning Carl and leaving a message, Peter took an acoustic guitar into the garden and played for about half an hour as The Paddingtons' equipment for the band was set up in the back room. The back garden was a weird two-storey affair and there was so little room that it was actually physically impossible to move; many spent their time making do with a glance of the top of Peter's head. Many more didn't even get that. He played songs including covers of The Smiths' 'There Is A Light That Never Goes Out' and The Coral's 'Dreaming Of You'.

Eventually, a severely disappointed Peter realised that Carl was not going to arrive. He proceeded to play the headlining gig with a ramshackle band in the tiny 10 by 8 room.

'Thank you, ladies and gentlemen,' he said before he and Wolfman went through a repertoire of unfamiliar songs, that the pair had written years before, that sounded in debt to soul and krautrock. There was of, course 'Wolfman', Peter's canonisation of his friend. People continued to push themselves through sheer force into the room. Peter was forced to back himself against a wall. A wall where I was stood. I tried to get out of the way, but the sheer numbers meant that I was pinned to the wall by Peter. The heat was oppressive, there was sweat running down the walls. People's digital cameras started to go on the blink as the temperature increased. The stench was like a male changing room with a dab of used netball kit.

The police arrived within forty minutes. Peter, rather than quitting, gave a cheeky shrug and unleashed 'What A Waster'. The whole crowd went mental. The Kirstys were convinced that the police were going to seize the equipment. After all, this wasn't Bethnal Green, Hackney or Whitechapel; this was a rich part of town, and the police weren't ready to let these things go.

A fan shrieked that it was 'one more song before they're in'.

'Fuck 'em! We're all having fun,' retorted Peter. But it was clear that the police really would have the equipment. The band stopped playing and Peter gave Kirsty Want the electric guitar to ensure it would be safe. Clasping it to her chest as people pushed and shoved she looked like a rock 'n' roll pilgrim with the highest religious symbol.

Without a focus, now that Peter had stopped playing, the crush of people eased up a little. But Peter was not defeated so easily. He spotted the acoustic guitar in the next room. 'Pass me the guitar,' he bellowed pointing vigorously, his eyes twinkling with devilment.

And so this massed crowd of people, barely able to stand in the heat, very tenderly passed the guitar over their heads, across the room. The guitar gently floated on a sea of hands and Peter, finally, carefully plucked it from the tips of outstretched fingers.

The police, with volume no longer being an issue now that there was no electric guitar, seemed satisfied and set off. Peter, on a roll, entertained the crowd with a bunch of new songs, which were already familiar to the people who'd downloaded the Babyshambles Sessions: 'Babyshambles', 'Albion', 'What Katie Did', 'The Man Who Would Be King',' Don't Look Back Into The Sun' and 'Last Post On The Bugle'. He asked for requests and even played his and Carl's glorious Razzcocks-era hymn to small-town scruffs, 'Bucket Shop'.

He was satisfied with the night, but stricken that Carl had not arrived. Couldn't Carl see that this was important? More important than normal gigs, these were people who, at the merest stroke of a keyboard, had come running to see them because they cared more than your one-CD-a-year-music-fan. These were people who genuinely realised that music was a way of life, not a lifestyle accessory or advertisement soundtrack. And as for Gary and John, well ... well, they really wouldn't understand at all.

The police returned at about 11.35 p.m. This time no explanation that it was a private party without amplification was going to hold any water. They were determined that this would not carry on in a road like this. They emptied the entire flat of people. Everyone stood around waiting for something to happen.

'The police were quite feisty, there seemed to be a real possibility of being arrested. They cleared the flat completely,' says Kirsty Ridout

I told Peter I was going. He replied, 'Nah, don't go. Don't worry, we'll wait until the police clear off. Carl'll be here soon and then we can get it going again.'

Most people went their own way, to get last tubes and buses, content that they had had the time of their lives.

Some people, however, did go back once the police had gone. A bunch of friends and fans snuck back in after the police cleared off. And the fans who remained had a truly magical night; they chatted through the night with Peter, forging new friendships. It was a fantasy come true – here was the source of their adoration sharing a flat for one night with them. And the interaction was on equal terms; it wasn't a rock star deigning to entertain some fans, it was inspirational. They listened to music, people wrote on walls, all their best literary quotes and songs. Among the people who stayed were Sophie Thunders, a talented, pretty teenage artist, and Dean Fragile, a smart but idiosyncratic music

fan with a habit of wearing pyjama bottoms underneath holey jeans – two fans on the cusp of turning twenty who would later prove to be key to the Libertines saga.

Early in the morning with the first rays of the sun sneaking into this basement flat, Peter played guitar and Wolfman recited his poetry. In one last moment of bonding, Peter stated that everyone would have 'Libertine' tattoos to celebrate and said they should meet in town in the King's Head in Soho that afternoon to get them. No one actually believed that he would really turn up. Why would he? A genuine musician with top-twenty hits? Not a chance.

But he did turn up. Five people got tattoos, including three who had 'Libertine' tattooed on them, two girls on their feet and one on her arm. Both Dean and Sophie agreed between themselves that they didn't want a tattoo like everyone else. After all, there was a possibility that either Peter would gift other people with the tattoo or word would get out and there would be copycat tattoos by fans across the Web. It was as if the pair of them could appreciate the important role they were to have and refused to be branded as part of an anonymous group. Libertines, yes, but not part of a group. So they had tattoos, but they had their own designs.

Peter told the tattooist that Banny would come back and pay for them. Needless to say, Banny didn't know anything about it and the tattooist never got paid. So a handful of people had Peter's handwriting forever inked on their bodies. For free.

Something significant changed after the Gunter Grove gig. Although other gigs would be important, this was perhaps the turning point for Peter and the band. This was the gig where the line between fan and artist wasn't just crossed, it was obliterated for good. Where previously Peter had sought solace in the band or in friends like Wolfman, Gunter Grove had opened up a new world of possibilities for him.

The Internet was no longer an indefinable mass of copper wires and fibre optics. It had become a real medium. But rather than a broadcast medium, it gave him support and encouraged him to go his own way. The support structure of the band, Banny, James

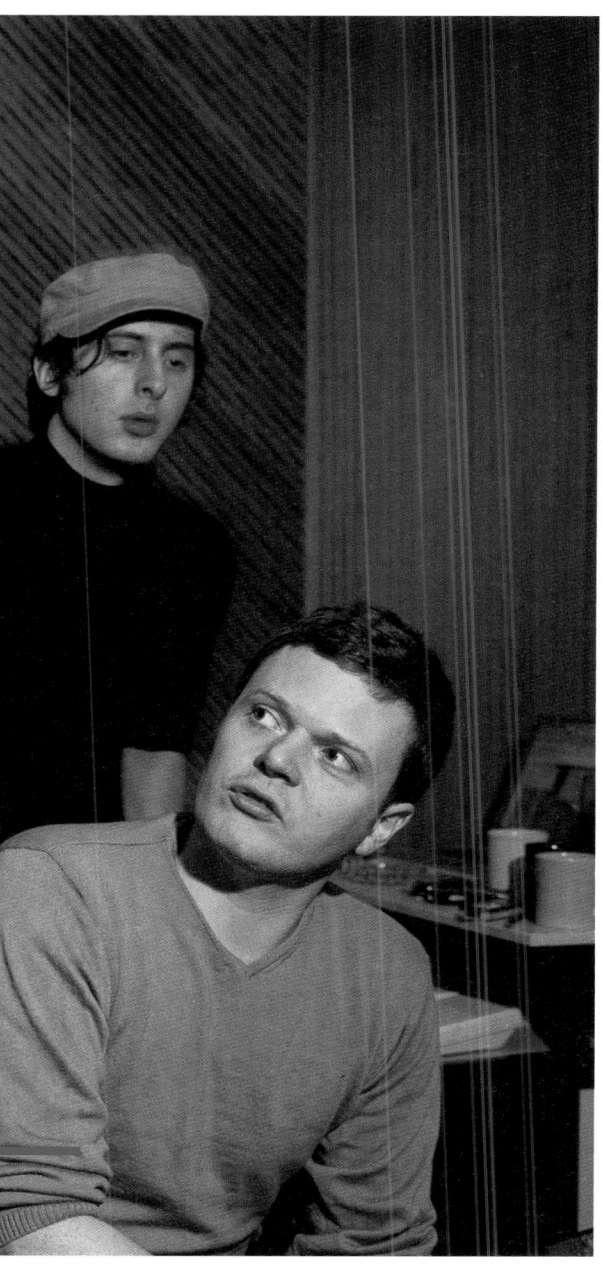

Endeacott, Tony Linkin – his friends who'd made it happen – suddenly weren't quite as important as before.

Peter had been quick to grasp the potential of the Internet – that all went back to the Charlie Wright's gig announced online – but what had been a dalliance and means of communication was now bolstering him and his version of the Arcadian dream. Best of all, perhaps, was how uncritical this new medium was. Unlike Gary and John, friends and the media, who always had the potential to disagree or upset Peter, the people who came to the gig were uncritical observers who wanted to be entertained and be close to their hero.

They didn't come with preconceptions or prejudice, or rather they did, but the ideas of what Peter was were all positive. Part bohemian poet, part rock star: Mick Jagger in *Performance* perhaps. He was a mixture of Morrissey and Joe Strummer, who was accessible – who had time for you.

There would come a time when the downside to all this became apparent: that people who had conversed with Peter on the Internet, or met him in person, believed that they had a stake in him, that they had an insight to offer that was important and should be heard. But that was months away. Months away.

Of course, the crucial thing about the Gunter Grove gig was what had gone on behind the scenes. On the surface this was a happy gig full of fans who wanted to get close to the source of music and poetry. Carl hadn't shown up, but so what? Carl would turn up next time without doubt. Carl would be there, no worries. At least, that's what Peter thought.

Peter had been due in the studio to record 'Don't Look Back Into The Sun' with the band – not to mention the cover of The Smiths' 'Jeane', B-side to their debut single – and instead he'd absconded to do a gig.

While within the band it was further evidence of Peter's deteriorating sense of priorities and his keenness to put the band second in favour of becoming a kind of 21st-century Internet minstrel – have guitar and Internet connection, will travel – across the net and in the media he was portrayed as an egalitarian troubadour, always on hand to do a quick version of 'Up The Bracket' or play you his latest acoustic sketch months before the radio, magazines or newspapers even knew it existed.

In reality, of course, gigs like these were feeding his addictions. And by the time of the next major gig, on a rooftop in Whitechapel, even the more naive members of the audience could feel that something was wrong.

The night of this gig was also Carl's twenty-fifth birthday celebrations. He had planned to go to a karaoke bar in Soho with friends and family and have a good old knees-up. He was keen to have a good time on what was also the night before they were due to hit Europe on a tour. This was going to be a tough tour, as it was comprised of rescheduled dates following Carl's feigned illness to avoid the last one after the trouble with Peter. CARL: 'I remember not getting on with Pete and feeling he didn't care about me. I was with a lot of people who actually turned up for my birthday do. And had put it on for me and it was all a surprise and it was all worked out – even Bernard [Butler] was there.'

In the meantime the gig in Whitechapel was arranged with a playfulness that reflected the heart and soul of The Libertines. Fans were told to assemble at a specific address at a specific time. Then, and only then, would they be led to a top-secret location, somewhere on foot, somewhere in Whitechapel.

And so everyone met. It was glorious. And after toing and froing around Whitechapel taking careful note to appear laissez-faire, while carefully keeping the trailing group of people in sight, it led to an artist's studio on a roof in Whitechapel. It was a perfect setting. Peter had successfully combined The Beatles' Magical Mystery Tour with their triumphant rooftop appearance. But he'd taken it one step further by making it democratic: if you knew the music and could be bothered to be there you'd have a place.

He circumscribed the music world of guest lists and who knows who and who's important that even The Beatles had had to adhere to, replacing it with a democracy of music. What was perhaps ominous was that, of course, when The Beatles played on the rooftop of the Apple building they never played live again. In fact, they bust apart soon afterwards.

But why would there be anything to bother about? Carlos would be there. The night itself was beautiful. You could see London laid out: a maze of side streets feeding into the main-road tributaries; it was a place where even neon looked beautiful and the gherkin building and Canary Wharf looked like totems of power, emblems of success towering above London. But it was as if the true character of London could be spied at last; the symbols of the very rich and the very poor had equal prominence. The entire tapestry of London and the way it tied together was there. It was revealing and beautiful – everything that fed into The Libertines could be spied on that rooftop and all of it from that height was liberally infused with glamour. The seediest side street became a Dickensian alleyway, the tower blocks probably had Harold and Albert Steptoe – rehoused by the council – lamenting the loss of their horse, Hercules, and the mighty office blocks were where Hancock's Rebel was plotting his escape to Peter 'n' Carl's adored Paris.

Peter had learnt his lesson since Gunter Grove – this gig would not start until Carl showed. He knew that Carl's birthday do would be difficult to escape but nonetheless he was convinced that he would make it. He had promised, after all. And Carlos made good on his promises.

And so everyone waited. Time slipped by at an unprecedentedly slow rate. Eventually, the remarkable view became banal.

In the karaoke bar, Carl was having a great birthday. The single was pretty much done, and sure there'd been some arguments recently, Peter was Peter after all, but this single was sounding brilliant; if only Peter wouldn't fuck off to do shows rather than record it. A simple shift of priorities would do it. Bilo and Biggles would nevertheless win out. They would show everyone what they were capable of. Tomorrow was the grand tour and tonight was drinks here at the karaoke bar, then over to Whitechapel for a bit of a singsong and then on to Death Disco, which they'd immortalised in 'Don't Look Back Into The Sun', for drinks, dancing to Alan McGee's idiosyncratic DJing and then who knows what?

Carl glanced at his watch. It was time to go. He was having such a great time, but he'd said he'd be there. So he stood to leave. The chorus of disapproval could be heard above the sound of the karaoke in the next room. 'Come on, Carl, you can't go now it's your birthday'/

'You can go in a bit'.

CARL: 'When I said oh I've got to go at seven, everyone was a bit hurt and pissed off and demanded an explanation. So I gave them the explanation and they were the same. They all looked disgusted and furious saying, "We're not going to let you go." They said, "How dare you be treated like that?" And it just felt good to know that people cared about me. So I didn't go in the end. And to be honest in the great scheme of things I don't think it changed that much really.'

So he stayed. So he stayed and sang his favourite Beatles songs and Blur and whatever took his fancy as he flicked through the karaoke bar's vinyl pages. People made the unlikeliest requests, just to see if he would do it. Across town Peter gave up hope of his friend coming and sang The La's and Chas & Dave in addition to Libertines songs new and old, before succumbing to taking requests from the throng.

Nightfall descended upon Whitechapel and the show, a pretty good one despite the desperate air, stumbled to an end. Peter was beside himself, though. He felt betrayed and broken. He had inadvertently staked everything on this night. On top of everything else he felt he'd been let down. His relationships with both Carl and Banny were at an all-time low – they just weren't getting on, his aunt Lil had died, he knew his drug use was too high. And now this. The fans didn't seem to notice that he wasn't his usual self and the chants of 'Carl, Carl, Carl' were extra torture. Surely they could see he was upset; hadn't they noticed that usually dapper if down-at-heel Peter was wearing a grey stripy sweatshirt that was more low-rent aerobics than literary Arcadia?

This is where Dean and Sophie from Gunter Grove came in. Dean, whom he'd met once before backstage at a Buff Medways gig in Chatham, saw his distress, and together they went to the house of his new friend Sophie Thunders. After all Peter had no idea what to do, he'd run out of ideas. It was the tour the next day, but Carl hadn't turned up to his tour. Twice now. Did they really want him in it? This was his band after all, well, his band as much as Carl's. And Carl hadn't turned up. Peter believed he'd made it known to Carl how important it was. Carl must have known had bad it was for him. Peter was convinced Carl must have known that Peter needed this to lift his spirits after losing a close member of the family, and the fact that within months he was to become a father brought new responsibilities. He wanted to get rid of the bullshit and for it to be about music and nothing else. Nothing else matters apart from music and yet, and yet, Carl hadn't come.

Through the night he sat up with Dean and Sophie and drank Jameson's whiskey and wrestled with what to do. Whatever he had to do, he couldn't do nothing – that would be admitting defeat. The coach at King's Cross had a seat for him in the morning and he had to do something. If he got on the coach it would be like admitting defeat, like saying that the gig on the roof wasn't important.

Eventually the tired, harried Peter Doherty made a decision. He wouldn't get on the coach. In fact, he would go away. Yes, if he went away they wouldn't be able to talk him round and make him go on tour again. He decided it was the right thing to do.

So early the following morning as the sun rose over London, no sleep yet had, Peter resolved to disappear. He'd get on the first train out of King's Cross St Pancras. By the time they noticed he wasn't there, he'd be gone. He'd show Carl how important it was.

Dean, his new compatriot and ally, went with him to the train station and waved him on to the train. He took a photograph of Peter, head bowed walking up the platform. Dwarfed by the station and the trains, he was a tiny lonely stooped figure walking away.

Peter's life was unravelling, the pressures were mounting; there was the death of a family member, the crushing tour of Japan and America, his problems with John and Gary, the constant squabbling with Banny, his escalating drug use, Carl's unwillingness to pursue what Peter thought was their dream, and this public snub on a Whitechapel rooftop. Peter was taking control of his life in the only way he knew.

Where was Peter? There was no sign of the itinerant sod. Sighing at Peter gave way to mild peevishness, which gave way to anxiety. They couldn't miss this tour, they'd knobbed it up once already and they'd be crucified if they didn't go.

Frantically the band began phoning around, trying to get hold of him. All leads were followed in an attempt to track down the wayward singer. Nothing. He'd vanished off the face of the earth. They tried all the usual people, all the usual dives, but he hadn't been seen at any of the usual hangouts. The last anyone had seen of him was on top of a rooftop in Whitechapel without Carl.

A snap decision had to be made. It wasn't easy. But they had no choice. Banny announced that they were going to Europe and they would play the gig tonight without Peter. The coach rolled out of London. All the usual high jinks of tour buses on the way to conquer the continent were absent; there was no queue to rush to the PlayStation or get a movie going. This was, to put it mildly, terrible.

The band were about to do a gig without Peter in Germany in a day's time. Their guitar technician, Nick Gavrilovic, said he could learn all the songs on the way to Dover. And so Carl spent hours teaching Nick all the songs he could. Some songs were frantically rearranged or dropped altogether from the set depending on the feasibility of just getting through.

Peter, meanwhile, was stewing in Leicester, he posted online; this featured words that would become part of 'Killamangiro', a song by his new band. He threw himself at the mercy of the messageboard. He was, he said, 'tearful, ravaged to the bone'. He wouldn't be on the tour bus with the band. Even then, at his worst, he still clung to the idea of Albion: 'I will not vent my rage and wonder and hope and Arcadian sublimities alongside Mr Barât for now.' Peter was convinced Carl had promised to come and resolved to travel Albion in words as desperate as they were poetic: 'If you live somewhere isolated and you have space for a lonely, broken soul intent on unstoning its core again in a beautiful morning, then let me know.'

There were dozens of positive messages of support for Peter, and plenty of offers of somewhere to stay. But in reality, the game, in a way that would become more serious over the coming weeks, was up.
CARL: 'Probably, to my detriment, I must have given Peter the impression that I was definitely going to go to the gig. In Pete's head that might have driven him to retaliate. Which in turn was to let down the fans again and more commitments on a bigger scale.'

The Kirstys pluckily resolved to track him down in a wondrous display of calm intelligence and assurance. It was as if Famous Five's George and Anne had grown up to be assiduous detectives. Kirsty Want went through the Yellow Pages and worked out the location of the Internet café where Peter was posting (by Leicester station). Kirsty Ridout phoned the cafe and asked if there was a man with a guitar case there.

There was. Kirsty spoke to him and confirmed he was OK and then texted a frantic Banny and Gary to confirm he was OK and told them the number of the cafe.

The schisms inside the Libertines camp were finally bubbling out into the real world – but in a distorted way

– and it was Peter who was busy communicating with the world, showing his emotional scars as the rest of the band slogged towards Germany with Nick working hard to learn his bits. It was miserable.

The Libertines played the *Rock Im Park* festival in Nuremberg on 6 June without Peter and with new guitar hero Nick Gavrilovic standing in on duty. Didz of The Cooper Temple Clause helped out on vocals, but it was a wretched affair: once again a European tour had been messed up.

The Internet messageboards meanwhile were swamped with well-wishers who wanted to know what was going on and couldn't understand why Peter had gone AWOL. Peter attempted to rejoin the tour, but it was time for the band to take firm action. Peter had to quit drugs. Immediately, they said.

CARL: 'Initially he was welcome to come back, but then after a point it turned into "we can't be played any more". The whole time I carried on doing these gigs because initially it was covering for Pete's absence and fulfilling commitments. Trying to keep it alive, give him something to come back to. And when he made it perfectly clear that he wasn't capable of understanding what I was trying to do, then it was just a matter of getting the commitments and the things we had to do out of the way and give each one the life and truth it deserves. That's what we were there for.'

After losing everything, including not only his band but his best friend, who'd previously stuck by him in Japan even after the Sapporo night, Peter threw himself further into the Internet and on the mercy of the fans, truly adopting the persona of the modern minstrel. But even the Internet bit back occasionally. Peter Snr, his father, logged on to libertines.org and informed Peter, and of course everyone else, that Peter had hit a new low and was 'crack-piping himself to death'.

Peter knocked back accusations that he was addicted to drugs, which some more knowledgeable messageboard users claimed. One claimed that, rather than pursuing the romantic pastoral vision of a troubadour he was projecting, he was holed up in a Paddington hotel room taking enormous amounts of smack and crack with Wolfman.

However, on the whole, he was buoyed up by the support, which was even greater than he could have imagined after the Gunter Grove gig.

On 11 June at six thirty in the morning, Peter gave thanks to the fans in a typically romantic way: 'A hell of a week it has been, and not much ado about nothing I'm sure, given the warm and surprising response from so many caring, genuine admirers of skiffly r&b punk and acoustic knavery.'

He described a week in which he travelled like a wandering minstrel, writing and playing. He attempted to dispel a claim his father had made in a post on the band, that he was 'crack-piping himself to death'. In fact, he said, Babyshambles would make a record shortly.

Behind the scenes, Peter begged to be allowed to return to the band. When Peter pleaded to be allowed to rejoin in their beloved Paris, Carl's determination wavered. Peter even planned to book an entire coach on the Eurostar and entertain fans on the way over to France. How could anybody reject such a magnificent gesture?

CARL: 'I had to make the phone call flanked by Gary and John who said I had to do it even though I didn't want to. They had their hands on my shoulders for the major call – this is horrible – Peter freaking out the other end fucking jumping out of windows and god knows what, y'know the burden was unbearable. But it was something that had to be done as far as I was concerned. I was very very hurt and very upset – it was murderous for me. It's something I never want to do again. The only thing that kept me going was knowing I was doing the right thing and that it would be over eventually.'

Peter turned to the friends he knew would be there for him, pouring out his heart on libertines.org. He described the phone call and pleading to play. According to the posting, he'd seemingly gone mad, karate-kicking a bus and smashing a building-society window before stealing a mate's car and overheating it in Hackney. Resolving to go to Paris regardless, he discovered his passport had been stolen by a 'minder'. Paris might as well have been the moon.

The idea that Peter had any problems with drugs, other than the usual level at which many bands function, was still largely unknown to the outside world. Peter daringly used this knowledge to present himself as a total innocent who had been harmed by his own band; a bewildered innocent who'd been knifed by his friend. Even that post from his dad claiming that he was piping himself to death could win over the fans on the website. The Internet messageboard had started as an amazing means of direct communication with the fans; now it was a home for solipsism and deceit. On 19 June, Peter, with the band in Paris, told fans that Carl had said he was definitely out of the band, while he remained in his 'current condition'. Peter professed to have no idea what Carl meant. His sign-off was uncharacteristically blunt: 'I'm getting on with things without any of them, though god knows I love him [Carl] . . . Fuck 'em.'

It was decided that since Peter had made no attempt to clean up he would have the thing he loved most taken away from him until he quit the drugs. But even now the band saw no benefit in going public with the real reason why they hadn't let him back. Peter spoke with Carl and the band on a ferry coming back to England as the Arcadian vision of Albion's white cliffs appeared out of a misty summer morning.

Carl remained resolute, but took pains to try and convince Peter he was doing it all for him, that he wanted Peter to be happy. Peter had tried everything that he could to change Carl's mind, but not even his most persuasive of arguments would work. He posted on the Internet that he would get a new band and start at the bottom again, signing off with a plaintive 'Bon voyage, Piggles.'

It was not until a day later – two weeks after Carl's birthday celebrations and the Whitechapel gig – that the stoical Tony Linkin was given a statement to release: 'Peter is unwell and the band are very concerned for his well-being, they have told him out of concern for his health that he needs to get better before he can rejoin them. They also want it to be known they fully support him through this difficult time.'

Even now they used a euphemism instead of saying exactly what they thought was his problem, that his drug use had grown out of control and that he was a danger to himself and that he was unreliable.

The problem being, of course, that the Peter who was in communication with the fans via the Internet didn't seem unwell to them at all. He seemed depressed and disconsolate, for sure, but not ill.

Carl, in the meantime, was about to face the trial of his life as the band were due to play the UK. Their first date was in Manchester – where Carl dedicated 'The Delaney' to Peter. It was, of course, a living, breathing nightmare of a night. Many confused fans started a chant of 'Pete, Pete, Pete', a brutal echo of the Whitechapel night. Those most vehemently shouting 'Where's Pete?' were convinced, despite the fact that Carl was clearly a man suffering, that there had been some kind of coup within the band to oust him. In wishing to do his utmost for his friend, he'd inadvertently become a target for hatred. He chose not to say anything rather than say the wrong thing and antagonise his friend.
CARL: 'They were chanting, "We want Pete" and I was saying to myself, well, so do I.'
GARY: 'The Manchester one – that's where I got a can thrown at my head. Nice.'

It hit him and a security guard marched over to stand right in front of Gary as a deterrent-cum-shield. Soon the aggressive section of the crowd had given up the idea of hitting the sitting target behind the drums.
GARY: 'Then the security guy walked away and *bang* another can, right in the head, fantastic.'

Although the Kirstys felt a loyalty to Peter, they couldn't bear for Carl to be put through this torture. So, somewhat optimistically, they attempted to punch everyone they saw engaging in chanting. But even with their Blitz-spirit determination, they couldn't tackle everyone.

Carl coped in a typically understated way, adding or changing lyrics on the tour so that 'Tell The King' had the extra lines, 'It's enough to drive your friends away' or 'It's enough to drive your love away' depending on his mood, and 'The Good Old Days' now had 'the Pigman's lost the source'.

The night after Manchester, the band supported their treasured Coral in Wirral for A Midsummer Night's Scream. It was to be The Coral's celebratory homecoming in a big top. In essence, it was a mini festival. And The Libertines were second on the bill below the headliners.

The gigs themselves were tight, although without Peter they lacked combustibility and unpredictability and they were hamstrung by Carl's obvious discomfort at having to lead the band on his own without his friend. He was frequently sick before going onstage.

The tour rolled on without Peter through Scotland and Leeds and then on to the London Forum. 'In a way I'm glad it's over,' Carl said at the time in the insalubrious surroundings of a back room at the Forum. 'All we're doing when we go onstage is try and do the songs justice. And I think we fulfilled that objective. Sometimes it feels like a public execution. It was walking up to the gallows walking on to the stage of the London

---

PETER WANTED CARL TO JOIN HIM IN HIS HEDONISTIC PURSUIT OF PLEASURE AND EXPERIMENTATION. HE THOUGHT IT WAS THE NEXT STEP IN GIVING YOUR ALL TO THE ARCADIAN DREAM.

Forum. I know Pete's started sailing on the *Albion* to Arcadia with the intention of being back on surf. He's got a bit of cabin fever. He hasn't lost his faith. He's getting better. We're very close. We're brothers. Some strong forces took him away. He's a dear friend. And he's such a good singer. When we play live without Peter he's a presence, like hands on the back of my neck. I miss my friend, god speed him back.'

There was some sense of relief at this gig, though, for Peter had entered rehab in a retreat outside London. The day before, with Rough Trade footing the bill. Peter's sister Amy-Jo even made it to the aftershow; she was introduced with the memorable Tony Linkin line, 'We've got a Doherty here, representing Peter!'

It wasn't to be a secret for long. Carl's mum Chrissie couldn't bear to see the fans suffer and posted online, informing the fans that Peter was in rehab and everyone was thinking of him.

When Tony Linkin saw Carl at the aftershow he greeted him with a grin and a raised eyebrow: 'I see your mum's been busy, Carl.'

But it didn't matter. Peter was in rehab, somewhere secret. He was going to be fine. Everybody was ecstatic; this was truly a chance to get him back together. And for some best of all, no more voyeuristic and vicarious need to follow the comings and goings through an Internet messageboard.

And then the worst thing happened. On the near-virgin messageboard of babyshambles.com a message appeared.

Peter described being dazed after a week's stay at a farmhouse with bars on the windows. He said he's been off the drugs for over a week and that a secret contact had said that Wolfman and Katy Bapples were to be married. He'd discharged himself against the wishes of the doctors only to discover the wedding was a fake.

Readers speculated that Peter was clean, and that he'd been tricked out of rehab by the malicious hand of Wolfman. People howled. How could Peter have been so stupid as to believe such obvious deceit? How could someone of his intelligence and perception not see what was transparently a trick?

Why indeed?

BURGLARY AND HEARTBREAK

'WANT OF MONEY AND THE DISTRESS OF A THIEF CAN NEVER BE ALLEGED
AS THE CAUSE OF HIS THIEVING, FOR MANY HONEST PEOPLE
ENDURE GREATER HARDSHIPS WITH FORTITUDE. WE MUST THEREFORE SEEK
THE CAUSE ELSEWHERE THAN IN WANT OF MONEY,
FOR THAT IS THE MISER'S PASSION, NOT THE THIEF'S'

William Blake

BURGLARY AND HEARTBREAK

SO PETER WAS OUT AND ABOUT. AFTER A BRIEF SPELL IN REHAB AFTER WHICH HE WOULD HAVE BEEN CLEAN FOR AROUND FIVE DAYS, HE SAID HE HAD BEEN CLEAN A TOTAL OF NINE DAYS. THE ATTEMPT BY THE REST OF THE LIBERTINES TO HARSHLY BRING HIM BACK INTO THE FOLD, TO SHOCK HIM INTO MAKING A STARK CHOICE BETWEEN MUSIC AND DRUGS, HAD STEELED HIM IN AN UNEXPECTED WAY.

Galvanised by the support of fans both online and in person, instead of crawling back to The Libertines he resolved, to go 'off into the mysteriously tomorrow to get a new band together and play the toilet circuit again'. The Libertines meanwhile, having finished recording the new single, were back on the road in Europe, without Peter.

And what's more he resolved to prove that he was the talent in the band, not Carlos and certainly not John and Gary, whom he went about mercilessly portraying as session musicians who certainly weren't Libertines. What had until now been kept within band powwows and the Books Of Albion was scrawled across Web messageboards. He never crossed this line with Carlos, though, he never went that far; not at this stage anyway. Communications about Carlos were full of confusion and betrayal and a need to understand what had happened, while simultaneously arguing that he had done nothing untoward and that his sacking had been random and unexpected. It was like the classic stand-off between recalcitrant lovers: with both refusing to budge in the slightest.

Starting as he meant to go on, he even scheduled a gig in Peckham on 2 July, an unloved corner of London where the eighteenth-century Albion seer William Blake

had a vision before he was ten years old ('I saw a tree full of angels in Peckham'). More parochially it was also the borough where *Only Fools And Horses* was set. The pub Peter chose, The Ivy House, was the perfect venue: a dour wood-panelled front bar gave way to a glorious huge theatrical back room, complete with splendid stage framed in Victorian gold and red. It resonated with a pre-war charm verging on synthetic. Despite the fantastic omens for the venue, he failed to show. This was the first time he wouldn't make an appearance.

While his non-appearance was a sign of how bad things were getting, for the fans gathered in that back room it was an evening of bonding with like-minded people. While Peter was starting to fall apart, the fans were forging friendships that would flourish into a desire to make music, write, DJ and put on gigs. The fans who'd believed in him unquestionably, who'd believed him when he claimed to be merely a wandering minstrel and the victim of his friend's treachery, were left bewildered.

Despite this, Peter was excitedly assembling a new band, featuring old cohort Scarborough Steve, the original Libertines singer, on vocals. He called the band Babyshambles, a name given to him by the Queens Of Noize. And a word that had its origin in a scrawl on the walls of the Albion Rooms. Similarly Carlos had been dubbed Papashingles, a name that remained, on the whole, unused.

He wanted to record a bunch of sessions and gave his new friend and ally Dean Fragile a call to help him. Dean headed up to what was transparently a crack house in north London where Peter handed him a tape.

'It's the band's new sessions, I want you to mix them,' said Peter. And so Dean sat in a back room with the instruction manual for the four-track recorder open on his lap and set about mixing it as the whiff of crack smoke wafted under the door.

'They were pretty awful sessions – or at least the other musicians were,' recalls Dean. 'I basically took the six tracks and eliminated everything, as much as I could, except Peter and his guitar.'

After the success of The Libertines' Babyshambles Sessions, Peter wanted it up on the Web as soon as possible. It was important for him that while The Libertines were out of the country, he made the most of media interest. Dean arranged for it to happen. Sophie Thunders was happy to provide artwork for what Dean dubbed the Sailor Sessions (mainly because his hometown was Chatham in Kent, a naval port).

By the time Babyshambles' first gig had come round, Peter was determined that this band was in fact going to be called The Libertines. The posting to announce the gig wasn't the usual happy-go-lucky Peter frolicking through London town on an innocent mission as an entertainer and troubadour, this Peter had something to prove: revenge was in mind. And what better revenge than to seize the name The Libertines for himself? He posted notice of a gig in Gascony Avenue in Kilburn and posed the question: 'Is London big enough for two bands called The Libertines?'

He would never play the gig. Fans who'd turned up in the area gathered in a bar just round the corner from Gascony Avenue. They were veterans; they'd been through the wars with The Libertines and had their faith tested. Many had been around since Gunter Grove, some had even been at the Albion Rooms. But even this bunch of stalwarts who'd weathered no-shows in Peckham and another in Camden were growing weary. Many had given up on The Libertines, believing that they weren't The Libertines without Peter. Others didn't want to put any more money into Peter's pockets.

So, rather than the excitable fellow-travellers of yore, this group had grown a little cynical. Even the news that Peter had recently become a father didn't raise spirits. The messageboard at libertines.org wasn't what it was before: an open forum where anything could be said, where poetry and short stories could be posted and where literature, classic television and films were discussed. Instead it had become factionalised. Innocent newcomers would be subjected to horrific putdowns because they dared to ask how to buy a military jacket like The Libertines'. The posting of poetry and short stories was labelled as pretentious and feverishly derided and there were arguments about the relative merits of Peter and his situation, and Carl and his. Frequently

PETER HADN'T PICKED A VICTIM AT RANDOM. HE HAD KICKED IN THE DOOR OF CARL'S FLAT.

messages would feature idle boasting about the poster's closeness to Peter, normally in a cruel and witless attempt to win an argument. What had been a place where writing and the exchange of opinions had blossomed had become ugly, graceless and malicious, with the more literary of contributors drifting away. It was as if the messageboard itself was a manifestation of the cancer at the heart of The Libertines, with anger and resentment turned inward.

Whatever the fans had gone through did not prepare them for what was to happen in this faux-Australian pub in Kilburn. Seven o'clock came and went and there was no sign of Peter. These fans made occasional trips up to Gascony Avenue to see if anything had been heard of Peter, if there was a final time when he was expected to arrive.

One such fan came back with absurd news. He'd heard that Peter had been arrested for theft and was probably being held. So it had come to this. After a call, police confirmed that Peter had been arrested and was in jail pending a hearing. Perhaps the most bizarre thing of all was that despite the immediate shock of hearing the news, the waiting fans reacted with tired resignation. In fact, they acted more like concerned parents who knew this terrible news would arrive sometime or another. Perhaps most surprising of all was that no one, not even the apologists, seemed to doubt the fact that he had done it.

The arguments were over, then. Peter was an addict and had fallen into the round of crime that everyone, as seasoned watchers of *The Bill*, knew happened to all drugs dabblers, even those, apparently, who'd sold thousands of records.

But there was a bigger shock than the arrest. Peter hadn't picked a victim at random. He had kicked in the door of Carl's flat. He'd bust in and made off with money, an antique guitar, video recorder, laptop computer, mouth organ and CD player. He phoned Lisa Moorish, the mother of his new baby, Estile, and confessed. She felt she could do nothing but report it to the police. She thought that if they arrested him, they would look after him. He was charged and released.

The rest of The Libertines were out of the country,

playing the Summersonic festival in Japan.

CARL: 'We were going to get sued if we didn't play it. It was probably a relief to be that far away from things. But even there I was copping a load of heart-rending opinions by people who really didn't have any idea. It was ever present in my mind.'

As they stepped off the plane, there was a message on the phone. It was blunt: Peter had robbed Carl's flat and been arrested.

CARL: 'It was the flat where I'd been trying to look after my sister who'd been ill. To find out that the home had been violated and there was all this panic and upset and all my family were involved … I'd found a new love in Annalisa and I wanted to step off the plane and go and see her. But I had to go to London and pick up the pieces. It was a dreadful mess. There was a lot of tears and a lot of worries and a lot of me thinking on my feet. Every waking moment was like having a panic attack and sleeping with the same feeling. I would have given anything to know what to do and what to believe in. I had to believe in myself and stand on my own two feet. All I had to get through it was an "all that doesn't kill me …" philosophy and knowing there's light at the end of the tunnel and the sun will come up the following day. And that was the only thing, and the love for people I loved and keeping sense in the truth and faith in people. Because if I hadn't kept that, then the end wouldn't have been long.'

All this served to overshadow the release to the Web of the six-track Sailor Sessions – Peter would refer to them as the Bang On The Bone sessions, slang for taking crack. Unlike the sprawling Babyshambles Sessions, this was focused. After Dean's production, Peter's fellow musicians occasionally appear as disembodied interlopers like Banquo's ghost, if Banquo's ghost had a drug problem. This was the first of a splurge of sessions that included the Chicken Shack Sessions, Branding Sessions, HQ Bethnal Green Sessions, HQ Second Wave and Whitechapel Demos.

By this time Peter had abandoned the idea of a fight over the name of The Libertines. Dean Fragile had arranged for Babyshambles to play their debut proper at the Tap 'n' Tin in Chatham. The band featured

Scarborough Steve on vocals, with Peter playing guitar. It was just like the old days. And Peter and his new band all had a new tattoo for the occasion: 'Babyshambles' tattooed in a circle around the right nipple. Their first photo session was with the Kirstys; Peter made sure that the tattoos could be seen clearly. The message Peter was sending out was transparent: Babyshambles were closer to his heart than The Libertines had ever been.

The band were awful. The veteran fans, who'd been dragged through heartbreak and disappointment, had taken so much, so so much. Deception, tears, break-ups and more. Sure the doubts were there, but the one thing they could not stand, the one thing they could not countenance, was bad music. Some fans fled the venue in tears. For many, the spell had been broken. They would not go to any more gigs – by staying away they would stop putting drug money into his pockets and the dwindling crowds would send him a message. And they would succeed where even Carlos and The Libertines had failed.

All of this was true, of course, except it was too late. If people had resolved not to show up for the rooftop gig in Whitechapel, it might have worked, but there was too much momentum to stop it, too many people had heard that they could see Peter Doherty play their favourite songs at close quarters and hang out with him afterwards. And there were still enough people convinced, even now, that Peter should not be deserted. That friendship was important.

At Horseferry Road Magistrates Court on 11 August he pleaded guilty to the counts of burglary at the preliminary hearing. Peter felt confident that he would get through the hearing relatively unscathed; there were mitigating circumstances and it was clearly a crime of, if not passion, then certainly passionate resentment.

His thoughts turned to other things. He was convinced that Babyshambles had it in them to be a great band. He approached Alan McGee, who discovered and put records out by Oasis and Primal Scream, with the idea of managing them. Alan was convinced that Peter was a great musician and singer but couldn't bring himself to manage Babyshambles when he knew how great The Libertines could be. He believed that

Babyshambles were Sham 69 to The Libertines' Clash.

Peter gave an interview to the *Evening Standard* that was, perhaps, the most honest account of his problems; it was printed a day after the hearing. In it he admitted to being addicted to crack and heroin and he recounted his version of the break-in.

Of the break-in, he said: 'I went to speak to Carlos about how I had a drummer and bass player living on my floor. They are on the dole and I needed to pay them because they are musicians. I was going down to Carlos's to say I can't pay them out of my own money and I found myself shouting at him and it turned out I was arguing with my reflection.

'When I realised, I booted the door in. I was engulfed by complete misery and despair. It wasn't revenge. It was more: why are you ignoring me? – a cry from the darkness. I do feel remorse, I feel sick.'

However, online he dismissed the article, but added, 'The disadvantages of being stitched up by the evening standard not quite outweighed by tapping the reporter for a few bob towards our own p.a. system.'

His denial of the truth at the heart of the *Evening Standard* story was bizarre; those quotes must have come from somewhere.

What mattered most, though, was that Peter had found a new source of income – the press. It would be something that, in the following years, he would come to rely on. The irony being, of course, that while he would begin to use the papers as twenty-first-century confessional booths, admitting his sins and addictions, the money from the interviews fed those sins and addictions. Oh happy day.

Amid all this there was the little matter of The Libertines' latest single, 'Don't Look Back Into The Sun', recorded as they were wrenching themselves apart. Produced by Bernard Butler, it was a distillation of everything that made them great, a perfect synthesis of controlled anarchy. There were no bum notes here, but it still fizzed with life as exemplified by Peter's yelps of 'Let me go' in the chorus. It was released on 18 August. Despite a strong midweek in the top five, it would eventually chart at eleven. It was their highest chart entry to date.

The weekend after its release, The Libertines played Reading Festival without Peter, with the New Yorker Anthony Rossomando on second guitar. It was an inspired choice of guitarist, he was Peter's opposite in almost every way: a mop of curls atop a body that seemed to torture the guitar to get the notes out in contrast to Peter's laissez-faire attitude to the instrument.

Unlike the earlier UK tour, Carl was no longer considered to be the bogeyman who'd kicked Peter out of his own band. He was a man valiantly trying to keep a band together – and tour commitments fulfilled – in the hope that Peter would have something to come back to when he was clean. Alan McGee roamed backstage watching the Libertines.

On 6 September, the eve of his court appearance, Peter played the Hope And Anchor on Upper Street in Islington, a venue famous for its central role in the punk days, when it played host to Albion fellow-travellers like The Stranglers, The Damned, XTC and Madness. He was pale and gaunt with a nearly shaved head – he frequently shaved it at peaks of crack use as it became unbearably itchy.

The following morning Peter pleaded guilty to burgling Carl's flat. Richard Locke, defending, asked for a community sentence to be imposed so that his client could seek treatment for his addiction.

The judge, Roger Davies, had no truck with this argument. 'He probably was suddenly earning too much money for his age and began behaving irresponsibly. Unlike most of us who have to study and work hard, they suddenly acquire wealth.'

Peter replied from the dock in a barely audible whisper, 'I have worked hard.'

The judge continued: 'Domestic burglary is always viewed seriously. You kicked down the door to the flat, which was ransacked. What's more, it's against a colleague and a friend. This is a serious offence.'

The judge wasn't interested in the defence counsel's asserting that it had been an impulsive act undertaken in a drug-addled state. Peter Doherty was sentenced to six months in prison. The severity of the sentence bore the hallmarks of Sir Mick Jagger's sentence in 1967 for possession of drugs. At that time the editor of *The Times*,

William Rees-Mogg, quoted Alexander Pope ('Who breaks a butterfly on wheel'); once again here was a judge ready to mete out the maximum sentence when perhaps rehab and the threat posed by a suspended sentence would have, in the long term, been more effective.

Peter hadn't expected to be sent down with a sentence as long as six months; it was a tremendous shock for him. As he was led away, he looked terrible. There was to be no attempt at rehab: he was taken straight to Wandsworth prison, where Oscar Wilde had been imprisoned following his prosecution for indecency and sodomy. (Wilde had then been transferred to the miserable confines of Reading Gaol, the place where he composed the poem that bore its name. As if it wasn't bad enough to be in prison, poor Oscar was in prison in Reading. It must have played havoc with his sense of aesthetics.)

During his stay in prison, Peter kept a diary in an A4 schoolbook. He was aware of the parallels with Wilde, and like Wilde he was painfully aware that he'd been incarcerated in one of the more severe prisons. He adorned the front cover of the exercise book with a Wilde quote – 'It is always the unreadable that occurs' – from 'The Decay Of Lying'. On the back, from *The Duchess Of Padua*, was this: 'Guilty? – let those Who know what a thing temptation is, Let those who have not walked as we have done, In the red fire of passion, those whose lives Are dull and colourless, in a word let those, If any such there be, who have not loved, Cast stones against you.'

The final reference to Wilde on the back cover was the date: 26th April 1895, the first day of Wilde's trial. Inside Peter would write a poem that is credited to Mr S. Melmoth, Wilde's pseudonym when he left prison.

The diary was different from earlier ones; he cast himself as the 'lonely villein' (it's not an Old English spelling of villain, it actually refers to a peasant landowner), and three times there's a motif of a prostrate figure with a wound upon his heart and the right arm dangling lifelessly. This motif is a line drawing of the figure in Henry Wallis's 1856 portrait 'The Death Of Chatterton'. Chatterton committed suicide at seventeen after failing to establish a literary career; he was later immortalised by the romantic poets, and by his own literary pastiches of ancient verse, which no one during his life could believe were the product of such a young talent. Peter felt that, like Chatterton, his aspirations were in tatters.

When he arrived at Wandsworth he was given a prisoner's pack including a Chomp bar. He shared a cell with a prisoner on remand for assault, firearms possession and 'a few other things it seems inappropriate to mention'. This big black fella with a '*Grange Hill*-style black suburban accent' had heard that someone else had been imprisoned for six months for robbery, but this one had burgled his band mate.

'That's me!' Peter spluttered and his cellmate laughed a big laugh.

During his time in Wandsworth he trawled up some old memories and wrote poetry in his book (including the lyrics to 'The Man Who Came To Stay', which was later recorded by Babyshambles). There's one sketch of him (with four books), his cellmate (clasping one of the window's bars in striped tracksuit bottoms) on the opposite page, and in childish handwriting at odds with his usual scrawl: 'I love heroin.' He was struggling with addiction and wanted out of it. In one frank paragraph addressed to himself he accuses 'Peter' of knowing exactly what he's going to do as soon as he leaves. 'I am shackled to this fate.'

He received many visitors, all wanting the best for him. All of Rough Trade visited. And Carlos sent a postcard adorned with pictures of pigs – a reference to their nicknames for each other. The Libertines PR Tony Linkin sent Peter a letter addressed to Norman Stanley Fletcher, the name of Ronnie Barker's character in *Porridge*. And once his address and prison number were helpfully posted on libertines.org, he received lots of post from fans offering support.

After a couple of weeks, Peter received good news: he was being transferred to the Isle of Sheppey, a lower-grade prison. Taking his kitbag he headed over. The new prison was better for the soul.

It was during this time that a friend successfully smuggled drugs in. It was a little cannabis and the smuggler felt that if he was clean of heroin and crack, it was both an adequate reward for his strength and something to make withdrawal easier.

So on the day in question, the visitor had precise instructions. He wrapped it up tightly and brought it along. Peter casually ate a Bounty bar during the visit, and left the wrapper on the table. The visitor then surreptitiously slipped the small bundle into the empty wrapper, avoiding the watchful eyes of the screws, and,

finally, Peter picked up the 'rubbish' at the end of the visit and pocketed it.

Peter's appeal was finally heard three weeks after he was sent to prison. Richard Locke told Judge Derek Inman that the burglary was an 'impulsive and unplanned' act motivated by 'feelings of anger and betrayal by his closest friend'.

Judge Derek Inman reduced the sentence: 'We feel that a custodial sentence was justified in this case but sufficient credit was not given for his timely plea of guilty which it should have been. We have reduced his sentence to two months, which will allow for his almost immediate release.'

Peter was transferred back to Wandsworth because, due to arcane laws, apparently you have to be released from the prison you were first admitted to.

Carl, after much soul-searching and attempting to build up the courage, resolved to visit his soulmate. Despite all Peter had done, Carl hadn't given up on him. He dressed in his finery and took presents with him. The journey was quite a long and arduous one and you had to have the right papers to visit him. It took ages to get there.

CARL: 'I went there going over every scenario in my head.'

Finally arriving there in plenty of time, he presented himself at the gates. And then went to the waiting room. CARL: 'I was stared at by everyone in prison and their families. I was dressed in a nice suit, I must have looked ridiculous to everyone else in the room. I had two teas and two sandwiches as I was waiting, before I was called.'

'I'm here to visit Peter Doherty,' Carl told the guard.

'One moment,' came the reply as the guard searched through the records of prisoners.

'I'm sorry, he's not here,' the guard eventually said with a sigh.

'What? Where is he?' said Carl, fearing where Peter could be and what had happened to him.

The guard at the desk in Sheppey leaned across the desk and said simply, 'He's been transferred back to Wandsworth. You have to be released from the prison you were originally locked up in.'

Wandsworth? Wandsworth? He'd never make it in

time. The ever-polite Mr Barât mumbled a courteous thank you and left. What an idiot he'd been, why hadn't he checked? Typical Peter, even when you know where he is and there's no escape, he manages not to be there: 'I went outside and waited for ages for a bus.'

On the night before the morning of his release, Peter considered what he could face the following morning. Cameras? Reporters? Friends? Family? Biggles? No, Carl was too much to hope for. He'd done his flat over and that was that. He jots into the exercise book: 'Bilo + Biggles go together like a cup of Earl Grey + giggles'.

Perhaps he would just lapse back into the bad old ways. But perhaps not. As he records in the book, he has been off crack for a full twenty-eight days.

The night before Peter's release, Carl didn't know what to do. Discussing it with friends in the flat that Peter had burgled – the skeleton of the door frame was still propped up by the front door – he wondered what to do. He knew this was a key time and that whatever he did tomorrow, even if it was simply oversleeping, would define his destiny for the foreseeable future.

CARL: 'People who knew nothing at all about it were trying to get involved, everyone had an opinion, everyone was trying to go through me. That didn't help things. I had to try and stay sane in that situation and not let everything in. There were people saying I would be wrong in going. A lot of people said I shouldn't go.'

The friends in the flat that night said that he should go, that if Peter had been clean in prison he'd be a different person, he'd be the old Peter, the Peter that Carl had formed the band with. But what if he wasn't? Carl knew enough about prison to realise you could get drugs there. Some people's drug problems actually got worse after a stretch in prison. Carl didn't know what to do. He went to bed.

RECONCILIATION

'THEY WANTED TO SPEAK, BUT COULD NOT; TEARS STOOD IN THEIR EYES.
THEY WERE BOTH PALE AND THIN; BUT THOSE
SICK PALE FACES WERE BRIGHT WITH THE DAWN OF A NEW FUTURE,
OF A FULL RESURRECTION INTO A NEW LIFE. THEY WERE RENEWED BY LOVE;
THE HEART OF EACH HELD INFINITE SOURCES OF LIFE
FOR THE HEART OF THE OTHER'
Fyodor Dostoevsky, *Crime and Punishment*

RECONCILIATION

WHAT THEY DON'T TELL YOU IS HOW LONG YOU'LL HAVE TO WAIT. THE SMALL GROUP OF WELL-WISHERS ASSEMBLED AROUND 8 A.M. OUTSIDE THE ENORMOUS, STARK, STUDDED GATES OF WANDSWORTH PRISON. A COUPLE OF COATS OF PAINT ASIDE, THESE WERE THE SAME GATES THAT OSCAR WILDE GLANCED BACK AT BEFORE BEING TRANSPORTED TO HIS MISERABLE PROLONGED INCARCERATION IN READING GAOL.

Despite his doubts after the previous night's conversations, Carl had weighed up how he felt and decided to greet Peter at the gates. This was it. He had to face Peter now if there was to be the slimmest of chances of sorting everything out. He arrived at 8 a.m. on the dot. A prison guard confirmed that 'that Libertarian bloke' would be coming out today. There was nothing to do but wait. And wait.

Then at 10.30 a.m. a tiny door opened in the massive gates and prisoner LL5217 stepped out into the light, a battered guitar case in one hand and a polythene bag stuffed with clothes and letters from friends and fans in the other. Among them Carl's solitary postcard has pride of place. The gaunt, shaven-headed prisoner-of-war look that characterised the weeks before his trial and conviction had gone. In its place was a healthier Peter, a little fuller in his once skeletal face, not quite yet ruddy but a little colour all the same. He'd had his hair freshly clipped that morning at his own behest – he wanted to look his absolute best. There was a solitary patch of near white behind his ear.

If he wasn't quite dapper – prison has a tendency to remove the confident air of even the greatest of clothes horses – he was certainly comfortable in Fred Perry polo shirt, a rosary ('I stole it from the chaplain, it glows in the dark!') and beige overcoat. Carl's similar outfit added

a weird frisson to the occasion as they stood mere metres apart. Peter was bowed by prison and, if not quite blinking into the morning light, then gazing into it with a mixture of trepidation and bewilderment.

Carlos had no idea what would happen. Thoughts ranged round his mind. He'd heard stories of prison and didn't know what would emerge – the place was more likely to have been *Scum* than his beloved *Porridge*. Peter, really, talked a good game, the streetwise so and so. But in reality he could have been crushed between the cogs of prison and substance withdrawal.

And Carl – despite his best efforts – hadn't made it to see him. Would Peter walk out and thump him, embrace him or the very worst of all – like the climax of *The Third Man* – simply walk directly past him, studiously avoiding eye contact, head held high, aloof at some unintended betrayal or another? Peter would then go and do anything. That would be the complete end of their shared vision and everything they'd fought for and, for some months, lost.

But Peter saw him, smiled a broad, broad grin, and

THE BOYS WERE BACK TOGETHER AND, AFTER ALL, AS PETER'S CELLMATE HAD DECLARED, THEY HAD OASIS TO SHIT.

with a wavering voice said simply: 'It's Biggles.'

Mutual doubts evaporated. Once again the strength of their relationship had won out. The soul brothers of Albion cast aside doubts, fears, issues and problems. They embraced.

'I'm not going back, that's for sure,' promised Peter.

All the vestiges of problems vanished. Forgiveness and fraternity were the order of the day.

'Well, not in a hurry, anyway,' he finished ominously.

And then, in true British fashion, they resolved to go and get extremely drunk. And then Peter had a gig to do, somewhere in Kent.

The pair went to Sophie Thunders' house to shower and get some food – where the menacing silhouette photograph of them that featured on the promotional album was taken. Then they found a pub and settled down for the long haul.

CARL: 'I just wanted to say I cared really, beyond the bounds and beyond anything. And I wanted that to be apparent.'

They spent the day getting hammered. The good news spiralled around family, friends and the Internet, courtesy of the ever-attendant NME.com: 'Today, Peter Doherty is a free man.'

But there was something else in the offing.

Dean Fragile, confidant and pen friend, had been in correspondence with Peter to sort out a gig. In the run-up to Peter's release, people had attempted to talk Dean out of the idea. Many friends of the band believed that a gig announcing Peter's precise location would attract the shadowy elements on the fringes of Peter's group of friends, who would turn up bearing bountiful supplies of opium and other narcotics. And to the more cynical onlooker it could be read that Peter had fallen straight off the wagon after prison and straight into the murky gutter of gigs and drugs.

It was a deep, troubling risk and Dean prevaricated but ultimately decided that, in order to lift Peter's spirits,

he should do it. Peter wrote to him on 20 September on paper with 'Libertine 4 eva' scrawled on the top and an anchor above, saying how joyous the news was that there was to be a gig with The Bandits in support and the dependable Rabbi ready to bludgeon the poor suffering tune 'Sally Brown' into submission once again. He added: 'Perhaps we should just make it me, you, Rabbi, Bandits + 500 birds (oh lord preserve me I'm corroding into a drooling con).'

Tony Linkin, James Endeacott and Roger Sargent had planned to accompany Carl on the train from Victoria down to Chatham as Peter went off to meet up with friends.

Two o'clock in the afternoon I received a phone call from Roger: 'Hey, Anthony, it's Roger. Listen, we're catching a train out of Victoria with Carl at 5.15. Be there, but I haven't told you, OK? You're there by accident. I don't want it to look like a set-up.'

I agreed readily and set my things in order. *NME* held

an editorial meeting to discuss what we would do. It was agreed that someone would go to Chatham, do an interview and write up the gig. This wasn't the easiest thing to do on the day of their reconciliation. They might be impossible to get hold of or they might not even be friends by the time I got to Chatham. I said I could do it. But could I write it that night and have it ready for nine in the morning? Sure, I lied. Won't be a problem at all. Transcribing the two mumbliest people in music and then writing a feature while the anticipated cartload of booze metamorphoses into hangover with nothing but King's Reach Tower's wheezing ventilation to keep me company. Pleasure.

Then there was another call. It was Tony Linkin. 'Anthony, don't tell anyone, but we're going to be at Victoria at 5.15 with Carl. You can do an interview on the way down. Don't let anyone else know, just make out you turned up … '

Ten minutes later there was a third call. It was Carl.

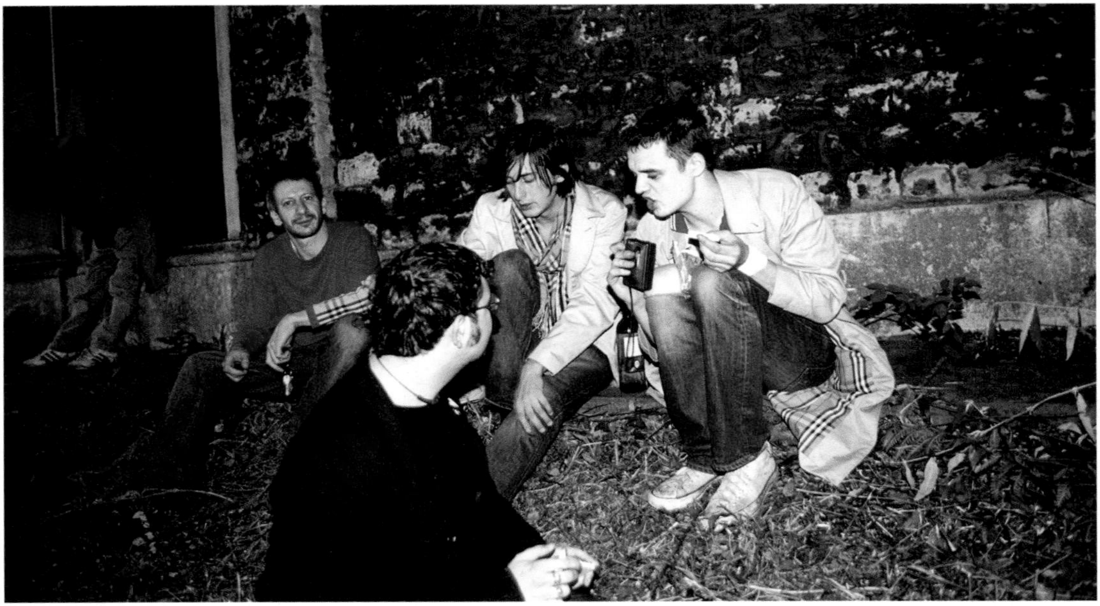

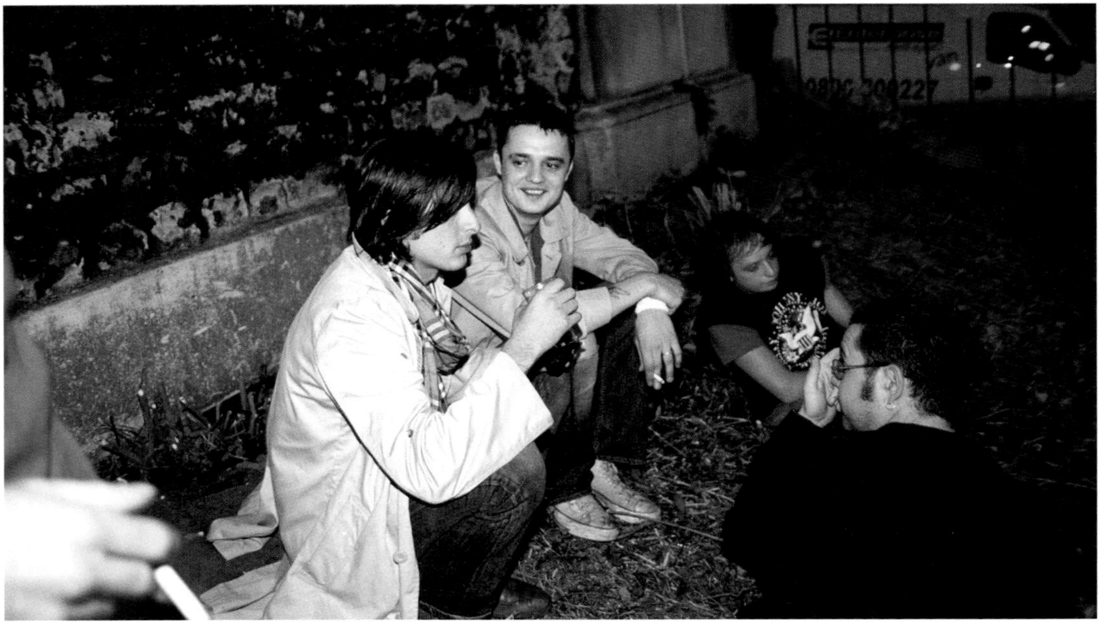

'Anthony, listen we're going down to Chatham on the 5.15 out of Victoria. You can do an interview on the way down. Please make sure that it looks like you've just happened to be there … '

I made it to the station and inevitably I couldn't find them anywhere. I had no choice but to get on the train and hope to catch them when they got to the other end. They weren't there. I'd got there too early. I had the first pint of the day while resolving not to drink too much too early. It was six o'clock.

Dean, meanwhile, who'd spent the day fretting over every detail, hadn't anticipated a sudden change of heart.

After weeks of planning and a fine start to the day, suddenly it seemed destined for disaster. 'About 6 p.m. Carl phoned me and was on the phone for half an hour,' Dean recalls. 'He said things like, "Dean you're a fucking idiot, I don't even know you. What kind of a person do you think you are that you can announce a gig like this as soon as he gets out of prison and you think you can organise a reunion?" And he kept the conversation going for so long. I was nearly in tears as I was walking around the pub with people staring at me. And then he went, "I'm only joking. I'm outside." I was so angry – but then I saw him and it was fine. And he was so pissed.'

The Yeah Yeah Yeahs' 'Pin' played on the finely stocked jukebox as Carl staggered into the Tap 'n' Tin: a picture of chronic inebriation. Cautiously making his way upstairs to the middle level, The Libertines started playing on the jukebox.

'They're all taking the piss out of me by putting that on,' an under-the-weather Carlos said to Dean. Dean assured Carl that it wasn't the case and went about getting him exactly what he needed: a drink.

James Endeacott arrived with John and Gary. But getting them there hadn't been so simple. Peter's rants on the Internet against them had hurt them both deeply. They couldn't face the Tap 'n' Tin as the fans began to circle, so instead went for a quiet drink at the pub up the road, a grim-looking edifice. Carl may have made up with Peter, but they hadn't and they weren't in a rush to do so, but somehow, for some reason, they'd decided to come. Here they were in Kent in a shabby pub wondering what was going on and what they were doing.

Dean had convinced them to come to give Peter the best possible start after prison, but although they were only yards from the pub, emotionally they had miles to go.

Also in the pub was Joe Absolom, formerly of *EastEnders*, who was there to see his girlfriend. He looked even more like a young Malcolm McDowell in the flesh than he did in *EastEnders*, with the same strange laser-beam intensity and winning smile. It was a good omen, as though O Lucky Man's Mick Travis had turned up to bless proceedings in person.

The Bandits drove for six hours from Liverpool to get to the gig; they weren't the main attraction, but they were going to do the best job they possibly could for their friends.

Peter arrived having travelled down independently. Peter and Carl reunited. Roger was keen to do the photos straight away – he knew that the chances of actually doing a photo session worthy of an *NME* cover was nigh on impossible. Meanwhile, I had an interview to do with a reunited pair of completely inebriated fellows whose faint grasp on sobriety had loosened still further. They were bursting with high emotion, flaunting their fondness for each other like reunited lovers. Roger looked concerned. Carl had already spent the entire journey threatening to beat up the gentle, friendly figure of Tony Linkin. The booze had made him aggressive – a busy commuter train meant he'd got the occasional knock as suited city gents pushed past. Tony got the blame for every single tap.

Dean had already scouted out the second room on the middle level. Somehow with a mixture of gentle cajoling from Tony ('It'll only take two minutes') and a more forthright declaration from Roger ('Fucking hurry up and get in there') they sat down on seats at the edge of a room designed for dancing. They were draped over each other, in serious danger of sliding to the floor. Tony Linkin was laughing. They were completely on each other's wavelength; their mumbles and giggles and sighs and shouts were incomprehensible to everyone but each other. Everyone else watching was outside their world – they weren't aware of anything apart from each other. Roger knew that this would be the only chance of

THE LIBERTINES ATTEMPTED THE BEATLES'
'SHE LOVES YOU' BUT THE FORCE OF PEOPLE
CLAMBERING OVER ONE ANOTHER IN AN
ATTEMPT TO GET NEAR THE BAND MADE IT
IMPOSSIBLE. AN ENERGETIC START BECAME
A PLAINTIVE 'YEAH, YEAH, YEAH' AS THE
STAGE WAS SWAMPED.

getting a decent picture of them together – he was familiar with their eccentricities and their ability to shut out the rest of the world, hiding under a carapace of shared jokes and catchphrases. He knew it was going to be difficult; he had to temporarily pierce the bubble surrounding them, if for no other reason than to get both of them to look at the camera at the same time. He coaxed in a way that he'd employed before. By shouting. Abusively.

'Peter! Carl! … Look at me. No, look AT me. Oi, Carl, Carl. No, look at me. Look at me. Bastard. Pete, LOOK AT ME. Stop being such a fucking knob. Look at me.'

They were both wearing rosaries by this time, which sadly didn't glow in the dark despite what Peter had claimed earlier. They also had a single plastic flower garland draped around both their necks binding them tightly together. The photo wasn't so much taken as plucked from the mitts of impossibility through a mixture of coaxing and good luck. Their grinning faces, deliriousness and cheery expressions proving that they could forgive and forget. Carl with a whisky and Coke in one hand and Peter's prison label in the other; Peter lost in the embrace of his band mate, unaware of the camera. They could put everything behind them. Naturally, later on Carl wondered if his smile was too cheesy. Whereas the cover in reality shows a beatific pair in each other's arms and ready to get going again. Roger only had about a minute. But he had the cover. He was happy and the boys were ecstatic.

And then Roger took the photograph. You know the one. The one on the cover of The Libertines' self-titled second album and the one that adorns the front of this book. Many many photos were taken by Roger, and many of them are classics. But this was the greatest photograph ever taken of the pair. Roger persuaded them to show their tattoos, both etched in Carl's handwriting in New York. A very simple thing really, but Roger caught Peter while he was still lost in the pair's interior world while Carl stared defiantly at the camera. Carl appears to be the tough guy gazing through a fringe, defending his delicate friend from an unseen foe or simply the harsh glare of publicity.

More prosaically, it could have been the effect of Roger dishing out a stream of swear words to tease the pair of them to look into the camera, with Carl finally realising what he was being subjected to. Whatever, it is one of the classic rock images of the past decade.

To their right, clipped out of the picture on the cover of the album, are the hands of the ever-dependable Tony Linkin with his fists held close together: P.E.T.E daubed in marker on his right hand and C.A.R.L. on his left. Naturally there'd be a point later on when Carl wanted to know why he'd only made the left hand and not the right. Once it was pointed out that C.A.R.L. had to be written first (with the right hand) all was fine.

Job done. It took less than three minutes in terrible lighting conditions and that was that, for Roger at least. I meanwhile had to get an interview and time was slipping away. Well-wishers were crowding the pair of them. I knew if I tried to wait until after the gig it would be too late.

We decided to do it on the grass outside, in the quiet. Roger shot a few more pictures of the pair of them outside with prison swag bag in hand as they sang a chorus of 'Any Old Iron' and a mauled refrain from *Treasure Island*: 'Ten Roger Sargents on a dead man's chest, yo ho ho and a bottle of rum'.

How do you feel at the moment?
PETER: The Libertines are united and at liberty once again. I remember my cellmate, he said (adopts 'heavy' voice): Yeah, Oasis you gotta shit 'em.
CARL: On the path of dalliance tread lightly/His new friends are quite unsightly/And that's the way it's got to be.
PETER: [Prison] was a horrid, glorious affair, it's no different from day one of The Libertines really.
How have you spent your first day together?
PETER: We've spent the day together lampooning, doing sketches … I asked for a real beer but he got me a Stella. We had a few things out.
CARL: We've had a marvellous day.
What's it like being out?
PETER: He hasn't been inside. He didn't go inside.
CARL: I did.

PETER (with a flourish): I done the time for Carl.
CARL (with equal flourish): I done the time for Peter.

What's prison like?
CARL (snoring noise): The rats were this big (holds arms apart).
PETER: I dunno – after the appeal and the sentence got knocked down, in a way I feel like a fraud talking about it in case it ends up glorifying it. Basically I went in – green, they call it. Spat in the face and all that but … .
CARL (Cockernee accent): Spat 'im in the face.
PETER: … there's a lot of talented people and my eyes have been opened. I've learned we search the heavens and the stars.

What were the people like in prison?
PETER: My cellmate was an armed robber. He said, 'Carlos, he's a shithouse. I'll wrap him up and put him in the car boot for you, Pete.' I said: 'If you do that you'll have to do it to me as well.'
CARL: I heard about that and I said if you do that to him, you'll have to do it to me. Again.

What was the one thing that you wanted to say to each other face to face in the four weeks?
PETER (without hesitation): I love you … I love you whether you like it or not.
CARL: I said that in last week's *NME* – I didn't intend to, but the buggers printed it already. They caught me off guard.

What was it like the first time you saw each other out of prison?
PETER: I think my nature … urchins go down quite easily but in prison I held up because people do long sentences. What I'm saying is when I got out I burst into tears 'cos I seen him and I know if he hadn't have been there the first thing I would have done is got myself a [crack] pipe. Carl was there though and that was it.
CARL: Don't you think you'll fall back into it?
PETER (to Carl): I've been off the pipe for 32 days and I don't intend to go back on while you're around.

What about you, Carl?
CARL: I feel the same. There was someone who'd been so constant in my dreams and my thoughts and my memories and my hopes. Seeing that face … every time I thought about it I nearly passed out. And then when I

did see him all I wanted to do was offer some kind of sanctuary, some kind of asylum. And work together on what's been said: Liberty, security. These things are subtle but it's freedom. I just wanted to hold my friend to make him feel better [adopts Scottish accent], to be there.
PETER: I felt I knew Carl but never understood him. Something dawned on me while I was inside, in the rigidity and mechanisation, about the truth of suffering. I felt like things Carl said years ago washed over me. I didn't understand them. I understand them for the first time. [It's] truth really. If Carl hadn't been there at the gate I wouldn't be sat here now. I think I'd be at the bottom of the river. I needed to know if it was more than a postcard.

How's the Albion*?*
CARL: You may well ask.
PETER: It's like a cross between *Porridge* and *Scum*.
CARL: We're not talking about that any more. The *Albion* didn't stop.
PETER: It did list a bit. He's tied me up with a knife to my throat and I never went to the police.
CARL: Yes you did, you phoned the police [adopts a whiny voice] 'Er … I'm a poet.'
PETER: Is that your impression of me being a poet?
CARL: Nah, you went, 'Go on, chop us out.' (laughs)

What's the future of the Libertines right now?
PETER: Trying to consummate the rage.
CARL [cheeky American accent]: I ain't got no rage!
PETER: Consummate the age.

Have you got anything special planned for tonight?
PETER: I'm looking forward to it … Just you wait and see.

And he winked a wink so theatrical it should have had a music hall built around it in its honour. Carl grinned conspiratorially.

Dean was sitting on the grass listening into the conversation. He was intrigued to see how much of the interview would be changed by the time it hit the pages of the *NME*. (He phoned me up a week later to confirm that what was written was exactly what had been said.)

What didn't make the pages of the *NME* was the appearance of a Dickensian-looking gent who, depending on whom you believed, was either a friend of Peter Doherty or one of his dealers. He was creepy and disturbing, he actually seemed to vibrate. What was most memorable about this scabby tramp, this Albion-like Fagin in Sunday best, was his neediness. He looked like a fallen gentleman who found himself caught between Whitechapel and an unpleasant habit. Later, with the facial tic doing overtime, he would proudly boast, 'I've been doing crack for twenty years and it's never done me any harm.'

As Roger sat on the slope, the Fagin character kept whimpering and making pleading noises to Peter. It was unnerving and more than a little distracting. Roger took Dean to one side and told him that he thought he was a dealer and should, under no circumstances, be allowed inside the Tap 'n' Tin. Dean nodded mutely.

And so we headed back in, interview done and my job still intact. And then the bouncers did their job as Fagin attempted to gain access. Two large and consummate professionals barred his entry to the Tap 'n' Tin.

Peter was already inside and disappearing from Fagin's vision. It was going to be fine.

'Peter, Peter,' he half croaked, half shouted.

And Peter turned around. 'What's going on?' he demanded, raising a quizzical eyebrow.

The bouncers said that he wasn't allowed inside as he was suspected of bringing in drugs. Peter looked appalled.

'He's not a dealer. He's a poet!' he said. 'You've got to let him in.'

Suddenly the celebratory atmosphere in the pub cooled: 'If you don't let him in I won't play.'

Fagin looked pitiful with his downcast eyes peering over the shoulders of the bouncers, pleading for Peter to intervene. The bouncers wouldn't budge though. He wasn't coming in. Peter attempted to coax them but they stonewalled him. This was getting out of hand. Roger intervened, explaining that there was nothing that could be done if they'd decided he wasn't coming in and that it would be foolish to jeopardise his big night over this. Peter wasn't happy but conceded. He shook hands with Fagin over the shoulder of the shorter bouncer.

Somehow disaster had been averted and the shadow of drugs had been repelled, for the moment anyway. A similar scenario would be played out ten months later, but with less happy results.

CARL: 'I remember some kind of shadiness going on. He was hovering in that wasteland.'

Meanwhile, upstairs at the Tap 'n' Tin where the gig would take place, anticipation was building. Fans from all over the country had flocked to Chatham. They knew by now that both Peter and Carl were in the building. They thought (and prayed) that Carl may join Peter onstage, but nobody dared believe that this would turn out to be a band reunion. Even when rumours circulated that Gary and John were in the building, it was too much to hope for. And then they appeared in the top room – people were in tears as soon as they saw them, were desperately hugging each other before they'd even taken the stage. Even as they pushed their way through the crowd to take strategic positions sipping pints with one eye on the stage. It seemed impossible that this was actually happening. Here. In Chatham.

CARL: 'I remember walking into the upstairs room and Peter had already gone in and coming upstairs. And there's these two Japanese ladies going, "It's true. It's true."' They were so elated.'

Dean had cleverly arranged for The Bandits to bring all their own equipment and let Peter or whoever use it after they'd finished. The equipment was all lined up and ready to go.

Bernard Butler was in the heaving upstairs room chatting to John Hassall, who, along with Gary, had finally agreed to brave the Tap 'n' Tin. At this point it seemed conceivable that Carl, a little more sober than before (after a haircut in the Tap's very own hairdresser's), would probably join Peter onstage. But there was no chance that the slighted John and Gary would share a stage with him. Insults notwithstanding, they hadn't even spoken to him since America, six months earlier.

Then, in an act of supreme selflessness, John and Gary got onstage with Peter and Carl. Peter leaned over to John and whispered a thank you and apology in his ear and did the same to Gary.

CARL: 'When he came out we managed to piece together everyone getting together and playing this so-called Freedom Gig. It was billed as a Pete gig and I didn't want him to go straight over to the dark side when he was released. Try again … give him a bit of love and try, and try to offer a different path.'

From the moment the gig started, the flash of cameras was so numerous it looked like there was a strobe light on them. For this gig, at least, Carl seemed more to the fore than ever before. Certainly the opening two numbers 'Seven Deadly Sins' (with his Django Reinhardt swing and picking) and 'Death On The Stairs' were showcases for him. From the outset the pair of them clicked back into what they'd always been, though, swapping vocals, sharing the microphone as Gary and John kept everything grounded and driving. There seemed to be an intensity as they sang and held eye contact. By the end of 'Death On The Stairs' they were bouncing off each other; the energy was high and they were back. The gig was a little rough around the edges but the emotion and energy would be remembered for ever by everyone who witnessed it.

Roger stood behind the stage photographing the band; on the verge of tears he put his arm around Dean and said, 'I can't believe this has happened.'

An exuberant Roger tipped an entire pint of lager over Carl's head in time for 'Boys In The Band'.
CARL: 'Apparently he poured a pint of beer over my head during the gig. The fucker. I think I must have been too overwhelmed by his uncommon generosity not to punch his lights out.'

And then there was 'Albion', a hymn to the Arcadian idyll of a Britain complemented with a touch of the kitchen sink. It never sounded more beautiful. It normally featured a virtual tour of unglamorous British locations, all in need of some love: Deptford, Digbeth, Watford, London Fields. This time, however, the tour included Wandsworth and Chatham. The cheers could probably be heard across the Channel.

'The Good Old Days', a celebration of the present and a rejection of nostalgia, was perhaps the most heartfelt moment. The couplet 'When you've lost your faith in love and music/Oh the end won't be long' seemed particularly poignant, and more tears flowed.

Then as 'Up The Bracket' finished the crowd surged forward on to the stage. The Libertines attempted The Beatles' 'She Loves You' but the force of people clambering over one another in an attempt to get near the band made it impossible. An energetic start became a plaintive 'Yeah, yeah, yeah' as the stage was swamped. And that was that.

Somewhat inevitably, it became *NME*'s Gig Of The Year. It would have taken a special degree of incompetence to pick something else.

The effect was extraordinary. Dozens of people couldn't hold it in any longer and started sobbing with joy. Everything had been put behind them. This was the best they'd ever been; there was no going back now. There was no way that anything could go wrong. The boys were back together and, after all, as Peter's cellmate had declared, they had Oasis to shit.

The band gleefully fell about as the booze kept flowing backstage. And Dean distributed thirteen specially cast medals inscribed with 'Peter Doherty Freedom Gig' commemorating the gig among the band, Tony Linkin, James Endeacott, Roger Sargent, myself and to some key people. Somehow, without anyone seeing, Peter found time to spray QPR on the wall of the wood-panelled dressing room. Nothing could go wrong. Falling out into the street, arm-in-arm shouting and singing, they were unstoppable.
CARL: 'I felt the world was good again. I had negative voices. And caution and paranoia. I chose to bash them away.'

But then, of course, there's a reputation to live up to. Carl bunnyhopped on to a plastic orange bollard, ready to deliver a monologue on the beautiful nature of friendship. The bollard crumpled under his weight and, after momentarily seeming as though he'd be able to spring free, he crashed chin first on to the tarmac with a distinct crack. Peter was horrified at the plight of his drunken friend and immediately borrowed a mobile off someone to phone 999. Shooing off medics, concerned at having two drunks in proximity to delicate medical equipment, he accompanied his injured bleeding friend to the ambulance. He had to make sure he'd be all right. They had plans to finish and put into action. Just as soon as they'd stitched up the hapless hero, the duo would remake *Albion*.

SELF-DESTRUCTION

*'EVERY REFORMATION MUST HAVE ITS VICTIMS.
YOU CAN'T EXPECT THE FATTED CALF TO SHARE THE ENTHUSIASM
OF THE ANGELS OVER THE PRODIGAL'S RETURN'*

Saki

SELF-DESTRUCTION

A COUPLE OF STITCHES ASIDE, CARL WAS PRETTY MUCH READY TO GET THE BAND GOING AGAIN. AND THE FIRST THING THEY DID WAS PERFORM A FLURRY OF GIGS, STARTING WITH A SPECIAL LUNCHTIME STRUM-ALONG IN REGENT'S PARK. IT WAS, NATURALLY, ANNOUNCED ON THE INTERNET, THIS TIME WITH ONLY A FEW HOURS' NOTICE. AROUND TEN PEOPLE MADE IT ACROSS TO REGENT'S PARK BANDSTAND WHERE PETER AND CARL ENTERTAINED THE ONLOOKERS WITH A PAIR OF ACOUSTIC GUITARS.

It showed that the Chatham gig wasn't a one-off gesture. Despite being burgled by his friend, Carl and indeed the rest of the band were working overtime to ensure that Peter was kept away from temptation. Everyone knew that it was always there, the threat of a return to the bad old ways, but they had to give their all to Peter, to give him every possible chance to leave it behind him for ever.

Somehow what had started as taking his child, Estile, for a walk, had turned into a wonderful, spontaneous day out. *NME*'s Marc Haywood and Phil Wallis went along. Unlike the flurry of solo Pete gigs at ten pounds a pop, this was free. The only money that changed hands was when Pete and Carl cajoled the *NME* pair to cough up for a pair of rowing boats. With everyone in lifejackets, there was an almost surreal quality to the situation, like *Swallows and Amazons* with guitars. They rowed to the island in the middle of the boating lake and more songs were played. Finally, they all retired to a Turkish shisha bar nearby for a last round of songs. In many ways it was the purest manifestation of the guerrilla gig phenomenon; no money was exchanged, and it was almost completely spontaneous.

Two days later Rough Trade celebrated its 25th anniversary celebrations at Neighbourhood (formerly Subterranea) in Notting Hill. The club was just around the corner from Rough Trade's Ladbroke Grove HQ and directly beneath The Clash's iconographic Westway. It was the music industry's worst-kept secret that The Libertines would be headlining.

Bizarrely, though, for what was ostensibly an industry gig, and therefore a self-celebration, the evening was extremely fraught. The band were magnificent, but the crush was unbelievable. The whole of London's music media were crammed in to celebrate the return of The Libertines.

The atmosphere was extraordinary, as was the sight of many level-headed music journalists losing it in the scrum. Bernard Butler was roadieing for the band, tuning guitars and making sure everything was going well. Mick Jones was also present, clearly enjoying himself and also clearly up for producing what was already an eagerly awaited album. However, it was Bernard and his mucking in that gave a fair indication of who would helm this album.

THEY FRANTICALLY SPAN AROUND AND BOUNCED OFF EACH OTHER, SWAPPING MICS AND SHARING MICS AND REVVED THE THREE SHOWS TO AN UNPRECEDENTED LEVEL.

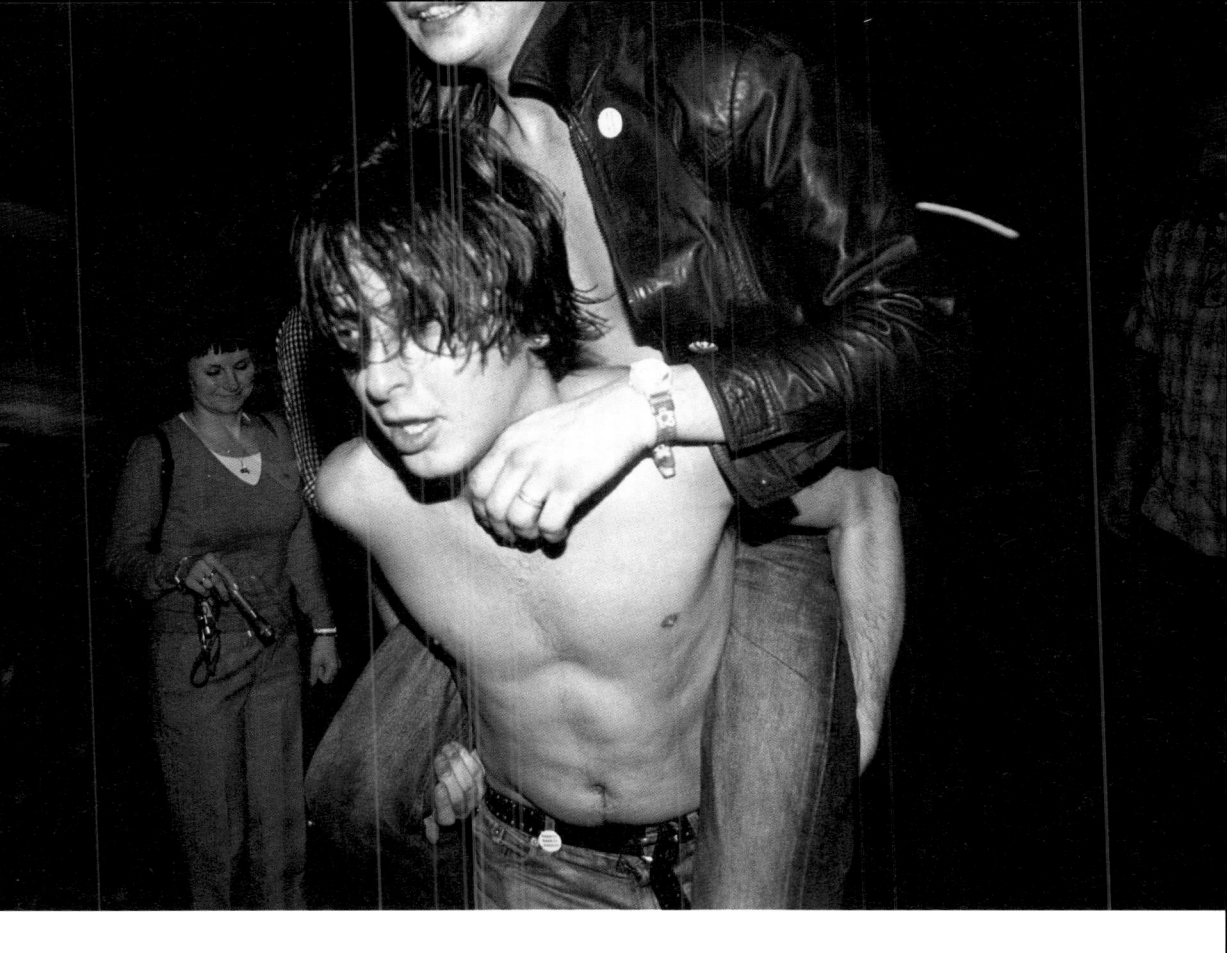

The gig itself proved to be a prediction of the following spring's UK tour. Bodies flailed around, glasses shattered, people shoved to the front not caring who was in the way. It was an orgy of thankfulness. It was like a pagan ritual, with The Libertines (and Peter and Carl in particular) as the deities.

The bouncers at the front took no prisoners as the force of adulation and curiosity thrust the body of the crowd forward; nothing could deflate the atmosphere.

Around this time, Banny, who'd devoted her whole life to the band, gave up the reins of The Libertines and handed them over to Alan McGee, who was only too pleased to pick them up. After discovering Oasis, Primal Scream and My Bloody Valentine, he was ready to pick up the band he would soon describe as the 'most culturally significant band he'd ever been involved with'. Banny slipped out of the picture, neither celebrated nor reviled. It was a shame, as she was the one person whose self-belief had got them signed; she was the one person

with the original vision that perhaps even Peter and Carl didn't have.

The Libertines were back together and on a roll. The *Guardian* even named them the Top Band in Britain Today at the start of October 2003. Initially they were interested in going to Paris to write new material. After much prevaricating they headed instead to Wales to stay in Alan McGee's holiday home just outside Hay-on-Wye, an old Victorian house with brass beds and sweeping staircase. Not quite as cosmopolitan as Paris, it was nonetheless aesthetically and spiritually the ideal place to renew old friendships. It was beautiful in the sunshine, and at night, with a little imagination could be viewed as a cross between *Rebecca*'s Mandalay and Wuthering Heights. It was the perfect place for a pair of British culture archaeologists to set up camp.

The idea, of course, was for them to restart their writing partnership and to ensure that Peter was kept out of temptation's way. Carl discovered, to his horror, that

Peter had brought a small amount of heroin with him to smoke. Carl was distraught. He knew what this represented; total abstention was the only way to quit drugs and small amounts had a habit of snowballing. But there was no sign of crack and this was all there was. It would soon be gone and then he'd know if Peter was addicted because they were stuck out in the country where the nearest town contained more second-hand bookshops than anywhere else in the world. It was no place of tenements and needles, to say the least.

To Carl's relief, he was right, the stuff went and that was it. No screaming fits, no 2 a.m. dashes to the nearest major city. Peter was, if not clean, then not craving. Carl could relax. Carl was fooling himself.

They set up mini amps and a Portastudio in McGee's library and played songs old and new and started writing 'What Became Of The Likely Lads?', its title pinched from the Clement and La Frenais 1970s Tyneside-based sitcom. Like the TV series, it dealt with the distance

between two best mates' juvenile dreams and the uncomfortable twenty-something reality. The difference, of course, being that this wasn't Rodney Bewes and James Bolam trying not to find out the result of the England football. It was about how communication becomes fogged, how mutual dreams seem to fork and about how deceit and betrayal win through.

Most interestingly it wasn't a song sung by one or the other; it was a song to be sung by both, to each other, about each other. It was the first time they'd successfully bound together so closely in a song.

What's more, the song's bittersweet nature captured their relationship perfectly: a relationship built on mutual distrust and on grand dreams that threatened to fly apart at a moment's notice, but which was ultimately united by a shared bond of music. The song offers no solutions or even an outcome ('We'll never know!') but its ambiguity is a snapshot of them at that time, tentatively getting to know each other again. The music

meanwhile was driven by a punkish riff touched with a little jauntiness in its trills that wouldn't be out of place in the soundtrack to the original 1970s sitcom.

Something had to give though. Following a night of heavy drinking with Carl abusing his favourite whisky tipple, all the things that had been left unsaid by both of them were unleashed. Heavy and personal accusations were tossed at Peter by Carl, and vice versa. Peter, appalled at the condition that Carl had drunk himself into, hid the whisky bottle before wishing his friend goodnight.

Carl locked himself in the bathroom and stared at himself in the mirror. He felt nothing but contempt. It was as if Wilde's epigraph from *The Picture of Dorian Gray*, detailing the rage of Caliban, was manifest in Carl's self-loathing.

Very deliberately he set about smashing his face against the side of the sink. He set about disfiguring himself, smashing his left cheek against the corner of the spotless porcelain sink repeatedly with enormous resolve, until after many blows he was at last satisfied. Having completed this macabre grisly mission, he went to bed.

Peter and Carl react to problems and situations in entirely opposite ways: Peter lashes out without thought for the consequences, attempting in that one instant to cause as much suffering as possible. An hour or so later as his temper subsides, he forgets everything that's been said and expects everyone else to as well. In earlier days this could be controlled. However, Peter's favourite medium of expressing outrage was now the Internet:

BODIES FLAILED AROUND, GLASSES SHATTERED, PEOPLE SHOVED TO THE FRONT NOT CARING WHO WAS IN THE WAY. IT WAS AN ORGY OF THANKFULNESS.

those outbursts, whether Peter liked it or not, became permanent. All those session-men jibes about John and Gary are still on the Internet preserved in virtual amber for people to greedily pore over. Carl, conversely, never had the cathartic Internet at his disposal; instead, stoicism and self-control in public were the order of the day. Not once, despite the goading and the temptation, did Carlos crack, not once did he allow himself to go on record with his feelings. Instead it was always a tireless succession of pleas for the return of his friend and for his friend to get better. He had always kept it together and kept it inside. That level of suppressed violence had to find a way out sooner or later and this act of supreme self-loathing incidentally destroyed one of the things that Peter had previously felt most threatened by – Carl's good looks.

When Carl woke in the morning he found blood all over his sheets. He was in a terrible state, dazed and out

of it, more as a result of the severity of the blows than the whisky still churning around his system. When Alan McGee saw it, Carl felt unable to talk. Alan went barmy; he thought that Peter had done it. Even more bizarre was Peter's idea, once he'd got over the horrific apparition before him, that Alan McGee must have done it. Neither could bear to admit the possibility that he'd done it to himself.

Alan took him to hospital. He'd come very close to losing an eye in his self-mutilating frenzy, and had stitches, an awful lot. He admitted that he'd done it to himself. He still managed to find the time to photograph his own injuries and give the camera to the *NME*. The picture was horrific; it seriously looked as though he could be disfigured for life. Along with the picture came a cock and bull story that he'd slipped getting out of the bath.

Peter stayed at home listening to the soundtrack to *O*

Lucky Man. He posted on the Internet about what had happened, making the best of something he was clearly shocked by. 'Sex symbol in an eye patch? Buccaneers indeed.' He went up to see Carl when he returned to the house: 'I told him he was my best friend and I care for him so much, am worried about him, and love him. He held me and said, "It's been a long time since you said that."'

Alan McGee was beginning to realise exactly what he'd let himself in for. 'Oh great, I've taken on a band with a genius songwriter with a penchant for crack and a sex symbol (another?) who likes to beat himself up.'

The writing holiday continued for a while, but Carl really had to go back to London to recuperate with his girlfriend Annalisa. With the holiday all over, all that was left was for Peter to attempt to nick some trinkets from Alan McGee's house. Carl told him that it probably wasn't wise to nick stuff off your new manager; well, not until he gets to know you. That's etiquette, that is.

Meanwhile Alan shrewdly set Peter up in a flat so small it couldn't be used for gigs, Peter's best source of ready cash. Or that was the intention, anyway. Peter didn't see Carlos during his recovery – Carlos' girlfriend had, unsurprisingly, banned Peter from the house after he burgled it.

On Bonfire Night, 5 November 2003, Peter joined Wolfman and The Side Effects onstage to sing 'For Lovers', 'What Katie Did' and 'Teenage Kicks' with the Rabbi. Wolfman looked, appropriately, like Guy Fawkes's emaciated brother.

Just under a week later, Peter announced that he would be doing a gig in the 'New Albion Rooms'. In other words, despite Alan's best efforts, Peter was going to put on a show in the tiny Whitechapel flat, at a cost of £10 a head, with a very special guest.

Peter suffered the shock of unexpected dissent when he announced it online. It stung especially because the Internet had become his cherished outlet: uncritical and supportive. But then, despite the homogenising effect The Libertines' messageboard appeared to have on people's opinions (you're a genius/when are you playing near my town), Peter hadn't considered the idea that his Stepford fans would learn, would have opinions that evolved.

Among the first couple of posts was a stark articulation of many people's fears by Billy Billy.

I hope you aint back on the drugs

Peter rebutted these suggestions. It was eloquent and heartfelt and on the whole the compass of opinion of the board clicked back into support of Peter, but something had changed. The veneer of innocence that Peter had displayed was scuffed and a new cynicism emerged.

More intriguing was that Wolfman's manager Jake posted a mysterious message under his realtimemanagement moniker: 'Please can I have my dog back as I think he may need some obedience training.'

It would appear that Peter and Wolfman had had a night on the tiles. And both had fallen off the wagon. The truth was that being inside hadn't cured Peter of his addictions, although it had at least slowed him down considerably and made him think about what he was doing. He wanted to quit the drugs permanently but the spectre of 'one more for old time's sake' dragged him, and a supposedly clean Wolfman, back in.

Why anyone would help Peter was obvious, almost irrelevant. Everyone wanted him to succeed; everyone was so blissed at the thought The Libertines could achieve their potential that they were always optimistic. People who'd experienced rock 'n' roll and all its pernicious paraphernalia couldn't help but want it to happen so much that they always always gave the benefit of the doubt.

Peter got over the problem of the size of his flat with a pretty astute application of logic: he played two sets.

Carl was soon recuperated, though, and before the end of November, the *Albion* righted itself. There was to be a gig at the Duke of Clarence. And not just any gig, it would act as a thank you to Mr Razzcocks; Peter made good on his letter from when he was in prison. This was,

for fans anyway, to be the gig to end all gigs. 'Legs 11' would certainly be played in full. More importantly it was Carlos's first time out since he nearly lost an eye.

Sure enough, the Duke of Clarence was packed to the rafters. Carlos, wearing an eye patch attached with a red bandanna, watched Babyshambles beforehand.

Gingerly he pushed through the massed throng. Despite the crush, they parted easily for him; many shook hands and nodded hello. Some moved to pat him on the back, but hesitated in case they do him any harm with a blow – in case that loose eye came popping out. There were so many people left outside that the semi-opaque, misted-up window at the front of the pub was full of faces pressed as close as possible, so that it looked like the gig was being witnessed by a league of delighted ghosts.

Then it was time for the main event, with Mr Razzcocks back on drums. One track in and with a dramatic flourish, Carlos whipped off the bandanna. Shocked fans held their breath for an instant but beneath the patch was a perfectly healed eye. They then dipped into the era of their early demos that made up 'Legs 11', including 'Seven Deadly Sins', 'Bucket Shop' and 'Love On The Dole'. They also played the swoony rejection strum of 'You're My Waterloo'.

Then Gary took to the stage and they played a glorious set of Libertines songs. 'Horrorshow', 'Death On The Stairs', 'The Delaney', 'Don't Look Back Into The Sun' and 'What A Waster'.

More gigs followed, all memorable for particular reasons. One at Filthy McNasty's was so crowded that they left with Carl on Peter's shoulders as a fan stood on a bar waving a Union Jack. At another gig at the Duke of Clarence the fans were so closely packed that at the end the only way out was to crowd surf over the fans, who very carefully ferried their heroes across the crowded room.

When it came to making the second album, it appeared that Bernard Butler had successfully wooed them. They attempted to get down 'Man Who Would Be King' and 'What Became Of The Likely Lads'. One night Peter excitedly phoned the Kirstys to tell them about the Phil Spectorish wall of sound that Bernard was creating, and played it down the phone to them.

Things weren't quite going quite as well as they appeared, though. Bernard and Peter just could not get on.

CARL: 'They had a funny old relationship. They were acting like schoolgirls together. I tell you there was always a drama.

'Peter was using again. Everyone was just trying to think that maybe it'd be all right. Maybe he would stop because he'd got everything he wanted or maybe it would just stay under control.'

The sessions were soon abandoned.

On the 16, 17 and 18 December, The Libertines were due to celebrate Christmas and their reformation. At the Forum the band got two bodyguards, twin brothers Michael and Jeff, who shadowed Peter and Carl all the time, and would for the foreseeable future.

Peter also got the chance to put on Chas & Dave, who were initially sceptical, believing that whoever this band

were they were taking the piss. But even in 2000, after hearing them in session on Radio 2, Peter had been impressed and inspired by them, believing they'd achieved what he wanted to with their blessed songs of Albion and London.

The three-day run was a massive success and is considered by many to be the high-water mark of The Libertines. For sure they were more focused than they'd ever been, but the passion remained as Carl and Peter's energy and co-devotion came to the fore. They frantically span around and bounced off each other, swapping mics and sharing mics and revved the three shows to an unprecedented level. Even the sceptical *Time Out* voted it one of the Top 100 London gigs of all time.

On the first night something astonishing happened, the likes of which I've never seen. For some reason, between songs someone threw an apple in the direction of a typically fumbling Peter with quite extraordinary

force. In one movement Peter almost absentmindedly plucked the apple out of its hurtling trajectory, took a bite, slammed it down and started the next song. This moment was an appropriate symbol of Peter's relationship with the 'real' world: one second he appears to be not quite aware of what's going on as people throw abuse his way, the next second he's neutralised the slings and arrows in spectacular fashion and started something wondrous.

The songs, though, highlighted the whole band, showing just how far they'd come: Gary was pummelling away with greater skill and force than ever before, the quiet John's bass lines powered the music like never before. These brilliant shows seemed to represent an inspired *Dads' Army* rear-guard action against the conquering American interlopers.

At the end of the first night, after Carl and then Peter leapt into the audience, the *Guardian*'s Maddy Costa noted the symbolic entwining of the pair's guitar leads. The last two nights ended with spectacular stage invasions and, like their recent 'secret' show at the Filthy McNasty's, Carl ended up sitting on Peter's shoulders surveying the crowd. Any residual doubts about whether they could keep it together or whether they were a truly sensational band disappeared.

On the way home after the third night, there was a party at the Duke of Clarence in celebration of the magnificent run of shows. After toasting their success over several hours, Gary set off home for Dalston, a walk of about fifteen minutes to his flat.

GARY: 'So we've got this security looking after Peter and Carl. Guess what happened after the third show, minus security? Gary gets mugged. I got mugged on the way home. I spent the whole of the next day in the A & E. Where was my security, Alan? Hahahah.'

ON THE ROAD

*'AND YET A LITTLE TUMULT, NOW AND THEN, IS AN AGREEABLE QUICKENER
OF SENSATION; SUCH AS A REVOLUTION,
A BATTLE, OR AN ADVENTURE OF ANY LIVELY DESCRIPTION'*

Byron

ON THE ROAD

CHRISTMAS WAS FINE; PETER WAS USING DRUGS AGAIN, BUT WINDING UP BERNARD BUTLER ASIDE IT SEEMED TO BE IN MODERATION. AND EVERYONE WANTED TO LOOK ON THE BRIGHT SIDE SO MUCH THAT THEY WERE WILLING TO TURN A BLIND EYE TO THE DARK SIDE. PETER AND CARL PLAYED SOPHIE THUNDERS' BIRTHDAY PARTY IN EARLY JANUARY AT THE DUKE OF CLARENCE. THEY WERE BOTH IN GREAT SPIRITS. AND THEN CARL HAS SOMETHING TO TELL PETER.

'What is it, Biggles? What do you want to say?' said Peter.

'Let's go to Paris and write, Bilo,' said Carl.

Peter was elated, he couldn't believe it: 'Of course, let's go, Biggles.'

Peter knew that he had to tell someone. Someone he could trust. He sought out the Kirstys, who he knew he could confide in.

'Biggles has asked me to go away to Paris, just the two of us. We're going tomorrow. Do some writing. We haven't told anyone yet so don't say anything, eh?'

Peter was ecstatic. He knew that Carl had been hurt by the breakdown of the sessions with Bernard Butler; but Peter felt too hemmed in by Bernard. Bernard had wanted to ban drugs in the studio but there was no harm in a little bit as far as Peter was concerned – it would just help him out.

In the Hotel France Albion in Montmartre they completed two new songs: 'Can't Stand Me Now' and 'The Saga'. The former had been inspired by Rhythm Factory maestro Mark Hammerton and the latter by a letter to Peter from a friend called Paul Roundhill. Carl had to return to Britain, though, with family problems, and Peter headed on to Italy to see his special ex-girlfriend, Francesca.

CARL: 'It could have been anywhere in Brighton, Blackpool or Wigan. But you know if we went to any of those places then outside influences might have crept in. We could have got pissed and gone out and milked our notoriety, met a hundred people and, next thing you know, the evil rituals are coming in.'

On 12 February it was time once again for the *NME* Awards, where they picked up Best Band. For the casual observer who only followed the normal release schedule it seemed bizarre – they'd only released one single that year, 'Don't Look Back Into The Sun'. Aside from that, though, they'd had managed to squeeze in tours, five CDs of new material released across the Web, gigs in their own house, a split, rehab, burglary, prison, a regrouping and three amazing nights at the Forum.

It was time to celebrate, it was justice of a sort. The band took to the stage and Peter and Carl swapped lines of the Siegfried Sassoon poem 'Suicide In The Trenches'. It was a magnificent gesture; at a place where most bands feel the need to be as 'rock 'n' roll' as possible, they subverted it with a stroke, and it felt right. It bewildered some, while others realised that there was, perhaps, more to this band than the druggy antics they'd heard about. It had a peculiar effect on the mostly cynical audience: a hush fell over them as they listened to the speech.

In the same way that when Bowie put his arm around Ronson on *Top Of The Pops* and outsiders across the land felt a purpose in rock, it would cause ripples across music for the next few years. This authentically and passionately relayed poem cut through the fog and hyperbole and shone with a beauty and simplicity. It spoke directly to music fans who wanted more than a pose, who wanted real heart in their music.

CARL: 'Well, I suppose that meant a lot to me, from what I remember. I taught it to Pete. And then me and Peter used to sing it all the time and play it on the guitar. And we talked about doing it for a speech – we really

---

PETER RETURNED FOR THE FINAL CHORUS OF 'THE GOOD OLD DAYS', SHIRTLESS, HAVING SLASHED HIS CHEST WITH A RAZOR BLADE.

didn't want to do speeches. And then we weren't going to do it. And then Peter started it and I had to match him really and then he got one of the words wrong. Still. I felt great togetherness with my great friend. And anything felt possible.'

With that recitation The Libertines crushed the tyranny of Oasis, who had ruled ever since they overthrew the quasi-intelligence of Blur in 1995. Although the momentum had been building for some time, this heralded the return of intelligence to British guitar music; something that, in truth, the British had always been most comfortable with.

That done, there were two more small jobs to do: take this show on the road and then record their second album. Ten months earlier both had seemed impossible. Now nothing, it appeared to those outside the circle of the band, could go wrong. They would make the best album of the year and they would become the biggest stars in the world. The shine was taken off the win though, almost immediately, as Peter headed off home early, leaving the rest of the band celebrating. It took the edge off what should have been a great celebration.

The first gig of the UK tour was at the Birmingham Academy. There was a huge line of fans queuing up; they were not going to miss this. It was like The Clash in 1977, they were inspiring unprecedented devotion. They had become a phenomenon.

They started with a brand-new song, which, unusually for The Libertines, hadn't been bootlegged and made its way on to the Internet. It was the song written in Paris, 'The Saga'.

DURING 'CAN'T STAND ME NOW', PETER SUDDENLY TOOK OFF HIS GUITAR AND SMASHED IT BEFORE LEAVING THE STAGE. THE BAND FOLLOWED.

The brutality of the crowd as they burst into song, with people shoving and punching their way to the front, was matched only by the brutal honesty of the lyrics. Even though it was only the first listen, it was obvious that this was about drugs and their deleterious effect on friends. The implication was that Peter had put all this behind him, this was something that could not be repeated. Even the softly spoken 'No, no, I ain't got a problem, it's you with the problem' seemed to be a snapshot of a past Peter, not one who was going to 'lie to your friends/lie to your people/lie to yourself'. However, it also signalled a new directness in their writing; nebulous tales of Albion and Arcadia were set to take a backseat to a thorough self-examination, particularly in Peter's case. To the average fan or pundit, it appeared to be a welcome confessional.

The other new song was even better, 'Can't Stand Me Now', a Peter and Carl two-hander, a merciless autopsy of the breakdown of their relationship. In turn, they put their point of view, although the lyrics were clearly penned mainly by Peter (with help from Mark Hammerton). It was a stricken plea for understanding. It sported a tune as robust and catchy as The Clash's 'London Calling', but was something far more personal. It was amazingly even-handed in its portrayal of the differences. It was sung by the pair of them with a hint of barely suppressed violence throughout.

In the auditorium, the crowd had no truck with suppressing the violence. It was the violence of repression let loose, but there was actually a nasty edge to it. And it wasn't just in Birmingham.

At this point, The Libertines were tapping into something that few bands had achieved. This wasn't merely some London band; they struck a chord with frustrated working- and middle-class youth nationwide. It wasn't just the music; The Libertines were the gang that fought the world and each other, and ultimately friendship and music conquered all troubles. They represented two important things: hope and escape.

The tour was the purest illustration of the 'Time For Heroes' lyric 'we belong to a class of our own', where middle-class, slumming toffs and working-class fans came together in a way not seen since The Smiths.

There was a desperate edge to fans' enjoyment; they knew how fragile this *Albion* ship was and that they weren't the sort of band that would necessarily be sailing back into town a couple of months later. They had waited a year for this, following The Libertines' every move across the Internet and in the papers, and they could have to wait a year or more for them to return, if they ever did.

Peter and Carl went outside the venue afterwards and signed things for hours and hours. Then after that they went upstairs and played guitar together.

Roger recalls: 'I remember the first night it was like the old days, they pulled out their guitars and started singing at the hotel. They played away and sang songs.'

They strummed their favourite songs backstage like human iPods, a constant stream of songs by Love, Donovan and The La's. They discussed the opening bands and what they liked about them, revelling in the fact they had handpicked the lot.

Carl told Roger that he wanted him to stay on the tour and photograph the band. John and Carl were chilled out. But after a couple of hours Peter suddenly fled. He told aghast onlookers that he had to catch a cab back to London to pick up a guitar. People were astonished; a few were used to the idea of claiming cabs on expenses and a second of mental arithmetic left them with the certainty that the bill for the cab would probably be over £500. But Peter needed the guitar and insisted fleeing the party.

Ever-dependable fan Gill was waiting outside with the car running. She drove him to London, parked, waited patiently for over an hour while he picked up what he

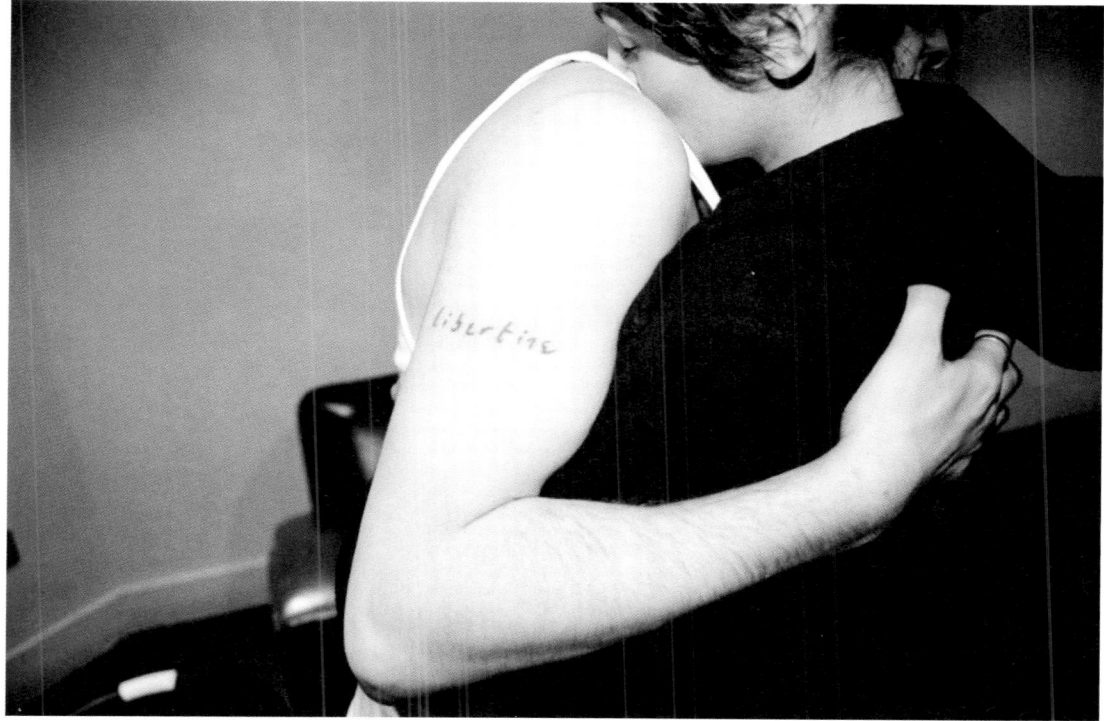

needed, then drove him back to Manchester. Bizarrely the press were informed of the 'taxi' ride. Gill, a music fan in her forties, was obsessed with The Libertines, and Peter in particular. She looked like a typical suburban housewife with a shock of black hair. Over the years, though, she would put up Peter and Wolfman in her flat and lend the pair of them thousands of pounds – money that she could ill afford and would have a long wait to see return.

PAUL BROWNELL (who runs Alan McGee's label's website www.poptones.co.uk): 'I saw Peter the following morning and asked him how was the cab fare and he sort of went, "hahaha".'

Peter had really fancied a decent fix and logic dictated that driving to London was the solution. Gill would later be named as his guardian angel by the *Sun*. Peter was so out of it he had to be carried on to the tour bus the following day, blissfully unaware of his surroundings.

In Manchester the violence wasn't abating; the atmosphere remained joyous but these fans required the same ritualistic outpouring as Birmingham.

PAUL BROWNELL: 'Someone told me he knew that Peter Doherty was Jesus Christ. It was mindless, people thrashing about, losing themselves in some kind of orgy of release. There was a man taken out of the crowd with a broken nose spread across his face and a look of dementia in his eyes before he grinned and said, "Fucking top show! Top show, wasn't it?"'

People were throwing bottles at bouncers, people were passing out, limp bodies were taken out past the sound desk. In the auditorium after the show, where you would normally see the usual discarded plastic glasses there were millions of plastic splinters glinting in the house lights, along with a dozen or so crushed mobile phones, mangled spectacles and blood. There was blood on the splinters.

The same night an exhausted Carl went to bed, but before doing so ensured that Peter was given Carl's last wrap of cocaine. Peter was nearly in tears, he was so touched by it.

GARY: 'Pete was playing guitar and stuff and me and Roger were there just drinking away and then I just said, "I've got to go to bed now – I'm done for," and I walked up to the door and Pete stops me and goes, "Gary, you can't go yet," and I turn around and I'm like, "Why?" And he picks up the TV and throws it out the window and I just stood there and went, "My job is done" and walked out. It was hilarious.'

ROGER: 'Peter was really funny and really nice. He thought throwing the TV set out the window would make a great photo and it was like a little gesture. It scared the life out of The Bandits who had also been on that night. Everybody tried to stop him, except me who egged him on.

'After the Birmingham gig, when Peter had gone back to London, he was in a frame of mind where it was like, let's do it again, let's go back to London, let's go back to London. I said, "Peter, you've had a really nice time and you're a bit tired – why don't you just go to bed?" And he paused and he says, "Oh, OK then." It's so tenuous: all he needs is the right girl, the right bar, right friend. Seriously.'

Glasgow was even better. The walls of the Glasgow

IN THE AUDITORIUM AFTER THE SHOW, WHERE YOU WOULD NORMALLY SEE THE USUAL DISCARDED PLASTIC GLASSES THERE WERE MILLIONS OF PLASTIC SPLINTERS GLINTING IN THE HOUSE LIGHTS, ALONG WITH A DOZEN OR SO CRUSHED MOBILE PHONES.

Barrowlands ran with sweat; the crowd were blitzed. The band went to a little club afterwards and were absolutely mobbed by people. Alan McGee, the local hero, returned and got the same amount of attention as the band. It was a great day. Fans were so used to the idea of their objects of affection being out of touch and unreachable that they couldn't quite believe The Libertines were so accessible. PAUL BROWNELL: 'Some girl tried to molest me in a Glasgow bar to get near The Libertines, and I'm going, you don't have to do this because I don't really want you to. If you're really that desperate to meet The Libertines they're just over there. And she was like, "What? You're not going to exploit me?" No, get off me.'

Bristol was equally successful, with one smitten reviewer declaring: 'I've been watching bands at the Colston Hall for 23 years – almost as long as the band members have been alive – and I can't remember a more exciting show there. This was a triumphant return for The Libertines and, if they're half as good as this at the summer festivals, 2004 looks like being theirs for the taking.'

Then it was back to London. They played the Brixton Academy for three nights; it was a masterstroke by the band, suddenly they were massive. This was a genuine grassroots band of the people and pundits were shocked. No one had quite conceived that they could be this big. Sure, plenty of people liked them but no one realised how big they actually were. They sold out all three nights within days.

The first show was great; perhaps not quite as good as

the run of shows at the Forum the previous December, but nonetheless marvellous. It culminated in Peter and Carl throwing themselves into the crowd as one. The second was even better: tighter, with improved sound, it was the equal of almost any show they'd done. The third, however, was the first clear public appearance that something was not right at the heart of The Libertines.

During 'Can't Stand Me Now', Peter suddenly took off his guitar and smashed it before leaving the stage. The band followed.

Out front, no one knew what was going on. Was that the end of the show? Of the band? Or what? It was more heartbreak for Libertines' fans, who'd had to cope with so much pressure on that tender organ that they probably couldn't bear any more.

The band waited ten minutes before returning to the stage as a three-piece playing 'Time For Heroes' and 'The Good Old Days'. Peter returned for the final chorus of 'The Good Old Days', shirtless, having slashed his chest with a razor blade. A bewildered and concerned audience had no idea what had happened. He apologised to the audience: 'Sorry about that. I had a bit of a strop.'

Backstage afterwards, Peter acted as though nothing had happened, which served only to wind his band mates up further. What should have been a grand celebration, officially the crowning of The Libertines as the best band in Britain, had been marred by Peter's behaviour. It was as if Peter could not handle the notion of fame – and the responsibility and pressure that came with it.

ROGER: 'I think it was the self-destruct button being pressed. It was a fear thing.'

It was as though every time they had it within their grasp, Peter would recoil in terror and sabotage the band, or his career. Although, ever the showman, he would do it in as public way as possible with a grand gesture.

Carl, John and Gary were so upset with Peter that they didn't contact him. On the morning of the Love Music Hate Racism concert at the London Astoria with The Buzzcocks and 80s Matchbox B-Line Disaster, they still hadn't spoken.

Peter stirred it up a little more by posting a note on babyshambles.com saying that Carl was hard to love. In language all his own ('Timeless boohooing about Biggles not being my mate'), he catalogued the sins against Carl: no birthday present or contact since Brixton. The Peter Doherty who, on stage, had casually acted like nothing had happened was transformed online into an emotional mess ('I need to speak to the boys before I go nuts.')

Peter Doherty needed the band and Carl in particular. The difference this time was that there was no quest to sack John and Gary. He was hollering into the virtual world of the Internet, displaying his emotional scars as deliberately as he'd displayed his literal scars adorned with red pearls of blood at Brixton.

The gig, however, did go ahead, with Peter. The band were on pretty good form, although it really took flight when, for an encore, Mick Jones joined them on guitar and vocals for 'Skag And Bone Man', 'Time For Heroes', What Katie Did', and then something truly monumental: The Clash's 'Should I Stay Or Should I Go'.

He hadn't played the song live since he'd left The Clash in 1984.

Chapter 13

THE
LIBERTINES

'MUSIC IS THE ART WHICH IS MOST NIGH TO TEARS AND MEMORY'
Oscar Wilde

THE LIBERTINES

WITHIN THE BAND THE PROBLEMS WERE MOUNTING AS PETER AND CARL TRIED DESPERATELY TO KEEP IT TOGETHER. THEY HAD A SHARED VISION, BUT IT WAS IN DANGER OF SLIPPING AWAY FROM THEM. OUTSIDE THE BAND'S CIRCLE THE WHOLE LIBERTINES STORY HAD A MOMENTUM OF ITS OWN. THEY'D REACHED THE EARS OF RADIO 2 TASTEMAKER AND BBC1'S PREMIER INTERVIEWER JONATHAN ROSS. IT WOULD BE HERE THAT THEY WOULD DEBUT WHAT WOULD EVENTUALLY BECOME THEIR FIRST SINGLE FROM THEIR SECOND ALBUM, 'CAN'T STAND ME NOW'.

Sharing a show with fine Englishman John Hurt, there to promote his portrayal of Tory reprobate Alan Clarke, and *EastEnders'* Alfie Moon (Shane Richie), this was an unannounced celebration of three generations of Britishness.

Peter's hair was backcombed in a way that wouldn't have disgraced Edward Scissorhands or The Cure. It gave him an appearance of permanent surprise, shock and exclamation. The wounds on his bare chest were still brutal reminders of the Brixton debacle. He seemed a little off focus but mischief was in mind, as ever.

Jonathan Ross introduced them and they launched into 'Can't Stand Me Now'. At the outset they made one of their great romantic gestures; holding their guitars at right angles they tenderly bashed them together: an electrifying cross that reverberated with a metallic clang that symbolised at once their togetherness and their enmity.

The chemistry between the band and Peter and Carl spoke volumes. It was as though the past two years had been distilled into the three minutes of 'Can't Stand Me Now'. After the recording was completed, Peter and Carl bundled Ross, who beamed as they set about leaping on his suit and ruffling his Wildean hair.

In the green room a couple of wily fans who'd dodged BBC security made an appearance. Peter, a picture of wounds, like St Sebastian in a leather jacket, spotted me and said: 'How did you get in looking like that? You look a right state.' And winked. Leaving shortly after the recording, he decided to avail himself of a piece of BBC furniture: an unwieldy pink bar stool. A very polite security guard informed Peter that while, yes, it was a lovely chair, it was unfortunately not his and would have to remain in the guardhouse for safekeeping. And yes, he would be able to come and visit it at a later date. Most assuredly.

Two days later, the band strolled into Metropolis studios in west London to start recording their second album. They'd booked a week's rehearsal before going in, but only John and Gary had made it.

From the outside they were still perceived – Brixton aside – as being in their honeymoon period. In reality, as had become evident on tour to those backstage, Peter had fallen back into the bad old ways. Hard. He'd begun to associate with Peter Perrett of The Only Ones, who was now more famous for his junkie habits than for the fact he'd written New Wave classic 'Another Girl, Another Planet' – a hymn, incidentally, to heroin.

Peter seemed to be ticking off the punk and New Wave legends one by one. With Mick Jones, an offer to tour from Joe Strummer and (via Crystal Palace) The Sex Pistols already in the bag along with the scalps of The Buzzcocks, there really weren't that many left. But in Perrett he found a deeper bond than the complacent

PETER, FED UP WITH THE SIGNING, INVITED FANS TO SIGN HIM. THE FANS OBLIGED WITH BEST WISHES, REGARDS AND THE OCCASIONAL CURSE SCRAWLED ACROSS HIS BARE, BARELY HEALED CHEST.

matery of playing on the same bill. They shared a taste in narcotics, and Perrett was more experienced than even Doherty. What began as a slow unravelling gathered momentum.

Peter thought Perrett was wonderful. But Perrett was a distraction; there was work to be done, and Michael and Jeff would make sure it happened.

GARY: 'Yeah. Peter Perrett – for somebody who wrote one great song – I mean, it sounds kind of nothing saying one great song, but to write one great song that actually stands the test of time, that is an achievement. But what a boner, what an absolute boner.'

Initially, the shock of getting into the studio meant that they weren't quite sure what to record. McGee was keen – as Banny had been before – that the band were recorded live, a feeling which James Endeacott and Rough Trade were agreed upon and which suited Peter's distracted state well. One song would be barely over as an almost indecipherable ' ... three, four' would emerge and they would heave headlong into a retake or completely new song.

Peter and Carl were bursting with new material. They raided the dressing-up box of the Razzcocks-era sessions for inspiration. It was all up for grabs: old songs were dusted down, new ones demoed. This wasn't quite the follow-on plan that they'd originally envisaged when they made Plan A to get signed. What they began to demo wasn't the pastoral acoustic snub to the record label that had been at the centre of Plan A; it was more developed. The time on the road had actually made them a much better band than the one that recorded 'Up The Bracket', so they demoed a range of songs from the insistent drama of 'Can't Stand Me Now' to the campfire strumming of Peter and Carl on their duet of 'Bound Together' which describes how the pair of them are united, by liquor, drugs but above all: 'We are bound together/We're bound forever/We're bound together by love'.

John and Gary were a solid bass which allowed Carl and Peter to improvise, while Carl's guitar playing had blossomed since the debut and his voice had developed into something powerful and unique, something that rather than merging with Peter's plaintive yelp was original and devastating and crucially his own.

PETER: 'We were like dogs out of the traps.'

They quickly got down a couple of versions of 'Can't Stand Me Now' At the end of the first day it was all going well. Mick Jones was happy. James Endeacott allowed himself a smile come six o'clock and cleared off home. The band were happy.

They decided to try recording 'Music When The Lights Go Out', from the old days, but tensions were building when a portable digital recorder arrived. Peter told me it happened like this:

I was going on and on at Alan [McGee] about getting myself a portable digital recorder. They'd had it for about nine months and hadn't fixed it; finally it turned up at the studio for me. And I think Carl must have been in a bad mood or something.

CARL: *Where's mine?*

PETER: *Let's share this one, mate. Why don't we set it up in your house and we'll do demos and that?*

CARL: *No, because you're not allowed round my house.* That crushed me a little bit ... took the wind out of my sails, but I soldiered on.

PETER: *Why?*

CARL: *Because my sister won't have you in the house, right, after what happened.*

PETER: *Why don't I sit down with your sister and talk about it and apologise?*

CARL: (fired up) *You don't know what you're talking about, you don't know my sister. I'm not going to let you talk to my sister, she don't want to talk to you.* We were really shouting at each other. And then someone came over and said, 'What's all this about?'

CARL: *Oh, nothing. Pete just can't handle the brown.* And I went absolutely mental and jumped across the glass table and started leathering him.

Michael and Jeff had their first intervention, plucking a ranging, swinging Peter away. Carl could not resist leaning back in his chair and with a deliberately antagonistic simple hand gesture said simply and firmly: 'Come on, then.'

CARL: 'And then Gary got right upset with me ... wanting to know why I wound him up.'

PETER: 'I was like Mowgli, picked up by Baloo the bear.'

Peter tried to do a runner then but Gary tried talking him round. It was at this point that Mick Jones intervened. He ticked them off equally, refusing to play favourites.

PETER: 'Mick Jones took me to one side and said, "You're like me and Joe [Strummer], you're brothers. You can't fight against each other, you've got to stick together."'

MICK: 'I think I told them the story of one Christmas ... '

PETER: ' ... about a bear watching telly on Christmas Day and hearing a knock on the door. Outside on the snowy path he sees a little snail freezing. He just picks it up and throws it as far as he can into the woods ... '

MICK: ' … then next Christmas the bear was sitting there and there's a knock at the door. He answers the door and the snail says: "What was that all about?" Hahahah … I said, what was that all about? They were cool after that.'

PETER: 'Hahaha … That's what he told me in my hour of darkness. So I went back down and go on with it, really'

That was that. The very worst of the recording experience was over. And, no, it wasn't 100 per cent happy from then on. Carl felt that Peter would occasionally try and stir things up, but he would ignore the come-ons. The fisticuffs were over. It was replaced by an atmosphere that was frequently happy-go-lucky and fun. There was lots of table football and fantastic meals.

Great meals, that is, until Carl took the chef on a night out.

GARY: 'We ate a lot of scallops and things were fine. Carl went out drinking with the chef and he put him out of action for ten days after one night's drinking. Hahaha. Carl absolutely killed him and in the meantime we had a sous-chef cooking and all he could cook was risotto. He was Lithuanian and all we got was risotto for five days … hahaha.'

CARL: 'To paraphrase Saki: the chef was a good chef, as chefs go; and as chefs go, he went.'

TONY LINKIN: 'There was practically a riot when the band realised there was no food.'

The songs, meanwhile, flowed easily. It was common to try songs out quickly, getting a handful of versions down until the band became bored and moved on to something else.

Peter insisted that Carl sang 'What Katie Did', a song that was considered to be the very best of his solo material, written during their estrangement. It was a massive gesture, a heartfelt desire to help repair old wounds. Carl, uncertain at first, took the song and made it, temporarily at least, his own. The version on the finished album is one of the most up moments of the entire record.

There were moments of great tenderness. On one particularly bad day, as Carlos sank into a gloom because of family problems, Peter made sure he was there for his friend to console him and cheer him up.

There was joy as well. On one occasion I visited them in the studio. Peter turned up with 'Cyclops' a new song, that he had sketched out on his acoustic the night before. The band worked through it over a period of two hours, adding new riffs, building up, swapping ideas and jokes, going into musical dead ends, escaping with a guitar flourish that was redolent of Elvis Costello's 'I Don't Want To Go To Chelsea'. All the time John remained his perma-silent self, but played the bass aggressively and fast. It was finished and would grace the B-side of the first single, 'Can't Stand Me Now'. It highlighted Peter's new fondness for ska, and while it could sound uncannily like two songs shoddily welded together, it was apparent that Peter and Carl had a future together; Peter the fast worker, tossing out ideas, whatever the quality, a trait he keeps to the day, Carl, meanwhile, stressing out on arrangements, the sound, individual notes and melodies. Although it must be said that Carl was capable of bringing his own take to a song: the rousing middle section of 'Don't Be Shy' was Carl's spontaneous strum.

This wasn't a band under self-imposed siege. Friends of the band would pop by; Geoff, Jeanette, James, Tony, Roger and the Kirstys all visited and watched a little magic unfolding in the studio. This was hardly the stuff of a band falling apart.

'So,' I said, 'why the security guards, Alan?'

'What do you think?'

'Well, it's either to keep people out, them in and unwelcome visitors away … '

'Or a combination of all three … '

However, the story that was to be printed was that it was to stop them from fighting.

I was at this moment complicit – not something I feel particularly comfortable with. I understand rock 'n' roll and the fact that journalists in the past have exaggerated events to make them appear more exciting. On balance it seemed such a small thing that would make very little difference.

I was wrong. The tabloids leapt on scraps like this, in a way they never would a year before. The story bounded across the globe as rubberneckers indulged in a game of when will it be over? In their eyes it was true; they took it to mean that their relationship, the album and the band was broken beyond repair. After the fact that Peter robbed Carl, it is the most repeated fact about The Libertines, a harmless tweaking of reality became gospel. I learnt my lesson.

On 13 April, Wolfman's debut single, 'For Lovers', was released. He had written it in 1997. Peter sang the tune and many suspected at the time that he'd written most of the song. How could Wolfman, who many considered a joke, write a ballad so touching? It had been recorded a year earlier at Britannia Row studios; Banny had blocked its release, concerned that it would detract from The Libertines. Carl had long since declined to tolerate Wolfman; a night on the tiles with him on the night before they recorded 'Radio America' for the debut album was enough to prove that Wolfman and friends were part of his friend's problem. But in the end, he capitulated, and recorded guitar for the B-side, 'Back From The Dead'.

Wolfman and Peter appeared together at a Virgin Megastore on Oxford Street for a signing. Peter, fed up with the process, invited fans to sign him. The fans obliged with best wishes, regards and the occasional curse scrawled across his bare, barely healed chest. He took to the stage for the launch party at the Café De Paris covered in scribbles, quotes and sayings. It was as if he became the human manifestation of libertines.org, a man covered in the words of his disciples, a modern martyr who'd given not just his words and music but his body to the fans. The fans were delighted. He didn't wash for days.

HOLDING THEIR GUITARS AT RIGHT ANGLES THEY TENDERLY BASHED THEM TOGETHER: AN ELECTRIFYING CROSS THAT REVERBERATED WITH A METALLIC CLANG THAT SYMBOLISED AT ONCE THEIR TOGETHERNESS AND THEIR ENMITY.

Two days later and McGee entered the recording studio. 'Peter was completely written on. He was three sheets to the wind. I walked into the studio to say something inane about soap that I was going to throw their way and saw that Peter had a pair of jeans on with one leg torn off and he had no socks or shoes. And he was totally written on.'

Peter looked terrible. He was beginning to stay up for days and his drug use was escalating. He appeared to be crumbling before the band's eyes and there was nothing they could do except hope for the best and especially for Carl to be there to catch him when he fell. But then a shower, teeth brushing and kip and he was fine.

This busy day saw Alan, James and Geoff in the studio to check progress and hang out. *Star Trek* was on in the lounge with Gary fully intending to watch five hours of it.

Radio 1 came down to record Peter and Carl's contribution to a documentary about the resurgence of British music called, appropriately, *Albion Rovers*.

Over dinner, talk turned to the fact that Peter Perrett was due to appear. Mick Jones had the final word on it: 'Peter Perrett, eh? The Only Ones, "Another Girl, Another Planet", a complete classic.' Pause. 'Just the one, mind,' and he chuckled.

Rock's very own Gollum duly arrived. I spotted the opportunity for a picture of punk legends old and new together and shouted at Roger to get his arse into the corridor. Something was wrong though; the composition was a little weird. It was fixed when Peter Perrett was persuaded to stand on a convenient box.

The rest of the evening was taken up with Perrett

rehearsing 'Don't Look Back Into The Sun', singing out of tune, mumbling and forgetting words, and, of course, 'Another Girl, Another Planet'. The band got frustrated, but Peter Perrett was tolerated.

PETE: 'Peter Perrett came down and did "Another Girl, Another Planet" and his strange harmonies on "Don't Look Back Into The Sun" – that was a joy. Yeah, that was a joy.'

The band were rehearsing for a gig to celebrate the second anniversary of the libertines.org forum. James Endeacott and I headed over to the Rhythm Factory for the gig, where 'Cyclops' was aired and the band were joined by Perrett and his two sons for 'Another Girl, Another Planet' (this was recorded for posterity and made up the Rhythm Factory album *Drink Your Own Poison*). The sound was awful but it was a great moment of rock 'n' roll. Actually hearing Perrett play was amazing, especially considering that a couple of weeks before rumours had spun round the Web that he was dead. Clearly not.

JOHN HASSALL: 'It was amazing. I mean, it was incredible because his sons played the song note-perfect, and obviously Peter Perrett can play the song as he wrote it, but I think that I was actually playing the wrong chords for half of it, hahaha. But it was wonderful to see him come back into his own really, seemed like he was at home playing it and back where he should be. He grew a few feet. And came into his own.'

Amazingly, as recording progressed they were packing in more and more of these gigs, including a show in Stoke-on-Trent on 21 April where they demolished a venue.

PETE: 'For me, that's it. At a certain age I devoured books and found expression that way but still for me I know inside me there's no fucking truer form of expression. There's the dark side of me that likes chaos and destruction. I'm still drawn to that. Because that was wicked – it was completely rammed and there was violence and that but the violence had a good cause. That's what I really fantasise, is to play a gig in thirtieth-century London while people are fighting the police.'

It was Peter driving this need to play, but Carl was keen to be there for fun and everything that came with it.

PETER: 'It was funny that Carl turned up 'n' all because it was supposed to be a Babyshambles gig and he turned up

and said, "What's going on here then, why aren't I playing?" And I said, "Carl, man, I've been asking you to play for the last two weeks." And he went, "Blurfffhghh where's the guitar?" He was supposed to be in disguise but he was wearing sunglasses and big luminous hood. Very fucking inconspicuous. And he had a big bouncer following him everywhere. Well funny.'

CARL: 'I wanted to go back on and Pete didn't so I went back on on my own. Then they wouldn't let me play so I told everyone there'd be a gig in the car park. So Pete came out and everyone was excited. The place got shaken up a bit and we played in the car park and they had to close the road off.'

Meanwhile, 'For Lovers' had gone in at number seven. Peter performed the song on *Top Of The Pops* without Wolfman, as Geoff Travis thought the haggard pipecleaner-doll figure of Wolfman would frighten children. Peter looked great in long black coat, with a hat stand on the side of the stage with scarf and flat cap.

It had been recorded the day before. Carl, John and Gary watched it on the television in the studio and cheered him on despite a slight unease that his latest effort had eclipsed that of The Libertines as a whole, with the single going in a full four places above The Libertines' last single. These feelings evaporated as the control room was filled with people ready to listen to a rough mix of The Libertines album. It burst out of the control at maximum volume as Mick Jones did his trademark jig, the one he did when he was excited by music, and the Kirstys hugged each other; it sounded great. Peter had scored a massive hit and the album was going to be finished.

There was James Endeacott, the A&R man who'd signed them; Geoff Travis and Jeanette Lee, Heads of Rough Trade; Don Letts, musician and filmmaker; Alan McGee, manager; Kirsty Want and Kirsty Ridout, heads of the fan club; Mick Jones, producer; Bill Price, engineer; John Hassall, bass player; Gary Powell, drummer, and Carl Barât, singer and guitarist.

Peter wasn't there, though. In fact, Peter would not return to the studio again. In a burst of activity they'd recorded the album, although there was still mixing and overdubs to do. That was left to Carl, John and Gary. Peter had flown.

DIRTY PRETTY THINGS

'IT IS DIFFICULT TO LIVE WITHOUT OPIUM AFTER
HAVING KNOWN IT BECAUSE IT IS DIFFICULT,
AFTER KNOWING OPIUM, TO TAKE EARTH SERIOUSLY.
AND UNLESS ONE IS A SAINT, IT IS DIFFICULT TO LIVE
WITHOUT TAKING EARTH SERIOUSLY'

Jean Cocteau

DIRTY PRETTY THINGS

EVERYONE KNEW PETER WAS OUT OF CONTROL AND ATTEMPTED TO BRING HIM
BACK DOWN TO EARTH AS MUCH AS POSSIBLE. IT STILL SEEMED AT THIS POINT
THAT HE WOULD RETURN TO THE STUDIO FOR EXTRA TAKES AND OVERDUBS, BUT
HE'D LOST THE WILL FOR IT. EVEN THE RELIABLE JEFF AND HIS BROTHER MICHAEL,
THE SECURITY GUARDS, WEREN'T ABLE TO BRING HIM IN ANY MORE.

Peter was indulging in everything, the drugs trough was overflowing and he wanted every bit of it. Meanwhile, A&R James Endeacott and PR Tony Linkin were fighting on two fronts. On the one hand they were trying desperately to help Peter, who didn't think he had a problem, and, on the other, they were trying to keep it away from a voracious media who had been successfully stirred up with the story of bodyguards being on hand to prevent Carl and Peter belting each other.

But then why would Peter think he had a problem? He'd performed a top-ten hit with 'For Lovers' and released the Babyshambles debut, a self-titled limited-edition single through James Mullord's High Society label.

Contemplating this, everyone tried to turn a good face outwards while working like mad to entice Peter down to earth. They were booked to play the Café De Paris

once again for John Richmond, a designer with a taste for rock 'n' roll. There would be £2,000 worth of clothes each up for grabs. And for a bunch of dandies who'd lived off second-hand threads from Camden Market, this was an offer that could not be ignored.

It was obvious at the aftershow that something was very wrong. It had gone further than ever before. As Carl helpfully manned the backstage bar and served friends and fans alike, Peter's ailing figure haunted the next room. He was out of control and looked terrible; too many drugs and too little sleep were damaging his increasingly fragile frame. The attractive cherubic minstrel was gone. He was gaunt, almost expressionless and in serious need of help. Even fervent apologists for Peter and his lifestyle were shocked. Fans were horrified at his appearance. McGee decided that something had to be done.

'IT'S GOT TO THE POINT WHERE CARL AND I DON'T SPEAK EXCEPT ONSTAGE. IT BREAKS MY HEART. HE TREATS ME BADLY AND EVERY TIME I COME RUNNING BACK LIKE A BATTERED HOUSEWIFE.'

Two days later, on 14 May, Peter was admitted to the Priory, the high-profile private hospital that has become a kind of country retreat for pampered celebrities and their smorgasbord of addictions. Peter was willing, everyone rallied round, there was hope. Much hope. Creation Management agreed to pay the extortionate fee for the health farm.

Peter posted on babyshambles.com that he was OK but full of various medicines the colour of gaudy confectionery. He said he was alone and confused but was pleased that his laptop was there, 'the only one who ever stood by me'.

He'd paraphrased The Smiths' 'Rubber Ring', although Morrissey's objects of affection were classic favourite songs, 'the songs that saved your life' rather than a humble laptop. Peter's message was written from a well of self-absorption, self-deceit, self-obsession and self-pity. In fact, during those days many friends visited.

And they came with gifts. Carl came over in a cab straight from doing overdubs on the album and brought a Tony Hancock DVD and a pair of QPR swimming trunks. The Kirstys brought mail from supporters. Many others visited. Some weren't quite as helpful as Carl, James Endeacott, Jeanette or the Kirstys.

Oh, and that laptop, that inert black thing. Peter took his laptop with him into the Priory to continue the dialogue with fans on libertines.org and babyshambles.com. However, the laptop wasn't quite such a good idea. This was less to do with the distractions and temptations of outside communication and more to do with the fact that, prior to admission, he'd meticulously stuffed it with heroin.

That reference 'to the only one who ever stood by me' suddenly seemed much less throwaway, less innocent. It was perhaps a little more revealing of his state of mind and wasn't just about lashing out at friends.

On 18 May he wrote a message on babyshambles.com entitled 'Still on suicide watch'. Despite its downbeat title it was upbeat ('I awake brighter-tailed and bushier-eyed than I have for many a year') and accompanied by some delicious black humour ('this place is probably full of celebrities in towelling robes. Enough to make anyone give up crack and smack').

Out of the blue came an offer for help from, of all people, June Brown, known to most people as Dot Cotton from *EastEnders*. Her godson Tim Arnold, who had been in a band called Jocasta, had travelled to the Thamkrabok monastery in Thailand to successfully cure himself of crack addiction. He had recently become close to Peter and thought Peter could be cured of his addiction. June Brown offered to pay for Peter's flight there. Certainly at first glance it appeared like The Libertines saga was a mixture of tragedy and farce: an *EastEnders* busybody offering to take Peter to the Far East for a cure?

The Libertines were confident that Peter would soon be cured of his addictions. The band cancelled appearances in a show of solidarity with Peter; they would not play without him. However, they were looking forward to playing Glastonbury as a band with him and announced a gig with Love Music Hate Racism at Finsbury Park, a couple of weeks before.

In the meantime, though, Carlos decided, at Dean Fragile's request, to return to Chatham's Tap 'n' Tin for a solo acoustic set on 22 May where James Endeacott was planning to DJ. Carlos, in contrast to Peter, was typically nervous of playing solo live; even in a small place he suffered terribly from nerves.

James Endeacott was DJing when I arrived at this scene that had housed the greatest of all Libertines events. He had devastating news; Peter had checked himself out of the Priory. James was attempting to look like he didn't care but he was noticeably tired and drawn. Carlos was distraught; all the hope that Peter would finally be able to put it behind him, and that The Libertines would be a united force with a fine record to their name was gone, snatched away again. He was disconsolate, but had a job to do, however nervous.

He played a superb show of Libertines tunes, focusing on the ones he'd had a greater contribution to, including 'Boys In The Band' and 'I Get Along'. The audience had no idea that hope had been crushed again earlier in the day. After playing the gig Carl apologised to Dean for not being any good. Dean was perplexed and a little miffed: 'Carl, you were brilliant, the crowd loved you and everyone had a good time.'

'Really?' said Carl. 'I thought it was all a bit ropey.'

Carl needed Peter to lean on, to give him confidence, even though his ability to perform without him was unquestionable. He looked to Peter for support and validation.

This time when Peter left rehab, there was no phantom wedding or excuse. Whether it was because he'd convinced himself it was simply a waste of money or that the heroin was running low is unclear; at the time Peter claimed online it was because staff at the Priory wouldn't let him watch the FA Cup Final.

On 24 May he agreed to sell his story to the *Sun*. Sean Hamilton was due to do it.

Peter felt that the Priory had let him down and was ready to flee Britain with his then girlfriend Renee. He opened his heart on babyshambles.com in a statement that reeked of self-loathing. He felt he was betraying himself in selling the exclusive story on 'Doherty Junkie Scum Quits Libertines'.

Peter was crying out for Carlos to come and save him. Carl knew he wasn't able and was frightened of what might happen if he did – Peter was always able to talk him round. In a mixture of demeaning candour tinged with a sneering malice, Peter said he didn't want to

be in a band when he wasn't allowed in his friend's house. In fact he still wanted to live in the Albion Rooms with Carl ('his highness').

He was sitting by his laptop tearing himself to pieces, recriminations seesawing between him taking aim at himself and Carl. Why didn't Carl want him, why couldn't they be the same? Twenty-one minutes later he responded to his own post, poetically detailing how he'd unshackled himself from his addictions ('laptop in the Thames, pipe over the wall, foil under compost soil'). Peter said he was going to escape to Paris, only to see his mother in Dover.

The whole thing has the whiff of one last indulgence, one last blow-out before he makes a run for it. Escape! And where else to escape to except Paris? There was one final posting five minutes later after Sean had texted Peter to say he would be there in twenty minutes, where he'd 'tarry awhile for a bob or so'.

He dressed it up as an Arcadian adventure, striking out, taking the King's shilling and then making a run from it overseas to the Arcadian idyll of Paris. This was to be the haven from The Libertines, who he paradoxically was annoyed at for not talking to him while simultaneously feeling shackled to them. He felt that if only Carl would come round – not The Libertines – everything would be fine.

Peter met the man from the *Sun* at Exmouth Market in London, just round the corner from the home of the *Guardian* and *Observer*. Money changed hands and the story was told. The whole of The Libertines' entourage was devastated; the *Sun* in their minds represented the very worst place, the one place they hoped he wouldn't go. And he was weaving tales – and revealing to the *Sun* that he'd left The Libertines. This was the

first time that Peter had appeared in a national tabloid. Everyone in The Libertines' camp braced themselves for the very worst.

Peter told the *Sun* about his plan to escape to France with his girlfriend, that he was convinced the Priory's rehab wasn't working. 'I was barely aware of what was going on in [rehab]. All these visitors were coming to see me and saying they were my family and my sisters – but really they weren't. I want to clean up but it's something I have to do on my own terms.

'It's got to the point where Carl and I don't speak except onstage. It breaks my heart. He treats me badly and every time I come running back like a battered housewife.

'I feel like I'm seeking the ghost of a former friendship but Carl gave up on me years ago. He did come to see me in the Priory but I hardly remember his visit.

'If [Carl] comes and grabs me by the hand, maybe we can reclaim the empire together. But for now I'm out of the band. Surely no one want to see me trapped in this

AND OF COURSE THE ONE THING EVERYONE KNOWS ABOUT REHAB, THE ONE FACT THAT ANYONE CAN PARROT, IS THAT THE POINT WHEN AN ADDICT LEAVES REHAB WITH HIS BODY SEMI-CLEAN IS WHEN MOST ADDICTS OVERDOSE.

cage that is only making me miserable?'

The story was desperate, but it could have been worse. Unbelievably, Peter had lucked out and in Sean Hamilton found someone in the tabloid press who was actually a fan.

At the same time as this was going to the presses, Peter toured all his regular haunts to pick up belongings ready to escape for good. Gill, who had driven him from Birmingham to London and back, drove him round and bought him tickets for the Eurostar. She was convinced that the best way to help him in the long term was to aid his escape in the short term, so that she could keep an eye on him.

He planned to meet his mother and then flee to France. Away from the stress and tension of the UK, away from the dealers, Perrett and the hangers-on, away from his band mates who wouldn't answer his calls, in short, away from the madness he felt was pressing down on him. France was the answer, it had to be the answer. Gill would lend him the money to travel and Renee would help him clean up and he'd be able to write. Away from numbers, like The Jam said.

Peter's mother met up with him. And then she revealed devastating news. She was seriously ill with breast cancer. Over the course of an hour, she cajoled him and coaxed him, made ultimatums and occasionally simply begged. She successfully persuaded him to return to the Priory. But things would be different this time. This time no one would know he was there. Employing the ancient stratagem of hiding someone in the most obvious place possible – Alan McGee, James Endeacott and Tony Linkin cooked up the idea – the story was spread that he'd been taken by his mother to a top-secret clinic in France to clean up. No one was any the wiser. And the unsavoury elements wouldn't bother going to France on a wild-goose chase, although most suspected him to be in Paris somewhere.

This time there was to be no laptop and they were much more careful with what Peter took in. The opportunity to indulge in drug taking was reduced to the minimum.

Peter's mum and the rest of them had pulled it off. He was back in rehab.

In the meantime, Carl had set up a weekly club called Dirty Pretty Things at the Infinity Club in Old Burlington Street in the West End. Announcements were made and he looked forward to a club featuring The Boxer Rebellion and Special Needs. Carl, John and Mick Jones were down to DJ.

Then on the morning of 7 June, a week after being admitted to the Priory, his third attempt at rehab, Peter checked out. Carl, Gary and John had no idea where he was or what he was doing. Every effort to help him and cure him had failed. They were at the end of their tether, things were getting desperate, completely desperate. And now he'd gone AWOL after failing to quit crack and heroin again.

A statement was prepared and Tony Linkin had the unedifying job of releasing it to the public. The French deception was dropped without comment; they'd failed after all and the whole reason to keep people at bay had vanished, along with Peter:

'Peter left the Priory this morning, his whereabouts are currently unknown although every effort is being made to find him. We are all very concerned for his well-being.'

The atmosphere that night at the club was brittle. It was the hottest day of the year. The other three Libertines were supposed to be celebrating Peter's slow recovery and having a bit of fun at a club. And here they were worried sick where he might be and in what state. And of course the one thing everyone knows about rehab, the one fact that anyone can parrot, is that the point when an addict leaves rehab with his body semi-clean is when most addicts overdose. And he could be anywhere. Anywhere at all.

All attempts at rehab had stumbled at the same point. Just under a week and Peter would flee. He would run back into the loving arms of heroin and crack. Something solid and reliable that never answered back and, money permitting, was always there. He loved Carl, sure, but Carl wasn't always there for him. Carl had got other priorities since the early days. He wasn't there all the time. He wasn't there for him.

So Boxer Rebellion came in. A filmmaker, Richard Harris, who'd taken to videoing Peter and had become quite close to him had a phone call from Gill. Peter was on his way – wasn't that good news, wasn't that exciting? How great was that?

A bunch of people celebrated with bottles of Coq, a French beer that while not champagne was fizzy and French and palatable. What the well-wishers and fans didn't quite realise was that rather than being a major breakthrough in Pete 'n' Carl relations, there was no way of knowing what condition Peter would be in, what he'd want to do or say. He was just as likely to strike out at Carl or the band as do anything else. He could do anything.

Carl was beside himself; here was this great force bearing down on him.

'Peter's coming,' he'd been informed by Roger, who'd been give the difficult task of breaking it to him after Kirsty Want received a call from Gill. But rather than celebrating he had no idea what he was supposed to do. Greet him as a friend, but send him back to rehab? Put up dukes for supposedly driving his friend out of the band? Just walk out of the first night of his own club?

To add to the tension; there were calls every five to ten minutes detailing Peter's current whereabouts, as though it was some contrived movie where imminent disaster is about to sweep in and that totem of stoicism David Niven has to face down his oncoming demise.

None of the options was the right one. None would guarantee the correct outcome. In the end there was nothing to do except wait and be anxious.

Finally the news arrived that he was at Oxford Circus, just two minutes from Old Burlington Street. This primal force was definitely coming.

Word circulated. He's here. Half the place erupted in celebration, the other half tensed and waited to jump in at an altercation or argument.

Peter was sporting a straw hat, brown leather jacket and happy expression – he was sober. Here was this great man who wanted to see his friend and he had big news for Biggles. Like an Ortonesque farce, one was upstairs and the other downstairs in the club that boasted two entrances. It was, quite simply, now or never. Carl was worried but ready. People went to speak to Peter to see if he meant ill or well. Carl finally ventured downstairs to see him.

It wasn't just the imminent meeting that bothered Carl, though; he was irritated: Why did Peter have to do it here? Why so publicly? Why not a discreet meeting in a quiet bar or cafe? It always had to be the grand gesture. Perhaps the reason was that publicly even with the addictions in the open, the fans knew Peter, they knew what a great soul he was, what a poet. Carl in comparison appeared aloof and distant. He wasn't, of course; it's just that he didn't make it his business to post on a messageboard every day. He kept his dirty linen in its place in the basket rather than posting it so that everyone could take a single impulsive posting as eternal truth.

Peter was always comfortable in this situation because it was anything but neutral ground; the hangers-on, the unctuous and the naive would be there. This was Carl's club, sure, but it was full of fans who'd spoken to Peter either on the Web or in person. Familiarity breeds contempt, but in contrast familiarity with celebrity breeds perpetual faith: well-meaning acolytes for a troubled deity.

But Carl steeled himself and wrested control as best he could. Ready to face the friend or nemesis in whatever form: Bilo or bile, Babyshambles or battering. And so a neutral ground was established. Paradoxically it was outside the venue, at basement level, away from the well-wishers and the voyeurs. Here at the foot of wrought-iron stairs faintly smelling of urine the two friends cautiously talked and embraced. The *Guardian*'s very own Betty Clarke guarded the fire exit to prevent voyeurs and photography.

'I'm going to Thailand, Biggles,' Peter told Carl. And that was that. Peter had rejected the Priory because it wasn't the place to get clean. He was ready to totally submerge himself in a regime that had succeeded where all others had failed, to put himself in the hands of monks, to be rescued, of course, by *EastEnders*' Dot Cotton.

And suddenly it was gig time. Rather than properly sorting out their differences, they ended up bonding and playing a gig. Music, like love, could conquer all. All four of them went up to play. Gary ebullient, John as poker-faced as ever, Peter uncharacteristically serious and focused, Carl relieved.

As they set up, Peter led the crowd in a chorus of Happy Birthday for Carl. From the debut song 'Don't Look Back Into The Sun', Peter sang the opening chorus as Carl hung back to play the riff – he was initially lost in the instrument: separate, detached. And then as they hit the first chorus all doubts evaporated, Carl thrust himself forward to share the mic with Peter. And that was that. Tension dissipated in The Libertines' traditional way, through music. What a send-off for Bilo – out to an isolated monastery to beat his addiction to drugs, the tabloids and the Internet. Carl made sure that Peter knew that if he came back clean the band was there for him. And Peter reassured him that he would.

The gig was just six songs long; it was sloppy at points but extraordinarily emotional. It ended with a magnificent version of 'The Good Old Days' that saw Peter and Carl share a mic for the middle-eight and Carl nick the fag out of Peter's mouth. Carl stage-dived into the audience with microphone; he managed to carry on singing even as he struggled free of the crowd. At the end Peter and Carl embraced warmly but not before Carlos had tripped over on to his arse. The staple of drama, music and farce was as present in these highly charged and emotional Libertines as ever before. What a glorious send-off, what a glorious night, what a band. It was to be the last time they ever played together.

BABYSHAMBLES

'*... YOU KNOW NOTHING ABOUT HOPE, THAT IMMORTAL, DELICIOUS MAIDEN*
FOREVER COURTED FOREVER PROPITIOUS, WHOM FOOLS
HAVE CALLED DECEITFUL, AS IF IT WERE HOPE THAT CARRIED THE CUP
OF DISAPPOINTMENT, WHEREAS IT IS HER DEADLY ENEMY, CERTAINTY,
WHOM SHE ONLY ESCAPES BY TRANSFORMATION'
George Eliot, *Daniel Deranda*

CHAPTER FIFTEEN

BABYSHAMBLES

THE DAY AFTER THE LIBERTINES PLAYED DIRTY PRETTY THINGS, EVERYTHING
WAS PUT IN PLACE. PETER WOULD FLY TO BANGKOK TO BE CURED OF HIS
ADDICTION. PETER TOOK BODYGUARD JEFF SHOPPING BEFOREHAND FOR SHORTS,
SUNGLASSES AND HOLIDAY PARAPHERNALIA FOR A HOT COUNTRY. AT 9.30 P.M.
THAT NIGHT HE BOARDED A FLIGHT AT HEATHROW FOR THAILAND, ACCOMPANIED
BY JEFF THE CIGAR-SMOKING BODYGUARD WHO WAS THERE TO PREVENT PETER
GETTING DISTRACTED IN BANGKOK, AND TO ENSURE HE REACHED THE DOOR OF
THE MONASTERY.

It was something of a coup getting Peter on to the plane.
The Priory hadn't worked because of the nearby
temptations and, perhaps more importantly, because he
hadn't wanted to be clean. But this regime was much
tougher and with a resoundingly impressive success rate.

Peter was seen to the door of the monastery. His
passport was taken off him by the monks. The place
itself was beautifully situated out in the country, miles
from Bangkok. There was a bunk for Peter and toiletries
and mouthwash all with unbroken seals to ensure no
drugs could be smuggled in. The treatment included
taking a herbal medicine and tablets that would induce
vomiting. A rapid detox can clear the body of drugs
within seven days.

From the moment he stepped across the threshold,
Peter hated it there. Living under the mosquito nets
reminded him a little too much of *The Bridge on the
River Kwai*. Although he had nothing bad to say about
the monastery, he had his own problems.
PETER: 'I got accosted in the steam bath for one … The
disasters came from other patients. The monks were
lovely … very wise people. But there were infringements
upon my liberty which I can't … It was no place, no
place … for a … for someone trying to find a bit of

space. I just thought that something was going to
happen. I was scared.'

Peter attempted to leave on the very first day he
entered the compound, but the monks refused to give
him his passport and stated that if he really wanted to
leave he had to wait for Jeff to return. A monk grabbed
Peter's face and squeezed. 'Peter – Fighter! You must be
stronger. Don't go to Bangkok.'

He managed three days, the same length of time as
before, then kicked and screamed at the door of the
monastery until the monks relented. He fled for
Bangkok. As Peter left, the abbot of the monastery did
not condemn him but bid him farewell.

This was the worst of all worlds. Bangkok is
notorious. It also has a deeply unpleasant footnote in
rock history; it's considered to be the place that drove
Richey Edwards of the Manic Street Preachers into a
headlong decline that led eventually to his unsolved

HE MANAGED THREE DAYS, THE SAME LENGTH OF
TIME AS BEFORE, THEN KICKED AND SCREAMED
AT THE DOOR OF THE MONASTERY UNTIL THE
MONKS RELENTED. HE FLED FOR BANGKOK.

disappearance in February 1995. It had also been the title of the B-side to 'Time For Heroes', with Peter singing through a megaphone. And here he was, his nose stuffed with the aroma that he wrote about so eloquently.

Peter checked into a hotel where he later claimed there was heroin on room service and that he indulged sexually in everything that took his fancy.
PETER: 'I went from the monastery, from that primitive, spiritual place, to Sodom and Gomorrah, Chinese rocks [heroin] on room service … outrageous, man … the girls … aaawwww … . I was skint so I thought I'd be no use to them but y'know … A pleasure-seeking individual always looks his best. They had cares too, those street girls ain't trash.'

Even in distant Bangkok he was an English colonial, quoting The Kinks' 'Dedicated Follower Of Fashion' to explain how attractive he was to Thai prostitutes. He indulged in heroin beyond his wildest dreams, in three days using an amount that would have cost thousands in the UK. Meanwhile, back home there was nothing to do but look on with mounting horror as the true legacy of the trip was revealed. He was stranded out there without anyone to bring him back.

The support for Peter on libertines.org ebbed away and it became seriously factionalised, as the fans exploded into arguments pro and anti Peter. Peter was frequently lambasted on libertines.org.

So ferocious were some attacks that Alan McGee himself, despite reeling from another failed attempt, felt the need to intervene to prevent Peter drowning in Thailand. He was under no illusions that Peter could overdose in Thailand, or, if caught in possession of drugs, find himself in prison, possibly with a death sentence. He also knew that if Peter were to enter a Bangkok Internet cafe and read the forthright views on his situation then it could push him over the edge.

Alan McGee wrote an impassioned personal appeal asking people to stop the attacks on Peter. 'No good will come of treating Peter like this. It will make him run away … Our belief in Peter as a person and his talent remains intact. The group will still put Peter into a clinic if he wants to return to these shores.'

And finally he appealed to their emotions: 'His

support of Love Music Hate Racism to trying to arrange benefit gigs for QPR only goes to prove he has a good heart. He may have lost the way at this point but he is a good person. Let him work out what he wants to do.'

For a moment at least the board settled down and went back to what had become its primary purpose for the past six months: the place on the Web to advertise gigs. Gill was beside herself; she planned to go to Thailand and rescue Peter.

He was at liberty in Bangkok – the drugs had fugged his senses like never before. He began posting on babyshambles.com once again, but this time the flights of fancy, the surreal images and the non sequiturs took precedence over lucid elegant prose. Despite the unusually oblique posts, some things could be discerned amid the wreckage. Contradicting his later statements, he blamed the monastery for opening all his letters and stated that 'one letter was too much to resist and through the rain we speed in a car to the finest bar in the world'.

And so on 17 June he flew back home. There were no recriminations. Everyone just crossed their fingers that he wouldn't try and bring back the heroin, a gram of which was cheaper than a pint of milk in Britain. Peter returned bearing gifts he'd picked up in Thailand. Most notably there was a flick knife he'd bought for Carl to accompany the sturdy Herr Flick from Germany. It was a bid to reconcile the pair, to explain what he'd gone through and where he was. To make things better again.

The night of his return, Gill was ready with her car at his disposal. She was happy to let him drive over towards the East End. He'd escaped Bangkok in one-ish piece, with his habit intact. He was free, though. Back in familiar territory, he resolved to meet up with Carlos and put everything straight. But first he would visit the Kirstys with the good news.

When he saw the blue light in the rear-view mirror as he drove down Hackney Road, he knew it was already too late. The police car pulled him over, suspicious at a car driving erratically late at night.
PETER: 'It's Carl's fault, y'know what I mean. He likes flick knives and things like that. I wanted to like heal the rift a bit. It was his birthday so I bought him a lovely flick knife.

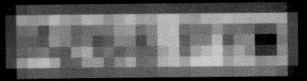

'I was going to get him a gun but … hahahah … I thought guns might be illegal in London, y'know. I ain't looked into it. Lucky I didn't … imagine that one?'

Peter had chopped the end off the blade, believing that meant it was no longer an offensive weapon. The policeman had other ideas. He was charged.

The Libertines gig at Glastonbury was cancelled completely. Carl managed to make it down to something he felt spiritually close to, particularly after his hippy upbringing. It was slightly odd, the urban dandy getting it together in the country. He was sanguine about Peter. Pleased he was back but uncertain what would happen.

Peter was distraught when he discovered that Carl had gone to Glastonbury with mutual friends while he sat in his flat alone. 'Seven o'clock in the morning I get a call from Chev going, "He really misses you, you didn't make it?" Why not phone me? Why not play Glastonbury? I didn't really believe it was happening to me again. I thought they would let me back in. I thought Alan was going to turn up and say, "Hi, let's go."'

The second Libertines album was in the can, and once again they'd blown their chance to play Glastonbury as a band. 'I just sat there playing along to the album. I felt like a fucking idiot. Then I thought back six or seven years to standing there in front of a mirror imagining playing Glastonbury and imagining it was real.'

On 29 June he made a brief appearance at Thames Magistrates Court accompanied by Alan McGee, Tony Linkin and James Endeacott. He pleaded not guilty and was due to appear on 10 August for a preliminary hearing. The band arranged to have a meeting with Alan later that day.

Peter believed that everything would carry on as before. After the Bangkok blow-out he would perhaps quit or at least cut down. Instead he was charged, and found that The Libertines camp were at the end of their tether. Having tried four times and spent extraordinary sums on rehab, it hadn't worked.

ALAN McGEE: 'Everybody had so much hope around Thailand. The Priory everyone knew wasn't going to work – I paid for both Priory visits, but getting him in the first time was me, the second time was his mum getting him in there – but we both knew it probably was not going to work. But when he took up the offer to go to Thailand we thought he was going to do it. Little did we know, he just fancied a holiday to Thailand!'

The band had had enough. He'd made them look stupid; they thought he'd had no intention of quitting. But that wasn't true. Peter always intended to quit, but always after one last indulgence.

The band needed to sort things out quickly. Their commitments were such that they couldn't carry on cancelling gigs. Gary and John were looking to kick him out. They had T In The Park in Scotland and the Reading/Leeds festival in the UK plus a massive American and European tour.

Gary had even gone as far as suggesting to Alan that they phone Anthony Rossomando ready for the tour. Carl would not budge, though. He wouldn't stand by and let his friend be thrown out of their band again. He proposed one last chance to thrash things out. They'd have a meeting and set the conditions on how the band would work with Peter and how he would work with them. Before the court hearing Peter had been told there would be a crucial meeting the same day.

Peter phoned Alan McGee's office to confirm that he'd be making the meeting. Peter couldn't believe how unlucky he'd been, being picked up by police straight after arriving back in London. For him, though, things could get back on track. He still wanted to dump the junk and make sure that music was centre stage. As Gary had suggested in New York, Peter wanted additional outlets for his music separate from The Libertines. He'd enjoyed the success with Wolfman, but for him it was time to get serious with Babyshambles.

The band were shaping up well, with Patrick Walden from White Sport on guitar, Gemma Clarke whose dad ran the rehearsal studio on drums and Peter Perrett's two

AS DOMINIC WAS TALKING TO THE POLICEMAN, PETER GESTURED TO ROGER TO JOIN HIM BY SOME STEPS JUST OUT OF SIGHT OF THE VAN. 'NOT NOW, PETER,' SAID ROGER. PETER IGNORED HIM, ENJOYING THE THRILL OF TRANSGRESSION AS HE PULLED HIS MARTELL-BOTTLE CRACK-PIPE OUT OF HIS POCKET AND PUFFED ON IT.

sons on bass and guitar. Peter had arranged to have a rehearsal the day of the hearing – the hearing had gone on for longer than he'd thought and, of course, he had this Libertines meeting to go to. He checked the time. He checked it again. It was a simple choice: meeting or rehearsal. It was no choice, really. As he told the Kirstys later: 'I'd rather make music than talk about it.'

He headed over to Babyshambles' rehearsal studio. There would be time for meetings later.

The Libertines sat in Creation's offices for a couple of hours in a room that began to ferment with a mixture of anxiety, in Carl's case, and resigned contempt on the part of Gary and John. Gary says: 'We waited around for a while and then it was just, forget it, we've had enough.'

Carl was crushed. Peter hadn't made it. He tried phoning Peter, but there was no answer. He'd tried brinkmanship, but he couldn't stop it any more. The potential compromises would never be uttered. Peter was out of the band.

Alan McGee repeatedly tried phoning Peter. He even phoned the Kirstys to see if they had seen him, impressing upon them that he had to talk to Peter as Peter had missed the band meeting and he was not going to be allowed to play with the band until he sorted himself out.

At about 2 a.m. the following morning, as a tube strike was about to hit London, the Kirstys had a call. It was Peter. He was obviously distressed and wanted to come over and talk. He'd often visit them when he was distressed. 'They calm me down,' he said.

Kirsty Want persuaded him that it was two in the morning and she had work the following day. She went back to bed.

Peter phoned again two hours later and this time the Kirstys relented; he could come over and chat. He arrived at 6 a.m. He looked terrible, he was fretful and he was high. The Kirstys, aware of what was going to happen to Peter later that day, endeavoured to turn the conversation away from The Libertines and on to other subjects, any subjects.

Peter pulled out his mobile and told them about the calls he'd had the day before and ignored. He confessed that eventually he'd turned his phone off. The girls were

statesmanlike in their composure, but inside they knew exactly what those missed calls were about. Peter finished the story with a flourish of his arm, brandishing his phone and turning it on.

The phone rang almost immediately. Peter answered it. It was Alan. The Kirstys looked at each other, terrified. What was Peter likely to do when he found out? After trying to get hold of Peter for twelve hours, Alan had to seize this opportunity.

Peter looked agitated; he began pacing up and down their small lounge. The conversation was short, but it was clear that the message was unequivocal: Peter was out of the band again.

Peter slumped into a chair and pulled out the mini

PETER: 'IT TEARS, IT TEARS, IT TEARS US APART ... CARL'S TEASING ME. WHY PUSH ME OUT OF THE LIBERTINES? WHY GO THERE? HMMM? HE HAS A HOLD OVER ME BECAUSE SOMEHOW HE'S GOT THE MACHINE BEHIND HIM THAT CONTROLS ALL THESE THINGS THAT ARE SO DEAR TO ME.'

Martell bottle he had had fashioned into a crack-pipe from his pocket, fiddling with it like it was a rosary. His demeanour was alien to everything they'd seen; he seethed and shook with hurt. The Kirstys were scared at what he might do but Kirsty Want put her arm round him all the same. He shrank back, shunning contact.

Glancing about the flat he saw and picked up a piece of paper with the 'Can't Stand Me Now' B-sides written on it. With petty precision he picked them apart. 'I wrote that. And that. Carl wrote that. I wrote that except for a tiny bit by Carl.'

Then he left their flat, still high on crack after neglecting for the first time ever to kiss the Kirstys goodbye. From their window they could tell he was veering all over the road, probably more so than when he'd been arrested on Hackney Road.

Alan had phoned from Paris where he was with Carl after catching the Eurostar to start the round of interviews. There were two reasons for being abroad. First and most obviously it was to promote the forthcoming album. Secondly, though, it was to keep Carl away from Peter, to keep him strong and stop him from buckling and caving in as he knew he would if he faced Peter in person.

Peter did the thing he knew best. He went out to play for the kids. He wasn't entirely sure what was going to happen this time. Would people still turn out to see him?

Peter was never your typical junkie. Unfeasibly charismatic, after so many attempts at rehab, robbing his friend and broken promises, why would anyone continue to believe him? If you were objective about it, it beggars belief that as Peter shed one confidant another would appear. But as Tim Arnold was falling out of favour, he had another guardian angel, Dot Allison. Formerly of One Dove; she'd sang with Death In Vegas and Massive Attack. They gelled, wrote a song together. She was convinced she would save Peter. He wanted to be saved. All it required was patience and it would be done. She would succeed where everyone else had failed.

But if he couldn't do it for Carl, for the sake of The Libertines, for Albion, for his lovers, why would he do it for Tim Arnold or Dot Allison?

As Peter set about clawing his musical life back in a bid to prove himself, many fans found the déjà vu too much to bear and dropped out, hoping that Peter would come to his senses. They had had their faith tested to destruction and certainly weren't going to put any money in Peter's pocket. The equation was clear. Little gigs equalled money for drugs. And they weren't prepared to put money into the destruction of their fallen hero.

There was too much momentum, though. A new wave of fans had become intoxicated by this man and with The Libertines' second album still almost two months away they wanted him. They wanted him badly, and they wanted to see it all first hand.

Ironically, Peter was out of the band just as interest surrounding The Libertines mushroomed. There was another group who confessed that although they thought Peter was spending the money on drugs, they had no choice, it was the only way they were going to see him.

Peter was determined not to let this version of Babyshambles become the source of mockery the last one had. This was no gimcrack band. He would sing. He would show the knockers that he could do it. And so the whirlwind of gigs started again. This proved to be a shrewd move. Typically, when artists leave bands they disappear to record a debut album for a year, and by the time they re-emerge no one really cares. In contrast, Peter rode the wave that The Libertines had created; and with Carl out of the country promoting their album, he was the only person the UK press and Libertines fans could get near. Peter Doherty's nascent band became the source of all news about The Libertines.

The Rhythm Factory – like Filthy McNasty's before – became Peter's spiritual home. He began to rebuild his career, if not from scratch, then from a precarious place – after all, he felt the world was against him.

Carl and the rest of the band resolved to dig their heels in. Peter could not be allowed back in the band until he'd cleaned up. He'd tried rehab four times now and none had worked.

As Peter decided to go it alone, to prove to everybody that he could do it, Carl, John and Gary had touring commitments they could not avoid. Due to the cancelled

European tours in the past the insurance to cover them was crippling; cancelling the tours that had already been booked would have bankrupted them.

The first gig without Peter was to be T In The Park on 10 July. Two days before I sat down and interviewed Peter for what would be the final Libertines *NME* cover.

Peter was confident, headstrong and full of bravado. For me, it was like intruding on a particularly gruesome and personal affair. Having spoken at length with both Carl and Peter, I knew Peter's ability to cast himself as a victim with the most hard-nosed of interviewers. It didn't make me feel any easier, though, in Exmouth Market above a mid-market pizza restaurant.

His self-belief at that point was extraordinary. He spoke about a Leeds gig with Babyshambles days earlier, and how great the gig was and how excited he was about it, talking animatedly as he showed me footage on his laptop. He spoke of his plans to record the Babyshambles album. As the interview was conducted, Wolfman sat in the front room in a dressing gown that looked mouldy and was a little too short for my liking. On the wall of Peter's bedroom were the titles of songs for the Babyshambles album, as he worked out the track listing.

With the future resolved and planned, the interview turned to the present and his predicament with The Libertines playing T In The Park in two days. He was adamant that he didn't know how they would play without him. I asked him why he wouldn't stop using drugs in order to return to the band.

Peter whispered, 'I don't shoot … I don't inject. Even if I started doing that or going into that kind of world … I think I was more unreliable before [going to prison]. It's all mixed up. Alan McGee promised me – he swore – that it would never happen again, they would never ever play without me.'

So what's going to happen when they do play without you?

All front evaporated in a second and his shoulders shook as he started sobbing. The ever-present sparkle in his eyes went out.

PETER: 'I'm gonna die. It means so much to me … I'm just gonna die … Something in me that was really badly, really damaged, yet somehow we forgave. Course you

don't forget, you forgive, y'know … They've got no right to play T In The Park and get onstage when I don't play.'

I was mortified; he'd crumbled so suddenly. I found the strength to stick to my guns. 'You do know they'll let you back in, if you give up drugs?'

PETER: 'How can I go back? I can't go back to that … It tears, it tears, it tears us apart. I can't live my life with that … Carl's teasing me. He's teasing me. Why push me out of The Libertines? Why go there? Hmmm? He has a hold over me because somehow he's got the machine behind him that controls all these things that are so fucking dear to me. He knows. He walked away. So much of this is my life.

'The door's been shut on me from The Libertines. Whether it was the management, whether it was the band, it doesn't matter to me. I don't want to hang around any place I'm not welcome.

'I can't betray myself. I feel betrayed. I don't want to go on about the drugs thing. I try and avoid it as best I can but to say it's about drugs to me is a cop-out.'

It was heartbreaking, but worst was yet to come. He asked me if he could review The Libertines at T In The Park for *NME*.

PETER: '"Three songs in I decided to get up onstage." Carl'll be, "Get 'im off." Can I go to T In The Park and review it? Can I actually do it? And to the man who would be king … I would ask only one thing … '

Then his demeanour changed again, like he'd worked out the ending to Margaret Rutherford's latest Agatha Christie film. 'Do you know something I don't?'

'Do I know something you don't? Well, no, I don't think so,' I answered, confused.

'Do you know anything?'

'About what?'

'About me playing at T In The Park with the band?'

'No, what? Are you playing, then? Have you sorted it out?'

'I want to … I dunno. I'm going to go there now.'

His hope, belief and faith was such that even then he thought he might be passed the message that he would be allowed to play by an *NME* journalist, of all people.

There was a knock at the door as a parcel was delivered for Peter. The parcel contained the drafts of

Sophie Thunders' cover art for the second Libertines album. It was astonishing for me that even with Peter out of the band Rough Trade ensured he still had a say on the artwork. Sophie had done a great job on the single for 'Can't Stand Me Now', but when faced with this complicated series of glued-down paper and cut-outs Peter reacted with a confusion that was an echo of Spinal Tap's Nigel Tufnel surveying the small breads and cold meats backstage and not quite understanding what goes where.

Eventually the cover art was worked up by Roger, and Jeanette Lee would bring the artwork over to Peter in person for his approval. He loved it at the time but later denied to *Newsnight* that he'd ever had anything to do with it: 'Unfortunately by that time all power had slipped away from my grasp. I was always so precious with the artwork and so for them to go on with the artwork and misprint lyrics and not to credit songs and to use a photo was like Stalinist Russia. All evidence of any of my contribution was gone now.' MICK JONES: 'I thought it was a lovely picture but I was worried about the connotations; that people might think it was someone showing track marks rather than people showing tattoos. I had a great picture by Wit of the Gordon Riots from Dickens' *Barnaby Rudge* for the cover.'

There was much debate over what the album should be called. There was one flippant suggestion that due to the amount of heroin that was imbibed during its recording they should take a hint from The Beatles' *The White Album* and call it *The Brown Album*. Peter was keen on calling it *Tomblands*. The more literary multi-meanings of *Consumption* nearly came through as well, but in the end it was to bear the name of the band. The lyrics were hastily typed up by Rough Trade by listening to the record and attempting to decipher the intricate enunciation. So hasty was this transcription that one line of the lyrics to 'Last Post On The Bugle' has written next to it: '??? Ask Mick Jones'.

On 9 July Roger was due to shoot Peter for a *Mojo* feature on The Libertines which PR Tony Linkin had arranged. Roger met the slight, delicate Tony and Peter at a rehearsal studio near Old Street. He suggested that they do the shoot in Whitechapel, in the same place as the first Libertines photo shoot.

In the taxi on the way over, Peter said to Roger and Tony in a concerned tone: 'How's Carl?'

They were both non-committal, saying he was fine; they tried to steer the conversation on to safer subjects.

'This should be a good photo shoot,' said Tony.

'Yeah, do you remember, doing those Libertines shots?' asked Roger.

That was it. Peter just started to shake and cry. Roger and Tony both welled up in sympathy. A few seconds after regaining composure, Roger and Tony tried desperately to talk Peter back up.

Roger said, 'It's gonna be good, it's gonna be well. Carl asks after you all the time.'

They stopped off at Dominic Masters's

house as it was nearby. Dominic was the singer with The Others, who'd made their name doing a ton of guerrilla gigs in places including the lobby of BBC Radio 1 and on a tube train on the circle line. He was also an unapologetic user of crack.

They headed over to the grim bridge where The Libertines had done their first photo shoot and took some shots, then headed down the other side, by a railway arch. The last time they'd been there, it had contained a burnt-out car.

Tony, looking for a little levity in these depressing surroundings, spotted a plank of wood on the ground. He picked it up and started swinging it round like a sword, before imitating a light sabre from *Star Wars* pretty convincingly.

'Neeeeeooooooow,' he wailed as he swung the plank in the general direction of Roger and Peter.

Suddenly a police riot van came screaming around the corner and stopped a foot in front of them. About ten policemen in full riot gear jumped out of the van like well-drilled action men.

The lead policeman screamed at them. 'What the fucking hell are you doing down here?'

Dominic replied, 'Doing a photo shoot.'

Tony casually tossed the plank to the floor in a way that could only be conspicuous.

'Right,' said the policemen. 'Well, you want to watch it down here, there's loads of whores and crackheads.'

I know, thought Roger. We're with two of them.

'Well, you carry on then,' finished the sergeant. The policemen all ran in different directions, disappearing in a second and leaving one kindly policeman by the van.

Dominic told him they were doing a shoot for The Others. He knew if he mentioned the name Peter Doherty, the chances were they'd be arrested.

As Dominic was talking to the policeman, Peter gestured to Roger to join him by some steps just out of sight of the van.

'Not now, Peter,' said Roger. Peter ignored him, enjoying the thrill of transgression as he pulled his Martell-bottle crack-pipe out of his pocket and puffed on it.

Roger took the photo, feeling the adrenalin pumping through him. Then Peter went to the side of the police van, on the opposite side to the policeman, and said, 'Let's do some more.'

'Don't be stupid,' hissed Roger. Peter pulled on the pipe once again. Beneath the van Roger saw the feet of the policeman begin to move as he inspected the van's tyres one by one. Peter pulled on the pipe again. The policeman drew level with Peter and saw him inhale from the mini brandy bottle.

Roger recalls: 'The policeman saw him pulling on the pipe … And he just … ignored it. He saw him but I'm sure his brain just couldn't comprehend what he'd witnessed, he couldn't believe that someone would do that, by a police van. He just looked at Peter in a spooked way and carried on walking around the van.'

Peter was freaked out and within moments started jogging away, saying to Roger and Tony: 'See you back at the studio.'

Tony and Roger went and bought a lot of beer.

The next day was T In The Park. It was clearly something Carl didn't want to do without Peter. He was broken and upset, and the return of Anthony Rossomando to The Libertines camp did little to lift his spirits. Every moment of those two gigs was hell. Every note a nail in the coffin of The Libertines. Carl couldn't cope. He struggled through after dedicating the first song 'Can't Stand Me Now' to 'my best friend, Peter'.

Once it was over he felt relieved and stronger. For a moment, backstage, he tried to put it to the back of his mind. Worse was to follow, though, as he was sent round the world to do press for the forthcoming record. He found it deeply distressing as he retold the story of The Libertines and the robbery and the need to try and get Peter back in the fold. After pouring his heart out, he would frequently be met with a blank stare and a question like: 'And tell me again, are you Peter or Carl?'

In the UK, Tony Linkin had decided that where possible he would like Peter to be available for interview as well as Carl. He wanted there to be a chance for both sides to put their voices across. He refused to play favourites even as The Libertines camp was growing increasingly divided along Peter or Carl lines. Of course, if they hadn't followed Tony Linkin's suggestions, Peter would have been all over the Internet putting his side of the story anyway, and the media would have been happy to turn what was a miserable experience for everyone into a much more fraught one. It would have become a slanging match that continued up to the release of the album.

In the middle of this, Roger's exhibition of Libertines' photographs took place at the Proud Gallery in Camden. This was supposed to be a photographic celebration of the band, or at least that had been the point when it was planned back in April. Four months later and the exhibition threatened to be a wake.

Carl was out of the country when Peter turned up to play the official launch on 23 July. Peter surveyed the pictures and was unhappy that perhaps Carl looked better than he did overall. Gary was also on hand, and hugged his friend onstage in a show of solidarity. It was touching and it seemed important for Peter to know that he was able to rejoin the band at any time, as long as he kicked the drugs.

Fans filled the hall as Gary walked round the venue inspecting the pictures. 'I was just talking to some people and I heard this music and I was like, whoa, where's that coming from? So I went out to the marquee out back, pushed through the crowd and it's Peter onstage and the first thing that went through my mind was oh my goodness. He hadn't finished off any of the recording with us, let us down with all the drug rehabilitation crap, and now he's taking all of the plaudits because Carl and John weren't there. I mean, this guy is a retard, but he's not stupid at all. He knew exactly what he was doing. I was forced to get onstage with him. Bob, a friend of Roger's, told me to get my arse onstage and I thought, what the hell. I'll just have some fun. And I stood there and banging along with his crap and I thought to myself, my god, I look like a total retard. And I was like, I'll love him and leave him, my job is done.'

Peter, despite nursing his betrayal, felt a little vindicated by Gary's appearance and hug.
CARL: 'That was a bit of upset, wasn't it? Because Peter thought he was in the clear again through no effort or recompense – or repentance or even admission of guilt.'

Two days later Carl himself made it to the exhibition; like Peter he was impressed with the pictures, but he felt that Peter probably had greater prominence.

On 2 August Peter was down to play a key gig at the Camden Barfly. It was full of music industry and media commentators, many of whom wanted to see if he could do it on his own. The heat was stifling and the place was packed.

Peter entertained friends and fans earlier at his flat with an acoustic set. Then he set out with the entourage to the Barfly. At the door the bouncers refused to let everyone in. In an echo of what had happened at the Tap 'n' Tin freedom gig, only Peter was to be allowed in, no one else. The ever-dependable Chev was shoved by a bouncer and Peter demanded an apology. When none was forthcoming, he turned on his heel and took the cheering entourage back to flat to entertain them some more.

It was another half an hour before the people inside were informed. This time the crowd was made up predominantly of people who hadn't paid but were on the list. These were sweaty movers and shakers who made a mental note never to include Peter in their paper/ radio station/TV show. This was something of a setback for Peter, eroding the image he'd attempted to cultivate as a wronged poet and minstrel who had been treated despicably by his friends.

He apologised for the no-show but then failed to show up for a gig the following day to support Wolfman. The Scala was sold out – this was supposed to be the platform to launch Wolfman's career. The night descended into a cringing event where every silence was punctuated with a chant of 'Where's Pete?', in a distant echo of Carl's similar experience touring with The Libertines the previous summer. It was, for many, unthinkable. Outside of Carl, Wolfman had been his closest confidant; they'd had a top-ten single together, for goodness' sake. But here Peter was deserting him. This was a scene he'd done so much to encourage, and he deserted them. To date Wolfman hasn't recovered from this setback, although he was nominated for an Ivor Novello Award for 'For Lovers'. Wolfman had shimmied his way to a certain level of fame that under scrutiny it transpired was fame in the form of notoriety. The show closed with Wolfman dueting with Chev on 'For Lovers'. His career essentially stopped there and then.

Peter, on this occasion, was unrepentant. Posting online in response to criticism, he savaged the fans who'd attacked him online. He admonished them for not believing in him and deserting him at the first opportunity. He said he planned to drive away all the fair-weather fans as he was inconsolable at their responses.

However, with a handful of great Babyshambles shows, the absent shows were soon largely forgotten. Some fans admonished those who complained about no-shows online, as a new breed of fan appeared. This was the fan that took pragmatism to a new level; they weren't Peter apologists, they had hardened into Peter celebrators. They saw the potential that he may not turn up as a part of the experience. In a curious mixture of macho and masochistic, they saw the possibility of a no-show was something to be endured or even enjoyed. They revelled in accusing complainers of being fair-weather fans. Suffering was part of being a real fan, they argued.

The nascent Babyshambles was under scrutiny at the time. Filmmaker Roger Pomphrey was making a documentary that would eventually become *Who The Fuck Is Pete Doherty?*, but Peter felt that he had only a limited time to make an impact before disappearing into obscurity. Around this time there was practically an open-door policy on filmmakers. Pretty much if you had your own handheld video camera you would pretty much be allowed into the inner circle – on some occasions there were as many as six video cameras being wielded onstage by a decidedly mixed group of documenters. Peter remained amazingly open and trustful of these strangers documenting his travails. He saw it as an extension of his generosity towards new bands – he was happy to give filmmakers a break. It was the spirit of Arcadia and the Filthy McNasty's scene: helping people's dreams come true. It was around this time that troubled documentary maker Max Carlish would film Peter smoking heroin in a north London studio, leaving Peter's trust perverted and exploited.

On 9 August 'Can't Stand Me Now' was released as the first single off the album. A day later Peter failed to make his court appearance because of a severe case of gastroenteritis (or because the no-show habit had gone to his head).

The nature of the song had changed completely since its first media out on *The Jonathan Ross Show* months before. Then it had been an honest declaration of Peter and Carl's differing views, ultimately turning to resolution and acceptance, and the hope that they could build on the partnership. Now it was bitter, a catalogue of accusations and counter-accusations. It stalled at number two behind 'Babycakes' by 3 Of A Kind.

At the postponed hearing at Thames Magistrates Court on 17 August, Peter pleaded guilty to possession of a knife. Speaking outside court, Doherty said: 'If the law was to send me to prison it wouldn't be able to look itself in the eye.'

The Libertines were due to play the Reading Festival. Peter was convinced that if he got near the band he could convince them to let him play, even if it was just for this one gig. The night before the gig, Peter's new Babyshambles, now without Peter Perrett's sons and with Drew McConnell on bass, played the Fez Club in Reading. Peter was keen to be reunited with Carl and The Libertines. A message was passed through Chev that Peter was not welcome and would be forcibly ejected if necessary.

Remarkably there were more pressing concerns than the possible appearance of Peter at the door of their tour bus backstage. Carl, John, Gary and Anthony had received anonymous death threats if they played Reading without Peter. There was no way they were not going to play, but they each had security. Before they went onstage the security guards donned bulletproof armour. Understandably, it was quite a tense set. A day later they performed in Leeds. There was still a grand tour to finish round the rest of the world, but it was the last Libertines gig on British soil.

Carl and Morrissey were snapped by the great photographer Andy Willsher backstage for what became the cover of *NME*. It was a great photograph. Morrissey

clearly thought a lot of Carl. But Morrissey had always been Peter's object of adoration, though, and when he eventually saw the cover he was inconsolable.

CARL: 'I felt bad for being on that cover [with Morrissey] but I have a genuine respect and appreciation for this man and if it's offered it's rude to turn down an icon.'

A day after the Reading/Leeds Festival, the eponymous second album was released. The reviews were unanimous: it was fantastic. Mick Jones's fresh, live production would win him that year's Producer Of The Year Award from Q magazine.

Living life ten times faster than anyone else, Peter's trial for possession of the Thai flick knife was on 1 September, the Wednesday after the Reading/Leeds Festival. He appeared at the court an hour before, driven by Chev. He stood with his head through the sunroof and serenaded the onlookers and reporters. Dressed immaculately in a suit and a pork-pie hat, it was startlingly similar to his style in the original Razzcocks-era Libertines. He couldn't resist quoting Hancock when asked how he felt. 'Innocent. What about the Magna Carta, did she die in vain?'

However, it wasn't just Peter with a heightened sense of the theatrical. On sentencing, Judge Malcolm Reid said that Peter was not suitable for a community sentence; he would serve four months in prison. Peter was aghast; he covered his face with his hands.

'However,' the judge continued, 'given the way the knife was found and that it was found shortly after you came back into the country, the sentence would be suspended for twelve months.'

Peter was free to go after paying £150 in court costs.

Leaving the court, Peter was relieved to the point of bravado, telling Andy Lee, a filmmaker documenting Wolfman's career, 'I just turned on the water works and he came round.'

But in reality he knew how close he'd been to a second spell in prison and his relief was unquantifiable.

The following weekend, The Libertines' album debuted at number one. Peter, meanwhile, was busy building his reputation with Babyshambles, and had a new manager as well. It was the return of James Mullord from the early days: Plan B, the man who was passed over for Rough Trade.

Somewhat strangely both Jake Fior and Wolfman's manager were worried about this new addition to Peter's business affairs, believing him to be a bad influence. But whatever they thought of him, a huge official UK tour was lined up and Peter hit the road with Babyshambles once again. The Libertines went overseas for foreign tour commitments.

So, taking away the one thing Peter cared about, the one thing he loved above all else, had backfired. Given isolation, he resolved to find friends and associates old and new who could help him. After the failed attempt to reunite at Reading, and the Morrissey snub, Peter was determined to show them. He would show them that he could do it without Alan, John and Gary. And most of all he could do it without Carl.

Chapter 16

TIME FOR HEROES

*'IT WAS THE SPRING OF HOPE, IT WAS THE
WINTER OF DESPAIR, WE HAD
EVERYTHING BEFORE US, WE HAD NOTHING BEFORE US'*
Charles Dickens, *A Tale of Two Cities*

TIME FOR HEROES

BABYSHAMBLES HIT THE ROAD ON AN EIGHTEEN-DATE TOUR. ON THE FIRST DATE IN BRIGHTON, I INTERVIEWED PETER ONCE AGAIN, WHERE HE WAS KIND AND COURTEOUS. I WAS INTERVIEWING HIM FOR A PIECE ABOUT THE MAKING OF THE LIBERTINES ALBUM. IT WAS INITIALLY UNCOMFORTABLE FOR ME AS THE FEELING OF BAD BLOOD WAS AT ITS WORST, BUT PETER WAS WITTY AND ENTERTAINING.

As we sat in a bunk on the tour bus, with Gemma the drummer watching *Finding Nemo* on DVD downstairs, a peculiar smell began to emanate from beneath the bunk. It was quite an unusual aroma and as the interview progressed, in a surprisingly upbeat way, the aroma grew stronger and stronger. It was weird, sort of brackish, not something I'd ever encountered. I assumed it was crack or heroin that he'd stashed under the bed that was assailing my nostrils.

Peter was just revealing how there could be another Libertines album. 'Mick Jones had a baby around the time of *Up The Bracket* and he had another little girl around the time of *The Libertines*. That's two Libertines babies. So I'm saying this to the world: you want another Libertines album? Then get Mick Jones to eat some

oysters or something!'

After I'd finished laughing he suddenly fixed me a look and said, 'Can you smell something?'

'Yeah, I thought it was … '

He glanced down and his eyes widened. 'Oh no, I don't believe it.'

I felt ashamed. I must have accidentally put my foot through the stash, wrecking it and creating the smell.

'You've trodden on the toothpaste,' he said. I looked over the edge of the bunk and sure enough, not only had I trodden on a tube of bicarbonate of soda toothpaste, but in swinging my leg absentmindedly I'd smeared the sticky discharge across the floor of the coach and all over my shoe.

Peter swung into action. 'Put your leg out,' he gently

instructed. I did as I was told. Then, very gingerly, he carefully removed the shoe and stomped downstairs to clean the worst of the toothpaste off it in the tour bus's sink. I followed, hobbling downstairs like a guilty child caught using a muddy shortcut. He returned my shoe, which bore a peculiar smell that's never quite left it. I made a mental note not to be so presumptuous in future.

Babyshambles were outstanding at that first date in Brighton. A new song, 'Fuck Forever', was a highlight. Peter had put aside his guitar for this tour, allowing him to move around. He was already displaying his trademark one-arm-behind-his-back stance. Dot Allison performed a short set in the middle, leading one disgruntled wag to state: 'It was pretty good until Yoko came on.'

The circus around Peter was growing. By the time Babyshambles headlined the Scala in King's Cross there were something like five people on the side of the stage videoing events. This show was a key show for Babyshambles.

Up until this point, fans had held out hope for a Libertines re-formation. And it always seemed possible. After all, the Scarborough Steve-fronted Babyshambles was awful, and fans felt that the chances were that the new one would be as well. It would be, most people believed, a shabby run-through of Libertines songs released and unreleased plus a handful of hastily assembled sketches. What greeted people instead was a proper band who, while a little frayed around the edges, were nonetheless pretty great.

The opening chords of 'Fuck Forever' swept away the last possibility of a Libertines reunion. There was only one possible response from the assembled Libertines fans: they cried. In a definition of bittersweet, highly wrought emotions competed for attention: relief that Peter had finally established himself as a reliable entity in his own right and utter despair that this crushed any possible Libertines reunion.

The notion of rehab had been all but been abandoned. But somehow he'd pulled it round; and rather than being a pariah, his momentum was building. People who'd read and imbibed the outlaw notions of The Libertines wanted to see what it was like at close range and flocked

to his side. And Peter, finding himself the centre of attraction, more than ever before lapped it up.

And the critics who came to bury them were pleasantly surprised and wrote pieces praising them to the skies.

Carl and the remaining Libertines hit the road on a world tour; they refused to play the UK, partly out of respect for Peter. Meanwhile Peter stopped saying that he would quit drugs if he was allowed back in the band.

This weird stand-off persisted. There could be no resolution; there would be no deus ex machina as there had been a year previously. The Libertines, meanwhile, were becoming a great live band; different from the Peter-fronted version sure, but great as well. They fizzed with an energy drawn from the frustration and resentment and driven into the music. Not once did Carlos criticise his friend. The very worst he could summon up was a wish that 'Peter would get better'. This antagonised Peter beyond belief, but the manner in which Peter tossed barbed comments around only served to underline the fact that he wanted a reaction. Carl would not bite, however great the temptation. But each comment rankled and upset him. Touring abroad was, if anything, a useful way to avoid this. CARL: 'I'd like to have [played a tour of Britain], but the reason I didn't was because I didn't want to upset Peter, really. I didn't want to rub it in his face. I believe I've done the right thing. I hope he understands it. Of course, I'd have loved to play Britain. I love the British crowds. I feel a loyalty, affinity and unity with him whatever plight he seems to have been trudged through.'

So Peter had done it. With Carlos and the Libertines out of the country, there were some who claimed Peter had been the subject of a coup by Carl and the rest of the band. But the fact remains that Peter had rebuilt his career. Here he was playing storming sets to loads of people. And if you didn't believe him, somewhere there were six sets of videos to prove it.

It had to come to a head. It did. Due to play a show in Aberdeen, he overdosed on the bus, passing out. The show was cancelled. The fans outside, in contrast to the uptight Barfly music industry crowd, rioted. Police were called and seven people were arrested. Peter recovered and the overdose was kept secret.

Meanwhile, Peter had successfully thrown in his lot with producer Paul Epworth, the hottest producer around after his work on records for Bloc Party and The Futureheads. The single 'Killamangiro', a pun on Kill A Man For His Giro, wasn't going to be produced like the last single or The Libertines album. It was going to be done with precision and control. There would be as many retakes as the song required, and Paul instructed Peter on warm-up exercises for his voice. During the making of the single, Max Carlish, the increasingly

IT HAD TO COME TO A HEAD. IT DID. DUE TO PLAY A SHOW IN ABERDEEN, HE OVERDOSED ON THE BUS, PASSING OUT. THE SHOW WAS CANCELLED. THE FANS OUTSIDE RIOTED.

eccentric documentary filmmaker, successfully interviewed Peter.

Max interrogated Peter in what he believed was an outstanding interview. However, the tragicomic gods must have been abnormally efficient because, in a scenario that could have been scripted by Galton and Simpson, Max's camera ran out of tape at the very beginning of the interview, just as Max observed 'You're very photogenic, the camera loves you—'

Fortunately Paul Epworth's attention to detail included making sure he got the single down on tape. The results were superb. The single, although perhaps not Peter's strongest song, nonetheless came out brilliantly. It was spiky and shrill, and amazingly precise for Babyshambles.

Patrick Walden was proving to be an able foil and an individual in his own right. A nice fiddly little oriental riff heralds the opening of the best recording session that Babyshambles had achieved up to that point.

While Pat's little squalls of guitar bring an individuality to it, 'The Man Who Came To Stay' boasted a similar driving bassline, but the beautiful ghostly backing vocals lifted it further, making it the best song that Babyshambles had recorded up to that point.

The Libertines themselves carried on with the tour, hitting quite a dynamic peak. Tight and burning with passion, the show they gave in Paris's Les Inrockuptibles festival was excellent. Carl, trying desperately to enjoy himself, went to an Irish bar down the road from the venue and chatted to fans before belting out a few choruses of Ewan McColl's ballad 'Dirty Old Town', a song about industrial decline that in Carl's hands – like The Pogues – became somewhat bawdy.

The third annual *NME* Cool List was due to hit the shelves in late November. The intention of this list is to pick out the most inspirational and important people in the world of rock, as chosen and voted for by *NME* staff. What had, in previous years, been a fairly sedate process of the staff and freelancers putting together a long (long) list of possibles and then everyone sticking their oar in to decide the final, wasn't so simple this time. The year before Peter had been noticeable by his absence; the consensus in 2003 was that awarding a reformed drug

addict any notion of 'cool' was untenable. In contrast, Carl's selfless act of accepting Peter back into the band after all he had suffered was awarded, and so despite the fact that only one single had been released that year Carl was awarded the number-five place.

Eventually, after much shouting and banging of the meeting-room table, in the interests of history rather than all the trouble it would inevitably create for the magazine, it was decided that Peter would make number one, along with Carl. So in an unintended piece of wish-fulfilment, Peter and Carl were reunited.

The issue hit the shelves on 24 November 2004. And the trouble hit the papers and the airwaves immediately. The pieces in the magazine made it absolutely clear that

Peter had been awarded the co-number-one slot because of what he'd done for music and culture, via guerrilla gigging and the Internet. In the interests of a good story, this even-handed approach was ignored and the wider media focused on what they perceived to be gross irresponsibility, given his drug taking and dissolute lifestyle.

CARL: 'WE HAD TO WORK REALLY HARD TO GET THE CROWD, WHICH TOOK SOME TIME, BUT WE EVENTUALLY SUCCEEDED. SO IN THE ONE SENSE IT WAS A GLORIOUS SEND-OFF, AND ON THE OTHER HAND IT TOOK US BACK TO THE VERY BEGINNING.'

The reaction was hysterical; the microcosm of the *NME* office was played out across the media and the Internet. BBC Online piled in like a concerned aunt while *The Times* stirred itself up in a froth of moral outrage: 'He's been jailed, sacked by his band and he's a junkie. How cool is that?' screamed the headline.

Peter took to it with disarming charm when asked by *Xfm* what he thought of being at the top of the Cool List. 'Why, who won? You can't take these things too seriously, but who am I to argue? I mean, I was git of the year, last year. I haven't changed that much.'

And in a sense he was right; he hadn't changed that much, but with his trekking to the far corners of the country with goggle-eyed followers professing their love

for him wherever he went, he was having a greater influence than anyone else.

Peter carried on down the road of endless gigging; while The Libertines were touring abroad as far afield as Brazil, Babyshambles kept going, building up a fanbase. The crowds were unbelievable, treating Peter like a saviour or deity. People who'd previously doubted Babyshambles and The Libertines suddenly understood what a charismatic and mesmerising performer he was. Some critics even proclaimed Babyshambles were much better than The Libertines had ever been.

Such was his skill and use of the Internet that on 3 December they announced they would be playing Brixton. This was after their second single had just been released. Even given that he'd been in a band famous enough in its own right to headline Brixton, it doesn't detract from the singular achievement that without an album they were headlining one of the UK's major venues with a capacity of 5,000.

Peter had proved that he could go out with a bang, play a great series of gigs and garner a huge critical response. But then his instinct to self-destruct reared its head again.

For everyone else, though, it was time to wind down for Christmas. Carl decided to have some fun back in the Tap 'n' Tin, where The Libertines had stormed it on the day of Peter's release from prison.

He put together a band featuring himself and The Charlatans' Tim Burgess on vocals, Duffy of Primal Scream on keyboards and Andy Burrows of Razorlight on drums.

With a healthy disrespect for their own back catalogues, they roared through what was the very definition of ramshackle. It culminated in a boozy rendition of The Pogues' 'Fairytale Of New York' that saw Tim and Carl collapse on the floor in an ungainly pile at the end. It was hilarious. It was wonderful to see Carl put behind him the problems of The Libertines.

Then Peter phoned Kirsty Want because he wanted to speak to Carl. Kirsty knew that it would turn a fun evening into an anxious one and was loath to get Carl. She gave the phone to Dean. Peter really wanted to come down. Dean spoke to him and persuaded him that it wasn't the time or the place. The Kirstys waited until after the gig to tell Carl.

Carl had, by this time, definitely resolved to dissolve The Libertines. He was well aware that he had an equal legal right to the name, and given Gary and John's involvement it's feasible they might have won a case if it was brought to court. But he was sick of the headache that it'd become, he was sick of the criticism and sideswipes. It was over. The one thing about it, the one satisfying thing was, he was the one who declared it over.

And so the band played their last gig in a secret location on the northern outskirts of Paris in a horrible-looking industrial estate. It wasn't even a headlining gig

– they were supporting P.J. Harvey in a venue which people got tickets for by texting a number given on the Paris metro.

The front line started with their backs to the audience. They played a sharp gig that highlighted how good a band they'd become. They were bright and exciting and tight in a way they never were with Peter. They even managed some spontaneity. After they played 'The Boy Looked At Johnny', Gary stood up behind the drums, stretched his arms and walked away from the kit. Carl seized his chance to take to the drums and Gary picked up the guitar and said to the crowd, 'You know I love you!'

JOHN HASSALL: 'I had a tear in my eye during "Death On The Stairs". It was the last time I was going to play these songs. It was very sad. It was happy as well.'

GARY POWELL: 'I never really thought about it. I was having a great time at the last show. And all of that was because it had come to a stage where we were kind of collectively thinking at that point in time, really we've all worked hard for this, why shouldn't we enjoy it?'

CARL: 'It was kind of ironically satisfying in a sense. In one sense it was P.J. Harvey's gig and the majority of the audience were her fans. We had to work really hard to get the crowd, which took some time, but we eventually succeeded. So in the one sense it was a glorious send-off, and on the other hand it took us back to the very beginning. Even though it was a bit of a bummer that we didn't get a red carpet – or any carpet.

'There was a lot of emotion. But I've still got faith that one day things could – it's going to take a lot of fucking work now – but I still have faith that one day we could play again.'

They didn't go out with a bang, but if it was a whimper, then after all the bangs, accusations, kerfuffles and more, it was a whimper of control and relief. If it was a whimper, it was a whimper by choice: Carl's choice.

And that was that.

There was an aftershow at a club in Paris in an extended wine cellar and Carl spoke there and then about the end of The Libertines.

CARL: 'It was inevitably poignant. It was laying a tombstone to what's been and gone and also laying a foundation stone for the future … it's cutting the ribbon into a different realm of freedom. Because The Libertines became constrained.'

He added: 'I intend to contact Peter. I'd like to embrace him on a level of friendship and maybe … I don't want him thinking I'm avoiding him … I want him to remember I love him. I get upset when he says things [to the media] that make me sad. I read it. And he knows I read it. I feel nothing evil towards Peter. I get angry sometimes but I know better than to spread it to the rumour mill and the gossipers, like some kind of virus.'

He spoke to John over a long period and wished him well, smoothing over the idea that some, and Peter in

particular, thought he wasn't a Libertine. John's new band Yeti, a Beatlesy pop band, was set to go already.

But perhaps most interestingly, Carl sent a message to Libertines fans: 'It's your turn, really. All the people who've come to our gigs and picked up a guitar, all the people who say they've liberated themselves … I look forward to what you come up with.'

Carlos then rounded up a handful of friends to escape the packed club and head up to the Sacre Coeur. There on the steps at the foot of the cathedral at four in the morning, with some of the club's battered red cushions, gazing over beautiful Paris, Carl, his girlfriend Annalisa, the Kirstys, Anthony Rossomando, Michael the bodyguard, Victoria Rees and I bid adieu to The Libertines.

Chapter 17

A RIOT IN LONDON TOWN

'CHRISTMAS IS GOING TO BE LIKE ANY OTHER DAY IN THIS HOUSE – DEAD MISERABLE. SO PUT THAT IN YOUR PUDDING AND STIR IT'

Tony Hancock, 'Hancock's Christmas', *Hancock's Half Hour*

A RIOT IN LONDON TOWN

ABYSHAMBLES WERE DUE TO PLAY THE ASTORIA, WHERE THE LIBERTINES HAD LAYED THEIR BREAKTHROUGH GIG LESS THAN TWO YEARS BEFORE. WHAT HAD AKEN THE LIBERTINES SIX YEARS TO ACHIEVE, BABYSHAMBLES HAD DONE IN LESS HAN SIX MONTHS.

s The Libertines were having celebratory goodbye rinks in a pub near Waterloo, the White Hart across the ver, the Babyshambles crew were setting up and oundchecking for their headlining gig. The rise of abyshambles had been inexorable. Despite some iccups along the way, they were set to eclipse The ibertines. In Patrick Walden Peter had found a istinctive foil, a tremendous guitarist who possessed an nusual style but whose precise shards of noise suited aul Epworth's clipped, post-punk style of production.

So, although this was supposed to be a landmark gig, nd for most bands it would have been of extraordinary nportance, to Peter it was familiar territory. He was living the rise of The Libertines but on fast forward; miliar milestones were zooming past at an xtraordinary rate. And this was just another of them. here was already a concert announced for Brixton cademy, a single gig, yes but nonetheless it equalled the enue that The Libertines had played at their height. nd this was a band who'd released only two singles.

The line-up was billed as a Christmas Special and the apport once again displayed Peter's philanthropic reak. Much like a Victorian explorer collecting bulous beasts and weird creatures into an eccentric useum, Peter collected bands and put them on show at s gigs. It didn't matter to him that many of them eren't ready; he was giving them a chance to reach eople in the easiest way he knew how, by being, if not eir patron, then certainly their fairy godmother. Of urse, it didn't hurt if the odd band he liked shared his

taste in recreations. It became a running joke among certain journalists that since drug use was at the heart of so many of his friendships, any user of crack was dubbed 'a friend of Doherty'. It was a crude nudge-nudge joke, updating the archaic code for gays; 'a friend of Dorothy'.

Come midnight and there was no band. Of course, this wasn't unusual for hardcore followers of Doherty's creed. However, an hour later and there was still no show. People had been drinking since seven o'clock and it was beginning to get a little rowdy. People were shouting out for Peter and this gave rise to chants.

At 2 a.m. it was announced that Babyshambles wouldn't play. The crowd's anger exploded. The stage was invaded by more than a hundred people who were intent on wrecking the entire band's kit.

It didn't help that people had heard that Peter had been at the venue. The crowd tore down the curtains and threw any missiles they had to hand at the small number of security guards. A couple of security guards panicked; one initially kept rioters away by wielding a vicious length of electrical cable. As they fled, this particular member of security continued to whip anyone within ten feet. There were some fans kneeling, covering their

---

PETER: 'ALL OUR DREAMS CAME TRUE. WE STUCK WITH EACH OTHER THROUGH THIN AND THIN AND THINNER. EVERYTHING WE LONGED FOR AND DREAMT OF … IT HAPPENED. WE STUCK BY EACH OTHER AND LIVED TOGETHER AND ACHIEVED SO MUCH TOGETHER.'

heads in defence as the guard whipped them with the cable indiscriminately.

The rioters destroyed everything onstage. Gemma's kit was totalled. A group of rioters surged backstage and were destroying the place, turning over tables and stealing anything of value. Babyshambles members who were backstage were terrified for their lives.

But perhaps the biggest betrayal was that Patrick's stolen guitar pedals ended up for sale on eBay. The Internet, the medium that Peter had so clearly been the master of, was the tool for people to mock him. The person responsible had no qualms about selling stolen goods; he felt he was morally in the right as he had spent a good deal of money to get there and had missed the last train home.

Odessa studios was quiet that night. There was no one in to record. Gwyn Mathias was idling his time away at his computer in the reception area of the studio. He was alone in the studio in the middle of Clapton on a road some have dubbed 'murder mile'.

There was a knock at the door.

'Who is it?' asked Gwyn, adopting his most confident voice, aware that if it's someone with trouble in mind it's best to sound like you know what you're doing.

'It's me, Peter,' a voice answered.

'Who? Peter who?' said Gwyn.

'Peter Doherty,' came the reply. 'It's me, Peter Doherty, don't you remember?'

Of course Gwyn remembered. Peter, Carl, John and Paul DuFour may not have been in the studio for four years but he'd followed the progress of the band, pleased for them but dismayed that the original songs hadn't made it out into the real world. And anyway, how could you forget someone who regularly turned up in all the music magazines, and was increasingly in the tabloids that were always by the studio's stained beige kettle?

Gwyn got up to open the door. There was Peter, thinner than previously, thinner even than the photos in the newspapers. He looked nervous, antsy, concerned. His eyes sparkled though.

'I've done a runner, Gwyn,' said Peter. 'I've done a runner from my own gig.'

'What?'

'I was supposed to play and I ran,' he replied. 'Can we make some music?'

'Of course,' said Gwyn remembering himself. 'Come in.'

'Can you give Paul a ring, get him in to drum?' Peter enquired, relieved to be crossing the threshold.

A short phone call later and Paul DuFour, aka Mr Razzcocks, was on his way over to Odessa studios to reacquaint himself with Peter Doherty. Peter repeated the fact that he'd blown out a gig and Paul shrugged as he took his drumsticks out of the bag.

For a couple of hours Peter played his latest compositions back-to-back, tracks like 'Music When The Lights Go Out', with Paul adding a little swing to bring them up to date.

Peter was happy smiling, telling jokes – adopting the Belfast and Noo Yoik accents as he showed Paul the new songs. It was time to get something down on tape.

'I've got to get something,' said Peter. 'I won't be long.'

Paul nodded. 'Don't be long. It's been too long already.'

'Don't worry,' Peter replied. 'I'll be back in a jiffy.'

He left the studio. Three hours later Paul decided to give up his vigil and go home.

On Tuesday 21 December, something extraordinary happened: the BBC's flagship current affairs show, *Newsnight*, broadcast an eleven minute and fifty-five second interview with Peter Doherty. It was the first of five interviews devoted to individuals who'd had an extraordinary year in the world of current affairs and beyond. He was in untypically rarefied company. The other interviews were with Otis Ferry, who'd led an invasion of the Commons to protest against the fox-hunting ban; Greg Dyke, who'd resigned as BBC Director General; Edward Chaplin, British Ambassador in Baghdad, and Kelly Holmes, who had won two gold medals in the Olympics.

The interview with Peter Doherty took place in the George Tavern, Whitechapel, and was sober and non-sensational, as befits the serious, analytical tone of the programme. Perhaps because of this, the programme was one of the few that seemed to get straight to the heart of the creative drive of The Libertines – that Peter and Carl drove each other on to greater achievements – dwelling more on their relationship than on Peter's addictions. KIRSTY WARK: 'There were two meetings. The first one, where he was more like I imagined he would be, was when I met him with James Mullord to talk about doing the interview and he was pretty out of it, frankly. I honestly didn't think we would make it through the interview.

'I thought it sounds like self-indulgent nonsense. There was no question in my mind that he would do it. He was really in no fit state. Are you going to do this next week? It's about camera crews, location, all sorts of things. I went away to do *Newsnight* thinking, it's not going to happen. The producer told me that after I left he put his coat over his head. I couldn't care what he was doing under his coat frankly.

'We had requested photographs of him from Pete's mum because I was quite interested in the fact he'd gone to Russia with the British Council at sixteen as a result of his poetry. And she wrote a really eloquent letter and it was a very heartfelt, "please can you give him some leeway? He's essentially a really good bright boy."'

Kirsty Wark wanted to use this letter as part of the interview, and received Jacqueline Doherty's blessing to do so. Kirsty Wark was determined that this was not going to be the usual interview, questioning the vague idea of glamorising drugs. In addition to exploring his youth and the nature of his relationship with Carl, she wanted to confront him with the supply chain of drugs. KIRSTY WARK: 'Actually the whole issue of whether he was going to influence other people and make people take drugs was not one that interested me that much because, when I was fourteen years old, Jim Morrison was my hero and there was no way I was going to kill myself. I thought that was a very naive view. There's certain things you should ask. I was far more interested in whether or not he had any idea of drugs mules. I think the whole distance from the crops to the user is actually one of complete exploitation of people.'

When he arrived in a suit and checked coat he looked marvellous, bright with clear eyes. He was polite and engaging, asking after Kirsty Wark's family and children. KIRSTY WARK: 'Then I said, I think we should get something to eat, so we got him a coffee and toast and marmalade and stuff. I'd been made up and then he got his make-up on and I went to talk to him. Suddenly I noticed out of the corner of my eye that he took a piece of red string out of his pocket. It was stretchy – I thought there was something happening.

'And the next thing he's up out of his chair, avoiding the gents and going to the ladies. I said to James, you've got to go and stop him. Apart from anything else, it's costing a lot of money to do this interview. I didn't want to lose the interview and I thought it's such a waste for Peter if he could not hold it together. Anyway, James persuaded him.'

Peter was used to defending his talent and being accused of glamorising drug use. It was Kirsty Wark's questioning about whether he had guilt about the people exploited as drugs mules that wrong-footed him.

Peter looked uncharacteristically awkward. 'I feel guilty about so many things. I don't feel guilty at the point of taking drugs, no, because I probably wouldn't take it

---

THE RIOTERS DESTROYED EVERYTHING ONSTAGE. GEMMA'S KIT WAS TOTALLED. A GROUP OF RIOTERS SURGED BACKSTAGE AND WERE DESTROYING THE PLACE, TURNING OVER TABLES AND STEALING ANYTHING OF VALUE. BABYSHAMBLES MEMBERS WHO WERE BACKSTAGE WERE TERRIFIED FOR THEIR LIVES.

because then the negative things that come from that outweigh the joys … I've never thought of it like that … the mules … '

She pressed the point. 'The drugs mules are the only way that … '

Peter replied, musing, 'The only way to get round that would be to grow your own poppies I suppose, but that would be too time-consuming.'

Recalling the interview, Kirsty Wark said, 'I think he seemed genuinely surprised, which really annoyed me in a funny way because, you're a bright guy. Why is this surprising to you? Surely you've thought in your saner moments, someone's stomach's been stitched up, someone's swallowed the stuff, someone's been hung out to dry. The people who are your dealers have dealt to kids, who knows? But to me that was the only thing I was interested in: the exploitation angle. And the devastation it causes, not just to the end user, because frankly the end user has a lot more choice than people along the way.'

In addition to this, the point of the interview was to produce a fully rounded portrait of Peter Doherty. Kirsty Wark didn't shrink from picking over the painful details of Peter and Carl's relationship.

PETER: 'All our dreams came true. We stuck with each other through thin and thin and thinner. Everything we longed for and dreamt of … it happened. We stuck by each other and lived together and achieved so much together.

'In the past, we were scrapping and would go for months without talking. We'd always be antagonising each other or winding each other up. Jealousy on both our parts, if you had a new friend or a girl got involved or chasing the same girl. Or, in the midst of a drunken creative session, come the morning you wouldn't be able to remember who wrote what line so we'd come to blows over that because I'd be so sure that I'd written something, but he would as well. What can you do … but fight or walk away?'

When asked if lyrics mattered that much, Peter responded, 'Yes, a lot. Always, it's the most precious thing really. It's our children. Whether or not a child loves his mum, which is me, or his dad, which is Carl, meant the world and it still does. The next time I see him will

probably be in court, fighting over a comma or something.'

It was an extraordinary interview, with a later broadcast of the entire interview even more revealing. Both featured a beautiful acoustic version of 'Music When The Lights Go Out' and spontaneous recitation of the poem that he wrote to earn his trip to Russia as a sixteen-year-old. In all, it was and remains the most accurate representation of Peter Doherty's talent and afflictions that has been broadcast on television.

Unknown to the general public and despite Peter's frustrations at trying to contact him, the relationship with Carl was thawing. Behind the scenes telephone numbers were exchanged via Chev. The pair of them would enjoy Christmas and at some point call each other. With The Libertines finished there was no reason for animosity, in fact this might give them the opportunity to rekindle their close friendship, since the issue of reliability, songwriting credits and everything else didn't apply any more.

They both left London to enjoy Christmas. Neither one of them called the other.

Peter decided to play four gigs in one night on New Year's Eve – people scoffed at the idea. 'He can't make one gig, let alone four.' The gigs were successful, however, each one boasting a crowd more animated than the last as they passed from Birmingham through Stoke and Oldham and delivered a show in Manchester to a crowd hysterical to a point that rivalled The Libertines' shows earlier in the year.

Carl, in contrast, was fretting about a forthcoming operation to remove a non-malignant growth. Without the operation, and without having it soon, he could end up with a serious facial twitch. It would be a twitch that would spoil those cinematic good looks. It was as if he was being punished for the events a year before in Alan McGee's house in Wales. This growth had to be cut out in order for Carl to be able to continue to record and play music.

Peter, long since cut out of Carl's life, was looking forward to what should be the greatest year of his life. He was a success, back on the road to great things. Nothing could stop him now. He'd proved to Carl he could do it.

SURGERY AND A SUPERMODEL

'HISTORY IS MERELY GOSSIP.
BUT SCANDAL IS GOSSIP MADE TEDIOUS BY MORALITY'
Oscar Wilde, *Lady Windermere's Fan*

SURGERY AND A SUPERMODEL

IN THE NEW YEAR, PETER FINALLY ACCEPTED THAT THE LIBERTINES WERE ALL OVER. CHRISTMAS CAME AND WENT WITHOUT EITHER PETER OR CARL CALLING EACH OTHER. SOMEHOW, DESPITE BEING IN LONDON, THEY'D MANAGED NOT TO BUMP INTO EACH OTHER. NEWS THAT CARL'S OPERATION WAS TO REMOVE A TUMOUR FROM BEHIND HIS EAR HIT THE TABLOIDS. CARL WAS EXTREMELY SCARED GOING INTO THE OPERATION, ONLY REVEALING LATER THAT, WITHOUT THE OPERATION, HE PROBABLY WOULD HAVE LOST THE SIGHT IN ONE EYE AND BEEN LEFT WITH A PERMANENT FACIAL SPASM.

On the weekend of 15 January 2005, supermodel Kate Moss threw her 31st birthday party. The year before the theme had been 'The Beautiful And The Damned' inspired by the bright young things of F. Scott Fitzgerald's novels. A year later, the theme was the more mundane 'rock 'n' roll', and the party was in her Cotswolds home. She had a stage set up in a barn. Guests included Mick Jones and Paul Simonon of The Clash, Pete Doherty and Bobby Gillespie of Primal Scream. Kate Moss was hopeful of a Clash reunion of some sort onstage, with Peter singing the parts of Joe Strummer who had died just over a year before.

The irony was that in an interview for Ireland's *Hot Press*, published shortly before the party, Peter had again criticised Carl for having famous friends, suggesting that Carl had lost touch with the ideas of Albion and Arcadia and that only he, Peter, held the legacy.

The party went as planned, a typically debauched affair. The only thing that didn't quite go to plan was that, come the end of the weekend, Peter and Kate were an item.

The tabloids had a field day – this story was a gift for them: the world's number-one supermodel stepping out with the UK's 'baddest rocker'. They indulged in a number of pleas of concern for Kate Moss to dump this outrageous, dangerous man. By contrast, several close friends of Peter's were concerned about the effect going

out with Kate Moss would have on him. It had instantly put him on the front pages of every tabloid and made him a subject of the chattering classes worldwide. Kate was an experienced operator in the rarefied world of the global media. Some, incorrectly, even suspected her motives, wondering if the whole thing was an attempt to reinvigorate her career, to make her appear more edgy and streetwise. Whatever, it appeared that Peter had not only met his match, but had met someone who could conceivably eat him up and spit him out.

Carl was equivocal about the relationship. He wished Peter well but was aware of the trouble Peter was bringing down on his head. He knew from personal experience that, while Peter would attract the attention of the media, Kate seemed to be immune to trouble. In the run-up to Christmas 2004 Carl had been out shopping with Pearl Lowe, wife of Supergrass drummer Danny Goffey, and Kate Moss when he realised he'd inadvertently brought his flick knife with him. CARL: 'We were in the middle of Selfridges and I

THE PARTY WENT AS PLANNED, A TYPICALLY DEBAUCHED AFFAIR. THE ONLY THING THAT DIDN'T QUITE GO TO PLAN WAS THAT, COME THE END OF THE WEEKEND, PETER AND KATE WERE AN ITEM.

suddenly realised Herr Flick was still in my pocket and I freaked out. And she said that she could look after it and no one would stop her, so, relieved, I unquestionably unhanded my burden.'

On 27 January Babyshambles drummer, Gemma Clarke, finally decided she'd had enough and left the band. At first, the decision seemed to be mutual, but it soon came to light that that wasn't the case. In a letter addressed to Peter she said she 'could no longer be part of a machine that I feel is destroying you'.

Peter, meanwhile, lost no time in finding a new drummer. Gemma's replacement was Adam Ficek, who'd played with Patrick in White Sport. A man of good humour with an addiction to flat caps, he was in many ways the perfect idiosyncratic addition to Babyshambles.

He wouldn't get an awful lot of chance to practise though. The night it was announced he'd joined the band, Babyshambles played the George on Commercial Road, Whitechapel, the scene of Kirsty Wark's *Newsnight* interview. On 31 January Peter was scheduled to play a gig as a tsunami benefit at the London Garage in Islington. The gig was arranged by Samantha Morton, Rhys Ifans, Pearl Lowe and Danny Goffey, the last two being part of the fashionable set that Peter had so vehemently decried only weeks before.

It was clear at this gig that things had changed for ever. Peter had gone from playing gigs in his own flat to being unable to leave his flat without the tabloids in tow. For the first time the coverage had stopped being about the music. The 'Libertine' was less free than he had ever been. The tabloid photographers were on hand in a pack, chasing Peter's taxi up the road. If their readers didn't know who Peter Doherty was, they would by the following day. It was at this gig that the *Mirror* took a photograph of Peter onstage with his eyes rolled back in his head. In an exceptional piece of juxtaposition, they put a picture of Kate Moss, taken at Paris Fashion Week the same day, next to the picture of Peter, rounded off with the headline 'The Living Dead'. Of course, anyone with enough time and a camera taking ten frames a second will be able to find a terrible picture of someone, but with this one they'd struck gold. It was a picture that

was printed again and again as proof of Peter's supposed insanity and unsuitability as a suitor.

The papers portrayed Peter as a hedonistic mess, out to drag the pure Kate Moss into his iniquitous ways. They begged Kate Moss to dump him and, over the course of the following months, reported that she had dumped him a multitude of times. Kate Moss was essentially still virgin tabloid fodder, having, on the whole, successfully avoided the attention of the front-page headline writers. She had also been litigious to avoid allegations from being published. The papers were loving it; they had longed to write about Kate Moss for years but were unable to do so – she had given only a handful of interviews in her career and had not courted publicity in the way other models had. At last Peter Doherty gave them the chance to print her picture and write extensively about her, somewhat disingenuously in the interests of her welfare. Given the loose gang surrounding Peter, who knew that there was money to be made by courting the tabloids, expensive drugs, the media's need for revelations and a world-famous model who had shunned tabloid coverage in the past, this was a volatile mix of impulses, needs and desires.

Things were about to get worse. Within days, Peter would be back in the press having punched Max Carlish, the documentary maker who had spied in Peter a way to lift his career. In his brief tenure as Babyshambles jester, he'd failed to get the necessary footage for his documentary. But, of course, what he had captured on film was Peter smoking heroin.

Max had contacted James Mullord several times but was unable to secure this much-needed interview to undo the previous year's embarrassment of a tape running out. Exasperated, but realising the value of the footage he held, he abandoned the people he'd claimed to be friends with. He approached newspapers with stills from his video footage that showed Peter smoking

---

EXASPERATED, BUT REALISING THE VALUE OF THE FOOTAGE HE HELD, HE ABANDONED THE PEOPLE HE'D CLAIMED TO BE FRIENDS WITH. HE APPROACHED NEWSPAPERS WITH STILLS FROM HIS VIDEO FOOTAGE THAT SHOWED PETER SMOKING HEROIN.

heroin. Although Peter's drug use was already out in the open, there had been very little documented and published evidence, and now that he was the partner of Kate Moss it was considered extremely newsworthy. Papers started a bidding war, which the *Sunday Mirror* won with an offer of £30,000.

For the first time the music was taking a back seat to sordid tales. Peter's passion for the Internet also dwindled; he no longer posted on websites, let alone released new tracks to the Web. Peter promised to quit the drugs for Kate – saying it was the only way he could keep her. He also revealed that they wanted to marry.

As music was becoming marginalised for Peter, it was once again becoming centre stage for Carl, as he recuperated from his operation. Unable to go out or bear loud noises, he began composing new songs on his acoustic guitar at home in London.

On 2 February, Peter and friend Alan Wass encountered Max Carlish at the Rookery Hotel in Clerkenwell. It's not clear what happened; all three protagonists were out of it by the time police arrived. The upshot was that Max ended up with a couple of shiners.

The sorry levels of Max Carlish's self-delusion were exposed when he spoke to the BBC. In Max's eyes he was a close personal friend of Peter's and their friendship had gone awry.

'I'm feeling bloody battered, but I'm bowed and I feel sorry for Pete. My heart goes out to Pete – he has screwed up big time now,' he said. 'Pete may be thinking, "I can't stand Max now," but I still love Pete and I want the best for him.'

What had appeared to be a simple case of a documentary filmmaker who had failed to finish his film was actually far more complicated. Max's behaviour seemed more like a delusional fan than a disinterested objective filmmaker.

Peter and Alan Wass were charged with robbery and blackmail and appeared in court on 4 February. The pair were bailed to appear at a later date, but there were problems raising Peter's bail of £150,000. Peter spent the weekend in the notoriously vicious Pentonville prison. Even when bail was reduced to £100,000, Rough Trade had problems raising it and an attempt to draw it against future earnings was dismissed by the judge. Peter hated Pentonville more than Sheppey or Wandsworth; he described it as hell

on earth. He had to spend a further night in Pentonville before the bail was raised, where he was looked after by a fellow inmate, his new friend the General, who would MC 'Pentonville' on Babyshambles debut album.

The bail conditions included a curfew between ten o'clock at night and seven in the morning. Peter was accompanied by security and forced to report to a local police station and give up his passport.

He was given the anti-heroin implant Naltrexone. This works by blocking receptors in the brain so that heroin has no effect. After receiving the implant Peter went straight to his dealer to check the implant's potency. It passed with flying colours.

Carl's post-op medication, meanwhile, was being reduced. He was slowly recuperating. The *NME* awards were about to come round again and The Libertines had been nominated by readers for Best UK Band – again. It looked as though Peter would be allowed to attend the actual awards ceremony and then return home in time for his ten o'clock curfew.

Peter was due to play a short acoustic set at the ceremony but Carl wasn't even going to go. Alan McGee, managing Carl still, was concerned that, with him still recuperating, he could upset his chances of a complete recovery. However, some of Carl's friends were outraged that he wasn't going. They felt that once again, Peter would be taking all the credit for The Libertines. They attempted to goad Carl into going, whether or not Peter would be there. Carl resisted these pleas, stating exasperatedly: 'Listen, I know Peter better than any of you. I don't want to upset him and you have no idea what effect it could have on him.'

Of course he was right. No one else did know Peter like Carl, even now as people flocked to sell their stories to the tabloids. Only Carl had an adequate insight into his psychology. Carl too couldn't avoid seeing the endless tales in the tabloids, and it hurt him to see the constant attacks on Peter. This commentary obviously informed the fanbase online and even if they, on the whole, rejected these stories out of hand, they were still nonetheless discussed. Their faith was being questioned daily, wearing down the resistance of some.

In the end, Carl resolved to go to the awards. His mind had been swayed by the haranguing of friends; even Alan McGee, who was convinced a shock could harm him, gave his blessing in the end. John was on holiday, but Gary would be there as well. The media prepared for Peter and Carl's first meeting since Peter flew to Thailand for his failed rehab attempt. Before Carl went to the ceremony, he had to sign a new record deal with Mercury Records.

Carl turned up at the awards. There was no Peter; his mother had phoned to say he was too sick to attend. His 'mother', as it happened, was actually Gill.

In a triumph of optimism over experience, The Libertines won Best Band for the second time, even though they'd been officially wound up the previous December. Carl went onstage with Gary and was presented with the award by former Blur guitarist Graham Coxon, who Peter had performed with just before Christmas. Carl's speech was typically heartfelt and to the point: 'We've been through a lot and I want to thank everyone who has remained objective. My heart goes out to Pete. I'd hoped he'd be here tonight and we would have had some kind of reunion.'

With The Libertines no more, both Peter and Carl felt a little warmer towards each other. Peter's savage attacks on Carl had subsided completely and Carl was more inclined to foster good relations. After the failure to meet up around Christmas, there remained some hope that they would meet again, not as musicians but as possible friends.

Peter's curfew conditions were extended for two nights on 21 and 22 February so that Babyshambles could play a warm-up show at the Garage, followed by the biggest gig to date at Brixton Academy.

At the second night, Mick Jones introduced them. Three songs in, however, during 'Stix & Stones', the pressure at the front became so tight that the show was stopped. Babyshambles left the stage and the crowd were told to step back.

Later on, Patrick and Peter came to blows during 'Gang Of Gin'. It was, however, put on – there was even a roadie in place to take Patrick's guitar off him so that he could swing a punch at Peter. The two of them bundled harmlessly. It was engineered by Peter, who wanted to make this appearance at Brixton as memorable as the last one with The Libertines, where he'd stormed offstage halfway through.

Two days later, in a move unprecedented in rock 'n' roll, the leader of the Conservatives, Michael Howard, decided to show his populist touch by barracking Peter. 'Here you have a man who takes drugs and gets locked up – yet ends up on the front pages,' said Howard, failing to appreciate that the reason he's on the front pages is *because* he takes drugs and gets locked up. Who was he expecting to find there, Coldplay's Chris Martin?

As a brief respite from being the tabloids' *bête du jour*, Peter appeared on Radio 4's poetry programme 'Bespoken Word', where he was greeted as a poet from Filthy McNasty's and the London scene first, and a performer with The Libertines and Babyshambles second. It was a chance to show where his passions really lay. He performed Siegfried Sassoon's 'Suicide In The Trenches'.

A few weeks later, Babyshambles headed to Twin Peaks studios in the Brecon Beacons in Wales. Peter was given special dispensation to leave London as part of his bail conditions, the logic being that it was difficult for him to come to any trouble in such a remote place. It is the highest fully residential studio in the British Isles, and is in the middle of nowhere. Mick Jones and Bill Price were back producing an album that they hoped to finish quickly in time for a late summer release.

Initial reports were good, with twelve songs recorded in a week. As Peter and Babyshambles recorded (with Mullord banned from the studio, as he was felt to be a disruptive influence), Carl Barât was less than twenty-five miles away in Alan McGee's house writing songs for his own solo career. It's quicker to get from Twin Peaks studio to Hay-on-Wye than it is to get from Peter's flat in London to Carl's. Peter didn't know that Carl was so close. Carl did, but he had to focus on his songwriting. It may have been the perfect place to meet, away from prying eyes, but Carl knew as Peter was finishing his solo opus that he had to work on his own.

On 10 April, the charges of blackmail and robbery against Peter and Alan Wass were dropped by the Crown Prosecution Service. Max Carlish was quoted as saying he was very pleased for Peter.

RECONCILIATION (REPRISE)

*'ONE MINUTE OF RECONCILIATION IS WORTH MORE
THAN A WHOLE LIFE OF FRIENDSHIP'*
Gabriel Garcia Marquez, *One Hundred Years of Solitude*

RECONCILIATION (REPRISE)

ON 18 APRIL 2005, CARL HEARD THAT PETER MIGHT BE GOING TO NORTH LONDON'S BOOGALOO BAR TO SEE SHANE MACGOWAN. 'PETER MIGHT BE THERE,' HE CONFIDED TO ME WITH AN UNUSUAL MIXTURE OF NERVOUSNESS AND RESIGNATION. 'IT MIGHT AS WELL HAPPEN NOW, BECAUSE IT'S GOING TO HAPPEN SOME TIME.' PETER'S FRIEND ALAN WASS RECEIVED A PHONE CALL AS WE STOOD OUTSIDE THE BACK OF THE BAR. AFTER A FEW MINUTES ALAN HANDED THE PHONE TO CARL WHO SAID HELLO TO SOMEONE IN A HUSHED VOICE BEFORE RETREATING FOR SOME PRIVACY.

'He's coming over,' he said casually as he passed Alan back his phone.

We watched Shane MacGowan perform a song with band The Lancaster Bombers before he retired to the edge of the bar with an Artful Dodger grin and magnificent top hat to match.

'It's cool,' said Carl, obviously anxious. And then Peter was there, Kate Moss in tow. Peter and Carl saw each other. Gingerly they approached. Roger and I were ready to pull them apart if it went down to fisticuffs. We needn't have bothered. They looked at each other and cautiously hugged. Retiring to the sofa beneath London's best jukebox, they chatted about niceties and complimented each other on their jackets; they even showed each other the labels – they were both Christian Dior jackets supplied by Hedi Slimane. Roger cautiously took photos of the pair of them, torn between wanting to record the moment and not wanting to invade their privacy.

Kate Moss plonked herself down next to Peter and moments later tried to stop Roger taking pictures of her. Roger was less than enthused, as both Peter and Carl had been happy to have the pictures taken and she had chosen to sit in front of the camera. Kate Moss appeared edgy, as though she was unhappy that Peter was devoting so much of his time to this foppish apparition from his old life.

They headed upstairs away from the main room where

IN A SHOW OF UNITY, BUT WITH AN UNDERCURRENT OF ONE-UPMANSHIP, PETER OFFERED CARL THE OPPORTUNITY TO PLAY GUITAR ON THE DEBUT BABYSHAMBLES ALBUM.

acoustic guitars were waiting. The two erstwhile friends quietly strummed snatches of songs for each other, including 'Can't Stand Me Now', 'Albion', 'Time For Heroes', Violent Femmes' 'Blister In The Sun' and Love's 'AloneAgainOr'. Peter was like a child showing off his Christmas presents after the holiday. He crouched down and showed Carl the chords for 'Fuck Forever' and 'A Rebours', named after J.K. Huysmans' nineteenth-century novel, a book so decadent that in Wilde's *Picture Of Dorian Gray* it drives Dorian into a life of debauchery and excess. Carl taught Pete a song and played 'Plan A' for him.

After ten months living less than five miles apart they had faced each other and although it had been nervy it had been fine. Carl carelessly tossed out a number of tunes. Kate Moss sat quietly listening, occasionally smiling.

In a show of unity, but with an undercurrent of one-upmanship, Peter offered Carl the opportunity to play guitar on the debut Babyshambles album, but Carl was scornful of what this represented. He wasn't keen to be 'the cabin boy on someone else's ship'.

It was clear this wasn't going to be the all-night session of songwriting and comradeship some had hoped for, but it was an ice-breaker nonetheless. In fact, it was enough of an ice-breaker for Peter to feel able to go in for a bit of gentle teasing. As he strummed though 'Time For Heroes', with a broad smile and twinkling eyes, he changed the lines, 'There are fewer more distressing sights than that/Of an Englishman in a baseball cap', to 'There are fewer more distressing sights than that/Of Mr Carl Barât'.

As the evening ended the pair were not really reconciled – too much casual abuse had been tossed by Peter in the past for that – but at least animosity had been tempered. It was a good start.

On 1 May Peter played his biggest gig to date for Love Music Hate Racism in Trafalgar Square. Peter and The Libertines had supported the organisation for a long time, and whatever problems occurred, they never disappointed at these shows.

The gig highlighted the split personality at the heart of Peter's burgeoning appeal. On the one hand, he was perceived as a junkie loser who was going to be bad for the world's number-one supermodel, and on the other hand he was a philanthropic poet who would turn out for a good cause and could hold the entire thronging Trafalgar Square in the palm of his hand. He played a clutch of Libertines songs, starting with 'Time For Heroes', 'Tell The King' and 'Don't Look Back Into The Sun'. However, a shimmering emotional 'Albion' competed with a cover of The Clash's 'Guns Of Brixton' for the best song of the day.

Peter played acoustic, accompanied by Alan Wass on guitar. With Alan in place, Peter took the opportunity to leap off the stage and crowd surf before extricating himself from the crowd's adoring arms to return to the stage for 'Can't Stand Me Now'.

As he tried to leave it was obvious that the manic fandom would prevent him. Hundreds of fans pressed as close as they could to touch and talk to him. James Mullord had assumed he would be able to hail a black cab at the end of the gig and Peter would be able to stride out through the crowd to safety. It wasn't to be and Peter was caught up in a sea of heaving adulation.

A couple of helpful people managed to hail a cab and the police cleared a way through the crowd for Peter to escape to the waiting taxi.

The contrast between the anti-fascist campaigner of Trafalgar Square and the spectre who appeared three and a half weeks later at the Ivor Novello Awards on 26 May, couldn't have been more stark. After a week in Cannes with Moss, he held court by telling journalists that his house was being bugged before admitting that he was 'a bit paranoid'. He had black marker pen drawn around his eyes. Wolfman and Doherty's 'For Lovers' was in the running for Best Contemporary Song, but lost out to Franz Ferdinand's 'Take Me Out'.

Both Carl and Peter had become the playthings of the fashion world by this time – they even had a photo shoot together for Italian *Vogue*. This voracious business that reinvents itself every season looks for inspiration at street level. That unusual dress sense of 2002 sported by Peter and Carl – a ragbag of suits and trilbies and whatever

AS HE STRUMMED THOUGH 'TIME FOR HEROES', WITH A BROAD SMILE AND TWINKLING EYES, HE CHANGED THE LINES, 'THERE ARE FEWER MORE DISTRESSING SIGHTS THAN THAT/OF AN ENGLISHMAN IN A BASEBALL CAP', TO 'THERE ARE FEWER MORE DISTRESSING SIGHTS THAN THAT/ OF MR CARL BARÂT'.

else they fancied – had gone overground. Male music fans cared about their appearance like never before and this had spread throughout street fashion. There had never been so many hats worn by men since the 1950s.

Carl had become the face of J. Lindberg, along with Hollywood actress Juliette Lewis. Carl, Gary, John and Anthony had been the subject of another Italian *Vogue* shoot, while Peter was the cover star of glossy men's magazines including *Arena Homme* and *GQ*, with, inexplicably, a bird of prey.

Perhaps the most enduring relationship has been between the head of male couture at Christian Dior, Hedi Slimane, and Peter Doherty. Hedi even produced a book of photographs of Peter Doherty in autumn 2005, *London Birth Of A Cult*. Hedi had been inspired by Peter and the coterie of bands that surrounded him. Peter was intoxicated by this top designer who wanted to see him and the storm around him up close. Peter was overjoyed to introduce the slender, discriminating Frenchman to the working-class environs of the George pub in the East End of London.

Hedi Slimane found Peter particularly inspiring. 'It's his freedom, as a utopia of course. It's utopia, poetry, romanticism.'

In July that year the *Guardian* published an extensive article on men's fashion where they highlighted Peter and Carl's influence and noted that the Glastonbury Festival was stuffed to the cowsheds with Doherty lookalikes.

However, despite the interest of fashion houses, these well-turned-out campers didn't peruse the fashion pages of the monthly glossies. In fact, they found it quite hilarious that their junk-shop chic was written about in such elevated tomes. This was genuine fashion that male music fans had taken to their hearts. If you compare the T-shirt 'n' jeans brigade pre-2002 with the scrubbed-up spiv look of 2005 it's like looking at two different planets. The effect, however, was even more subtle than first appears, for there was a paradigm shift in the male music fan's attitude to dress. It's less a particular style that has taken hold and more a genuine concern to look good, to look right. This had always been the cornerstone of Britain's mod culture, which was not so much a prescribed uniform but more of a generational development of a personal aesthetic. Clothes weren't just something to be worn, they were meant to say something about you: T-shirts and jeans were for the middle-aged ex-clubbers of the 1990s or Jeremy Clarkson – looking good was as modern as you could be.

Peter and the band were invited to Hedi Slimane's birthday party in Paris. The Paddingtons, who had played the key Gunter Grove gig just two years earlier, played for the party. On the way back Peter and Kate Moss rowed publicly on the Eurostar. As a result of arriving in London late, Babyshambles failed to make it to a support date for Oasis's tour.

Liam Gallagher was furious. 'It's not a question of professionalism. It's much more simple than that. This is the greatest group in the world and what we're not going to do is let anyone, Pete Doherty, Liam Gallagher or Elvis, fuck it all up.'

The outburst wasn't met with Oasis's usual groundswell of support. It was rank hypocrisy from someone who'd absconded from several gigs, and in invoking 'professionalism' for the first time he inadvertently sounded less like a rock star and more like a quantity surveyor. Somehow Peter had done something that had not happened since the early days of acid house. The Libertines, and particularly Peter, had created a schism, a generational divide. Paradoxically, Liam's surreal comparison had also elevated Peter to the level of rock 'n' roll's high table.

Peter represents freedom. Freedom of expression and, rarely in music, freedom of intelligence. All the arguments for the counter-culture of the 1960s, before it became the establishment, were true of The Libertines a thousandfold. The difference was that the critics sitting atop their vast canons of work, from Dylan to The Beatles, Oasis to The Clash, were happy with historical rebellion and rebellion served up in a four-CD box set. They had much more of a problem dealing with something that was genuinely different, even though they were born of the same lineage.

This schism was completely exposed with Peter Doherty's performance with Elton John at Live8 of Marc Bolan's 'Children Of The Revolution'. The song's title alone should have been sufficient to make people question their knee-jerk condemnation of Peter Doherty. Arriving with a lighter in his mouth and wearing Kate Moss's military jacket with the flesh of his arms protruding a good four inches from the sleeve, he performed as though he was playing the Boogaloo bar to fifty eager punters rather than a global audience of millions.

He was crucified for the performance. Epithets such as 'unprofessional', 'shambolic' and simply 'rubbish' were rained on him. However, his performance overshadowed everything else on the day and it held the public imagination much longer than U2 and Paul McCartney performing together or even the eternally acrimonious Pink Floyd getting back together. Those people yelling at the TV sets that they couldn't hear the words and that it was a disgrace and that he looked a right state forgot that they laughed at their parents when they were outraged by The Sex Pistols on the *Grundy Show* in 1976. Music, for a few minutes at least, had reasserted its long-lost right to upset the middle-aged, even the middle-aged who fancied that they were still in middle-youth. Even Elton John himself, the grandmere of the middle-youth, locked into a role of older sibling to the stars from Robbie Williams to Robert Downey Jr, felt the need to explain away the performance.

Carl watched the performance on a TV set at home with one eyebrow glued to the ceiling of his front room. Leaving the stage Peter saw Johnny Borrell of Razorlight. They chatted in a friendly way and Peter left Hyde Park with Kate Moss.

The highlight of Babyshambles' live show was set to be released. 'Fuck Forever', borrowing its title from a print by Sex Pistols' designer Jamie Reid, articulated his frustration and had become a classic live anthem. It also possessed an unusual directness.

There was trouble brewing, though. There were disagreements over the mix of 'Fuck Forever' that had been completed. James Mullord handed it over to Soul II Soul and Massive Attack producer Nellee Hooper. Peter went ballistic when he found out and sacked everyone and everything: James, Tony Linkin, Drew, Patrick, Adam and the tour. For good measure, with the tabloids finally getting to him, he hit a *Mirror* reporter at the Boogaloo bar.

As Peter's band was falling apart, Carl was assembling another. The band featured Gary Powell of The Libertines, Anthony Rossomando, Peter's replacement, and Didz of The Cooper Temple Clause. They were rehearsing in secret on London's South Bank, with Carl, as ever, biding his time and hoping to make everything right before taking it out to the world. It was clear though, as he insisted on the umpteenth replaying of the chorus of 'Deadwood', that this band would be tight and structured in contrast to Babyshambles.

Within a week of their break-up, Babyshambles were back together, playing a gig at Stoke. It was, and it was supposed to be, like the old days – admittedly those days were only a year previously but it seemed much longer – a last-minute date at a small venue. James Mullord, however, wasn't reinstated.

It was typical Peter. Just at the point where everything seemed to be unravelling for good, he pulled it back together. Sure he'd had Kate Moss performing with him in the Duke of Clarence and had his equipment seized by

police, been caught with drugs in Oslo, and headbutted former band mate and Razorlight frontman Johnny Borrell. Essentially, though, it was back to business as usual. Peter was buoyed up by the news that his intermittent flatmates, Libertines superfan Gill and Wolfman, were working together. Gill was managing Wolfman.

Then Peter's lifestyle inevitably caught up with his girlfriend. On 15 September 2005, the unstable situation of an international star model, drugs and the tabloids boiled over. Kate Moss was exposed in the *Daily Mirror* using cocaine with the band. Six months previously it looked as though Peter Doherty would be crushed between the cogs of the tabloid wheels because of his association with such a big star: the reverse at first appeared to be happening. Kate Moss lost a number of high-profile fashion campaigns, including Chanel and Burberry. Chief of the Metropolitan Police, Sir Ian Blair, said he intended to bring Kate Moss in for questioning. The double standards at play were dazzling: on the one hand a model in an industry where drugs were common became a pariah, while on the other top fashion designers were being influenced by Peter Doherty in their autumn collections with people applauding the new 'edginess' of their designs. Drugs in fashion, then: love the romanticism, hate the reality.

You would have thought, given the people around Babyshambles at the time, that it wouldn't have been too difficult to isolate the culprit who had videoed the event. The footage was taken by someone wandering round the studio who knew exactly what they were looking for. But who was it? The extended Babyshambles family looked set to tear itself apart; no one was above suspicion. On the wall of his flat, where once he wrote potential track listings of the debut Babyshambles album, Peter used his marker pen to write a long list of everyone who could have been in on the videoing of this. Meticulously he scored through one name after another, leaving just two.

However, despite the Moss saga, music was centre stage again. On 27 September, Babyshambles' debut album *Down In Albion* was mastered and finished. On the same day, Carl Barât settled on a name for his new band, the same as his club, Dirty Pretty Things, and booked their first gigs in Italy.

EPILOGUE

IN JANUARY 2004, AFTER PETER AND CARL'S RAPPROCHEMENT IN OCTOBER 2003 AND BEFORE THE FINAL SPLIT IN AUGUST 2004 WHERE THEY WROTE 'CAN'T STAND ME NOW', CARL BARÂT DASHED OVER TO PETER DOHERTY'S HOTEL ROOM IN THE HOTEL FRANCE ALBION IN PARIS IN A STATE OF SOME ANXIETY.

'That's it, Peter,' said Carl. 'The band's all over.'

'What is it, Carl?' said a nonplussed Doherty attempting to calm his fretting co-frontman. 'Has Gary left?'

'No.'

'Has John left?'

'No.'

'Have you left?'

'No.'

'Have I left?' Peter quizzed. 'Again?'

'No. It's Franz Ferdinand. They're at number two in the midweek charts. The good British people have made their decision. They want Franz. They don't want The Libertines.'

It was typical of Carl to see the worst. Sure, Franz Ferdinand had had a massive hit single but it was The Libertines who'd laid the groundwork for them, Bloc Party, Kaiser Chiefs, Arctic Monkeys and a host of other bands. All of them, inspired by The Libertines, finally rejecting the nonsense and platitudes that had cursed British music since the arrival of Oasis.

Peter and Carl revitalised a hopelessly moribund British music scene. In 2001 it was still suffering a Britpop comedown and was in the worst state it had been in since the birth of rock 'n' roll. They made music that was as informed by literature and movies as it was by their musical heroes and instilled a sense of British pride in music that had been lost in the rush to market third-rate bands.

They made music something to believe in, they made it dangerous again, in an age when the media had tired of rock 'n' roll and compartmentalised it as a minor adjunct to the arts behind movies and computer games. They created a generational divide in music that hadn't existed for a decade and a half.

There simply wasn't a British music scene prior to Peter and Carl putting pen to paper in the tinsel-strewn Rough Trade offices in December 2002.

They didn't sail the *Albion* to Arcadia, but they sure got it out of dry dock and out on the ocean waves in the right direction. The Libertines' pioneering spirit in the live arena with guerrilla gigs, their influence over fashion and the use of the Internet to serve the fans and expose the creative process was unique. The mark of their accomplishments, like most artists, is that in retrospect everything they did seemed obvious, but no one had done it before. Even after the end of The Libertines the waves they caused in Britain continue to ripple through music, fashion and culture, as those influenced and inspired by them become musicians, writers and artists. It remains to be seen whether Peter and Carl's own bands, Babyshambles and Dirty Pretty Things, can achieve what The Libertines did. Certainly it won't be by attempting to replicate the chemistry of the past. They're both too canny for that.

Even as Peter and Carl seemed to shoot off in separate directions, they were still inextricably tied together. Peter phoned Carl on the Monday after the 2005 Reading Festival to see if he wanted to meet up, play guitar and sing. Peter was outside the hotel he assumed Carl would be at; Carl had checked out of it just two hours before.

These two rapscallions, dizzy with ideas, music and literature, came together to take on the world. They saw in each other something that could help them escape the narrow boundaries imposed by circumstances. The fear of death on the stairs – curtains drawn in mid-afternoon, baked beans out of a can and a fuzzy television – has been vanquished. They succeeded in avoiding their preordained destinies because they were heading out jointly – them against the world. Meanwhile, the people who accompanied them – Paul, John, Banny, Gary, Anthony, Alan, Patrick, Gemma, Drew, Adam and Didz – all deserve ample laurels for keeping it together.

In 1977 Neil Young wrote 'Hey Hey My My (Out Of The Blue)'. Apart from containing a celebration of The Sex Pistols' Johnny Rotten – a snarling cynic at the forefront of the vanguard determined to overthrow the hippies – it contained probably the most succinct evocation of what rock 'n' roll should be about: 'It's better to burn out than fade away.'

The Libertines did burn out, avoiding the trap of longevity. Sure, drugs and misunderstandings quickened the end of their relationship, prematurely snuffing out the most creative music partnership in two decades, but it just fast-forwarded the inevitable.

They might have got one more album out, an album that would probably have overshadowed the first two, but after that they would have split or gone into artistic decline.

Their relationship was by turns tempestuous and totally creative. In the end, they broke each other's hearts, but made the hearts of music fans beat as though it was for the first time.

They were and are emotionally bound together, but temperamentally they were always bound to part.

APPENDIX

THE LIBERTINES
DEMOS
Early Demos 1997–2001
Odessa Studio Recordings
(First demo)
1. 'Breck Road Lover'
2. 'Pay The Lady'
3. 'Music When The Lights Go Out'

Odessa Studio Recordings
1. 'Music When The Lights Go Out'
2. 'Hooray! For The 21st Century'
3. 'Love On The Dole'
4. 'Anything But Love'
5. '7 Deadly Frenchmen'
6. '(TAG)'
7. 'France'
8. 'You're My Waterloo'
9. 'Men In White Coats'

EMI Studios Demos
1. 'Bucket Shop'
2. 'Sister, Sister'

River Audio, London (Rehearsal)
1. 'Lust Of The Libertines'
2. 'Kitte'
3. 'Glee Maloyer'
4. 'Lean As A Runner Bean'
5. 'The Domestic'

Legs 11 – Compilation by Carl Barât
1. 'Music When The Lights Go Out'
2. 'Hooray For The 21st Century'
3. 'Love On The Dole'
4. 'Bucket Shop'
5. 'Sister Sister'
6. 'Anything But Love'
7. 'France'
8. '7 Deadly Frenchmen'

Early demos (Date not known)
1. 'Smashing' (feat. Lula Camus)
2. 'Never Never' (Hancock version)

Endeacott's Demo
1. 'Mocking Bird' (Steve Bedlow vocal)
2. 'Thru The Looking Glass' (Steve Bedlow vocal)

Rough Trade Demos
Nomis Demos 1,
7 December 2001
1. 'I Get Along'
2. 'Time For Heroes'
3. 'Never Never'
4. 'Horrorshow'

5. 'Boys In The Band'

Nomis Demos 2,
13 February 2002
1. 'Up The Bracket'
2. 'Begging'
3. 'What A Waster'
4. 'Skint + Minted'
5. 'General Smuts'
6. 'Bangkok'
7. 'Mayday'
8. 'Mr Finnegan'

Rak Revisited, 26 July 2002
1. 'The Boys In The Band'
2. 'Horrorshow'
3. 'Time For Heroes'
4. 'I Get Along'
5. 'Death On The Stairs'
6. 'Death On The Stairs' (Alternative guitars)
7. 'Skag + Bone Man'

French Sessions, January 2003
1. 'Narcissist'
2. '_ Cocked Boy'
3. 'The Ha Ha Wall'
4. 'Through The Looking Glass'

2 June 2003
1 '8 Days A Week Monitor Mix'
2 '8 Days A Week Monitor Mix' (Less Guitar)

INTERNET SESSIONS
Babyshambles Sessions,
The Libertines
CD 1
1. 'Babyshambles' (Take 1)
2. 'Road To Ruin'
3. 'Babyshambles' (Take 2)
4. 'Don't Look Back Into The Sun' (Version 1)
5. 'What Katie Did'
6. 'Don't Look Back Into The Sun' (Version 2)
7. 'Last Post On The Bugle'
8. 'Side Of The Road'
9. 'Back From The Dead'
10. 'The Man Who Would Be King'
11. 'I Got Sweets' (Instrumental)
12. 'All At Sea' (Take 1)
13. 'All At Sea' (Take 2)
14. 'Do You Know Me (I Don't Think So)'
15. 'Campaign Of Hate'
16. 'Love Reign O'er Me'/'Bilo Song'
17. 'In Love With A Feeling' (Version 1)
18. 'Instrumental'
19. 'In Love With A Feeling' (Version 2)
20. 'I Love You

(But You're Green)'
21. 'That Bowery Song' (a.k.a. 'Merry Go Round')

CD 2
1. 'Albion'
2. 'Albion' (Intro)
3. 'Albion' (sans Biggles)
4. 'France' (Take 1)
5. 'France' (Take 2)
6. 'France' (Take 3)
7. 'The Good Old Days' (Acoustic)
8. 'Skag & Bone Man' (Acoustic)
9. 'Instrumental'
10. 'Instrumental'
11. 'Oh pigman where art thou?' (Early version of 'Likely Lads')
12. 'What A Waster' (Acoustic, sung by Adam Green)
13. 'Who's Got The Crack' (Moldy Peaches cover)
14. 'Back From The Dead' (0,00)/'Jeanne' (0:55) (Smiths cover)/'Bollywood' (3.03)/'Dilly Boys' (4:37)/'Black Boy Lane' (6.02)
15. 'Love reign over me'/'Through The Looking Glass' (1:12)/'Callin' All' (2:35) (La's cover)/'Son Of A Gun' (La's cover) (4.28)/'Deep Pile Dreams' (Ian Brown cover) (6.50)/'Ha Ha Wall' (8.37)/'I Love You (But You're Green' (11.02)/'Don't Be Shy' (13.35)/'Time For Heroes' (15.00)/'Well I Wonder' (15.52)/'Rubber Ring' (16.18)/'Everyday is Like Sunday' (16.42)/'Albion Instrumental' (16.55)/'Everyday Is Like Sunday' (17.33)/'Shooting Stars' (18:19)/'Unchained Melody' (La's cover) (19.09)/'Huckleberry Grove' (Ocean Colour Scene cover) (20:18)/'What A Waster' (21:20)/'Ballad Of Grimaldi' (22:28)/'Road To Ruin' (23:27) /'Delaney' (24:55) /'The Blinding' (26:45)/'Back From The Dead' (28:17)

CD 3
1. 'Playing around with a piano' (a.k.a. 'Back From The Dead')
2. 'I Got Sweets'
3. 'The Coral Medley': 'Dreaming Of You' (The Coral), 'New Love Grows On Trees', 'I Remember When' (The Coral), 'You're My Waterloo', 'Killamangiro'
4. 'Killamangiro'

SINGLES AND ALBUMS
Singles
'What A Waster', 3 June 2002. Highest UK chart position: 37
CD Single (CDS)
1. 'What A Waster'
2. 'I Get Along'
3. 'Mayday'

7"
1. 'What A Waster'
2. 'I Get Along'

'Up The Bracket', 30 September 2002. Highest UK chart position: 29
CDS 1
1. 'Up the Bracket'
2. 'Boys in the Band'
3. 'Skag and Bone Man'
CDS 2
1. 'Up the Bracket'
2. 'The Delaney'
3. 'Plan A'
7"
1. 'Up the Bracket'
2. 'Boys in the Band'

'Time for Heroes', 13 January 2003. Highest UK chart position: 20
CDS 1
1. 'Time for Heroes'
2. 'General Smuts' (Demo)
3. 'Bangkok' (Demo)
CDS 2
1. 'Time for Heroes'
2. 'Mr. Finnegan' (Demo)
3. 'Sally Brown' (Demo)
7"
1. 'Time for Heroes'
2. '7 Deadly Sins' (Demo)

'Don't Look Back Into The Sun', 18 August 2003. Highest UK chart position: 11
CDS 1
1. 'Don't Look Back Into The Sun'
2. 'Death on the Stairs'
3. 'Tell the King' (Original demo version)
CDS 2
1. 'Don't Look Back Into The Sun'
2. 'Skint and Minted' (Demo)
3. 'Mockingbird'
7"
1. 'Don't Look Back Into The Sun'
2. 'Death on the Stairs'

'Can't Stand Me Now', 9 August 2004. Highest UK chart position: 2

CDS
1. 'Can't Stand Me Now'
2. 'Cyclops'
3. 'Dilly Boys'
4. 'Can't Stand Me Now' (Video)
7"
1. 'Can't Stand Me Now'
2. '(I've Got) Sweets'

'What Became of the Likely Lads', 25 October 2004. Highest UK chart position: 9
CDS1
1. 'What Became Of The Likely Lads'
2. 'Skag & Bone Man' (Live, Brixton, 6 March 2004)
3. 'Time For Heroes' (Live, Brixton, 6 March 2004)
CDS2
1. 'What Became Of The Likely Lads' (Re-worked)
2. 'The Delaney' (Live, Brixton, 6 March 2004)
7"
1. 'What Became Of The Likely Lads'
2. 'Boys In The Band' (Live, Brixton, 6 March 2004)

Albums
Up The Bracket, 21 October 2002. Highest UK chart position: 35
CD/LP
1. 'Vertigo'
2. 'Death on the Stairs'
3. 'Horrorshow'
4. 'Time for Heroes'
5. 'Boys in the Band'
6. 'Radio America'
7. 'Up the Bracket'
8. 'Tell the King'
9. 'The Boy Looked at Johnny'
10. 'Begging'
11. 'The Good Old Days'
12. 'I Get Along'

CD/DVD, 8 September 2003
As above plus:
13. 'What A Waster'

DVD:
1. 'Up The Bracket'
2. 'Time for Heroes'
3. 'I Get Along'

Unreleased *Up The Bracket* Monitor Mixes, 12 July 2002
1. 'Breck Road Lover'
2. 'The Domestic'
3. 'Never Never'
4. 'Sweets'
5. 'Wolfman'

The *Libertines*, 30 August 2004.
Highest UK chart position: 1
CD
1. 'Can't Stand Me Now'
2. 'Last Post On The Bugle'
3. 'Don't Be Shy'
4. 'The Man Who Would Be King'
5. 'Music When The Lights Go Out'
6. 'Narcissist'
7. 'The Ha Ha Wall'
8. 'Arbeit Macht Frei'
9. 'Campaign Of Hate'
10. 'What Katie Did'
11. 'Tomblands'
12. 'The Saga'
13. 'Road To Ruin'
14. 'What Became Of The Likely Lads'
Hidden track: 'France'

Reissued 15 November 2004
with DVD
Chapter 1
1. Live Footage From Shows At Summer Sonic, The Factory and Filthy McNasty's
Chapter 2
2. Scenes From The Forum Shows, December 2003
3. 'Can't Stand Me Now' (Video)
Chapter 3
4. On The Road With The Band During Their Trip To Madrid
Chapter 4
5. Interviews
6. Photo Gallery
7. Footage From NME Awards

Unreleased *The Libertines*
Monitor Mixes
1 'The Delaney'
2 'Bangkok'
3 'Bound Together'
4 'Plan A'
5 'Hooligans On E'

PETER DOHERTY/ BABYSHAMBLES

INTERNET SESSIONS
Sailor Sessions, Peter Doherty/ Babyshambles (mark one), July 2003
1. 'Black Boy Lane'
2. 'The Ha Ha Wall'
3. 'Campaign Of Hate'
4. 'Killamangiro' (sic)
5. 'Music When The Lights Go Out'
6. 'The Whole World Is Our Playground'
7. 'Hooligans On E'
8. 'What Katie Did'

Chicken Shack Sessions, Peter Doherty, September 2003

1. 'Begging'
2. 'Campaign Of Hate'
3. 'Curtain Call'
4. 'Curtain Call' (Gaks And Enob Mix)   5. 'The Man Who Came To Stay'
6. 'My Darling Clementine'
7. 'Stix & Stones'
8. 'Pay The Lay'
9. 'Don't Look Back Into The Sun'
10. 'Bucket Shop'

Whitechapel Demonstrations Sessions, Peter Doherty, February 2004
1. 'Anything But Love'
2. 'Dilly Boys'
3. 'Love On The Dole'
4. 'Another Girl, Another Planet'
5. 'The Whole World Is Our Playground'
6. 'Smashing'
7. 'I Love You (But You're Green)'
8. 'What Katie Did'
9. 'Skag & Bone Man'
10. 'Pipey Magraw'

HQ Sessions Second Wave, Peter Doherty, February 2004
1. 'Black Boy Lane'
2. 'I Love You (But You're Green)'/'Tomblands'
3. 'Sheepskin Tearaway'
4. 'Killamangiro'
5. 'Through The Looking Glass'/'Love Reign O'er Me'
6. 'Stix & Stones'
7. 'Pipey Obrady'
8. 'Lust Of The Libertines'
9. 'Do You Know Me'
10. 'Wolfman'
11. 'Babyshambles Instrumentals'
12. 'In Love With A Feeling'
13. 'The Last Of The English Roses'
14. 'Sheepskin Tearaway'/ 'Conversation Diva'

HQ Bethnal Green Sessions, Peter Doherty, February 2004
1. 'At the Flophouse'
2. 'Babyshambles'
3. 'Pipey Magraw'
4. Random chit chat and wolf raps (inc. 'Don't Be Shy'/ 'Ask'/'Back From The Dead')

Branding Sessions, Peter Doherty, March 2004
1. 'Can't Stand Me Now' (Drum Machine Version)
2. 'Stix And Stones' (Trumpet version)

Acousticalullaby Sessions, Peter Doherty, April 2004

1. 'A Little Death Around The Eyes'
2. 'Arcady'
3. 'Un Bilo Titled'
4. 'I Love You (But You're Green)'
5. 'Albion'
6. 'In Love With A Feeling' (10 seconds)
7. 'East Of Eden'
8. 'He Will Fall'
9. 'New Love Grows On Trees'
10. 'My Darling Clementine'
11. 'Back From The Dead' (25 Seconds)

Shaken And Withdrawn Megamix, Peter Doherty, August 2004
CD1
1. 'My Darling Clementine' (Version 1)
2. 'Back From The Dead'
3. 'Lady Don't Fall Backwards'/'Bollywood To Battersea'
4. 'The Whole World Is Our Playground' (Version 1)
5. 'Hooray For The 21st Century'
6. 'Curtain Call'
7. 'There Is A Light That Never Goes Out'/'32nd December'
8. 'Conversation Diva'
9. 'Never Never'
10. 'East Of Eden'
11. 'My Darling Clementine' (Version 2)
12. 'There She Goes (A Little Heartache)'
13. 'Can't Stand Me Now' (Version 1)
14. 'The Ha Ha Wall'
15. 'The Ballad Of Grimaldi' (Version 1)
16. 'Stix & Stones' (Version 1)

CD2
1. 'Can't Stand Me Now'
2. 'Pipey Magregor'
3. 'Music When The Lights Go Out'
4. 'The Whole World Is Our Playground'
5. 'Albion'
6. 'Arcady'
7. 'Black Boy Lane'
8. 'Scouser In Space'
9. 'Ballad Of Grimaldi'
10. 'Love Rain O'er Me'/'The Saga'
11. 'Killamangiro'
12. 'Stix And Stones'
13. 'My Darling Clementine'
14. 'Curtain Call'
15. 'Don't Look Back Into The Sun'
16. 'I Love You (But You're Green)'
17. 'If You Fall'

SINGLES AND ALBUMS
Singles
'For Lovers', Wolfman feat. Pete Doherty, 12 April 2004. Highest UK chart position: 7
CDS
1. 'For Lovers'
2. 'Back From The Dead' (feat. Carl Barât)
3. 'For Lovers' (Video)
7"
1. 'For Lovers'
2. 'Back From The Dead' (feat. Carl Barât)

'Babyshambles', Babyshambles, 10 May 2004.
Highest UK chart position: 32
CDS
1. 'Babyshambles'
2. 'At the Flophouse'
3. 'What Katie Did' (Limited edition, 2000 copies)
7"
1. 'Babyshambles'
2. 'At the Flophouse' (Limited edition, 1000 copies)

'Killamangiro', Babyshambles, 29 November 2004. Highest UK chart position: 8
CDS
1. 'Killamangiro'
2. 'The Man Who Came To Stay'
3. 'Killamangiro' (Video)
7"
1. 'Killamangiro'
2. 'The Man Who Came To Stay'

'Fuck Forever', Babyshambles 15 August 2005. Highest UK chart position: 4
CDS1
1. 'Fuck Forever' (Original)
2. 'Monkey Casino'
CDS2
1. 'Fuck Forever' (Original)
2. 'East Of Eden'
3. 'Babyshambles'
4. 'Fuck Forever' (Video)
7"
1. 'Fuck Forever'
2. 'Black Boy Lane'

Albums
Down In Albion, Babyshambles, 14 November 2005
1. 'La Belle Et La Bête'
2. 'Fuck Forever'
3. 'A'rebours'
4. 'The 32 Of December'
5. 'Pipedown'
6. 'Sticks & Stones'
7. 'Killamangiro'
8. '8 Dead Boys'
9. 'In Love With A Feeling'
10. 'Pentonville'
11. 'What Katy Did Next'

12. 'Albion'
13. 'Back From The Dead'
14. 'Loyalty Song'
15. 'Up The Morning'
16. 'Merry Go Round'

YETI (feat. John Hassall)
'Never Lose Your Sense of Wonder', 18 April 2005. Highest UK chart position: 36
CDS
1. 'Never Lose Your Sense of Wonder'
2. 'Working For The Industry'
3. 'Midnight Flight'
7"
1. 'Never Lose Your Sense of Wonder'
2. 'Working For The Industry'

'Keep Pushin' On', 29 August 2005
CDS
1. 'Keep Pushin' On'
2. 'In Like With You'
3. 'Carpet Road'

NOTABLE COMPILATIONS
Blackball Soundtrack, 1 September 2003
'Lazy Sunday' (Small Faces cover), The Libertines

Observer CD, 26 September 2004
A free five-track compilation featured the unreleased song 'All At Sea'

Bring Your Own Poison – The Rhythm Factory Sessions, 18 October 2004
Live tracks from The Rhythm Factory featuring:
'Up The Bracket', The Libertines
'Killamanforhisgiro' (sic.), Babyshambles
'Back From The Dead', Peter Doherty
Hidden Track: 'Another Girl, Another Planet', The Libertines/ Peter Perrett

Warchild – Help: A Day in the Life, 24 April 2005
Charity Compilation
'From Bollywood to Battersea', Babyshambles

Under The Influence, Carl Barât, 27 June 2005
A compilation of some of Carl's favourite artists

Please note this is not a complete discography as it doesn't include either live tracks or stray leaked tracks.